THE LIBRARY BOOK

learwater | Cambie | Port Moody | Camosun College | Malaspina College | Enderby | Gold River | Sointula | Nazko | Ea
ls | McBride | Powell River | Kitimat | Tumbler Ridge | Surrey Centennial | Port Coquitlam | Aldergrove | Burquitlam Plaza
stbank | Whistler | Port McNeill | Douglas College | Castlegar | McLeese Lake | Poirier | Salmo | Peachland | Bowser | I
anagan | Strathnaver | Cloverdale | Ridgeway | New Westminster | Parksville | Royal Roads University | Townsite | Montro

THE LIBRARY BOOK

A History of Service to British Columbia

DAVE OBEE

CONTENTS

Page 1: The Carnegie library, completed in 1903, has been a landmark at Hastings and Main in Vancouver for more than a century. *Vancouver Public Library*

Page 2: Fraser Valley van in the 1940s had sides that opened to allow access to the books. *Fraser Valley Regional Library*

Page 3: The Burnaby Public Library's Tommy Douglas Branch at night, 2010. *Burnaby Public Library*

FOREWORD

My first visit to a library was memorable on two fronts as I encountered an old friend and a new concept of furniture. The Collingwood Branch of the Vancouver Public Library was just enough of a walk from our house to qualify as an expedition. When my mother and I arrived I was gobsmacked to see *Curious George*. It was exactly the same as the *Curious George* I had at home. How was this possible? I checked carefully. Yes, George had blue striped pajamas and he was walking on the telephone wires.

Somebody had made exactly the same pictures in the library book as were in my book. Libraries were obviously places where some kind of deep magic was at play. My other delighted surprise had to do with the chairs. They had small chairs just for children. I had had no idea that such small chairs existed except in Goldilocks' house. Who were these people who accommodated me so thoughtfully? Kindness and magic. My preschool self was hooked.

Histories of libraries tend to focus on buildings. New buildings make a splash. All those local worthies with shovels in their hands, turning sod. In my early days as a public librarian I quickly got fed up with buildings. Plugged toilets, the annual summer ant invasion, mutant air conditioning systems. I dreamed of a world in which we could just deliver the materials, services and programs to the public without benefit of buildings. Collections and people, that was what mattered, not bricks, mortar and the leak in the underground parking lot. Little did I realize, of course, that such a world would become possible during the course of my career.

When historian Dave Obee asked me to write this foreword, however, I looked back over my life in libraries as a reader, student, writer, librarian and teacher, and realized that, in spite of my professional exasperation with buildings, my strongest memories actually were of the structures themselves, of specific places in those buildings where I found inspiration, refuge, friends, amusement, challenge,

delight, and a chair just for me. In the historical spirit of this book I'm going to indulge in one more snapshot from the past.

Another neighbourhood and another library: My elementary school was Lord Roberts in the west end of Vancouver. Its library was the place where I felt most like me. Every day after school I dropped in and chose one book to take home. If it was raining, and it was almost always raining, Miss Fletcher the librarian would let me come into the workroom while she wrapped my book in brown paper from the huge, luxurious roll that lived there, along with book mending tape, ink pads, date due cards and a teapot. I once heard a chemist admit that he was initially drawn to science because of the laboratory glassware. I'm like that about library paraphernalia. I grew to admire libraries for their defense of intellectual freedom and their commitment to inclusive public education and citizen empowerment through information but really, at the beginning, it was the rubber stamps.

In the current stage of my patchwork career I've taken up some casual volunteer tutoring. My student and I like to tackle our homework sessions in the public library. Her local branch is the Collingwood Branch of Vancouver Public Library so there I am, full circle, half a century later. Why do we bother to meet there? My student has Internet access at home; we could find all we need electronically. It's like *Curious George*. We had that at home too. My ESL student and I go to the bricks and mortar library because it is an expedition. We go because sometimes a girl needs to get away from her kid sister. We go because we like to browse shelves and check out the displays and people-watch. We go because it is free and fun and because the folks there seem pleased to see us. When it comes right down to it, we go there for the chairs.

Sarah Ellis

INTRODUCTION

Readers gaining access to reading through more than a century and a half of library development makes a compelling story. *The Library Book: A History of Service to British Columbia* isn't just a compendium of dusty dates and past times; it brings to life some of our more memorable predecessors who quite simply loved books and sought to share them. *The Library Book* traces the history, growth and political evolution of B.C.'s libraries, across time and through the lives of diverse peoples, commencing when books were tucked into trunks and packing cases of the first arriving offshore settlers. Books were considered essential to new lives being forged in what was then regarded as an "isolated outpost" of the British colonial empire. The creation of libraries here was a life's work to many often-forgotten men and women who personally modeled the value of reading and who were determined to share the experience.

Millennia of oral histories had preceded the first literature written in this territory. Tales of high drama and hereditary importance were told and re-told to generation after generation of First Nations Peoples. These stories took in the form of creation myths, heroic histories and cherished legends, explaining their world and their places in it. The fearsome smallpox epidemics of the 1860s left more than half of the original peoples of this land bereaved, if not broken. They suffered unimaginable losses, including much of their historic continuity; a fact that proved almost as devastating as the disease itself and that has coloured our history and much of our indigenous literature. Among the decimated and traumatized peoples who survived the several epidemics of death, some First Nations original stories remained. Rich in detail, they were suffused with magic and mystery and possessed the added distinction of having risen from this land and from nowhere else on earth. In time, some essence of pre-contact British Columbia was to be incorporated into the widely diverse literary arts and a poetic canon that today enriches us all in works by many admired and respected B.C.-based authors, writers and publishers.

Literary arts would not form such a rich vein of education and knowledge and enjoyment as they do today if the works had not become accessible and widely distributed. From the earliest post-contact period, when the first private library was brought to Nootka Sound, it was apparent that libraries were to play a pivotal role in creating the province that we live in today. The first of the professional libraries were somewhat random. For instance the canoes of Simon Fraser carried books as well as furs to B.C.'s first capital at Fort St. James; while another Nor'wester, Daniel William Harmon, encouraged his trappers to promote the value of books as a constructive influence on the emerging new society. Sir James Douglas of the Hudson's Bay Company, the first Governor of Vancouver Island and later of B.C., appointed B.C.'s first judge, Matthew Baillie Begbie, who was reputed to "use words as weapons," and was known to carry the classics along with his law books in his saddlebags as he rode the circuits of this nascent province. Both men were close associates of B.C.'s first Lieutenant Governor, Colonel Richard Moody, who earlier, as commander of a small band of Royal Engineers, used professional manuals from England to set out the first roadbeds and basic infrastructure of our province, some of which remains today.

The latter half of the 19th century was an exuberant time. Great trees were felled and lumber shipped abroad while towns emerged from what once been primeval forest. In 1858, the *British Colonist* newspaper began operations in Victoria. Shortly afterward a commercial library opened there and by 1863 a rudimentary legislative library had been established as an "official institution" deemed to add a measure of decorum to the occasionally raucous proceedings within. In 1891 the Legislature passed a Free Libraries Act and in New Westminster a year later, the first public library proudly opened its doors, only to be burned to the ground a mere six years later. In 1903 Victoria College opened, and by 1915 the University of British Columbia opened its doors with some 20,000 books in its library. The "Great War" of 1914-18 intervened but public libraries continued to expand. The floodgates of literary demand were opened across the length and breadth of the province as new towns sprang up and soon afterward added library access to their amenities. Institutions, professional associations, businesses and citizens established libraries, reading rooms, professional libraries, travelling libraries and small, innovative lending establishments to encourage the circulation of books.

There were library associations, archives, the Andrew Carnegie offers (some of which were refused) and a host of supportive actions that included the revision of the Public Schools Act in 1919 setting out the duties of school librarians. Towns, villages, hamlets and islands small and large from Kaslo to Prince Rupert opened libraries and were so popular that even the Great Depression of the 1930s did not slow but rather increased their progress.

As with most stories about our province, the history of library services reads like a novel. It is a testament to individual determination intended to overcome all challenges associated with B.C.'s difficult geography, complicated history, sparse population and ever-shifting economy. People volunteered too, as has long been a positive pattern here. Through their own love of books and reading, men and women worked hard to enrich the unique culture of this precious province of ours. They knew the value of the gift of learning, education and knowledge that was to be found in libraries and they knew the simple joy of being able to borrow literary works of history, fiction, poetry, drama and criticism to experience a "really good read!"

As you read this carefully researched and well-written, even exciting, story of British Columbia's libraries, you will naturally question the role of information technologies in the library. You can be forgiven for wondering what the impact will be of innovations in audiobooks, Amazon's gargantuan Kindle books, Librivox or any of the whole panoply of "free" online applications to reading. If we have learned anything from *The Library Book: A History of Service to British Columbia*, it is that whatever direction libraries may take in this 21st Century, there will always be dedicated women and men to guide and protect our heritage of library services to, as they say, "provide equal access to information and information services for all British Columbians, which is as important and crucial today as it was when B.C.'s first public library was established in 1891."

Iona Campagnolo

PART 1

1786 – 1926

Knowledge is what you need to have any chance to be equal in
this world. This is a non-threatening place, where you can get the
information and knowledge you seek to help you make the right
decisions. It is also a public library. Anything we have is open to view.
Aileen Tufts, librarian

1

WORKING TOGETHER FOR THE COMMON GOOD

What is a library? It could be a building, a collection of books, a service or even a website. Many libraries in British Columbia began as shelves with books, but modern ones have much more — films, digital resources, Internet access, databases and web portals accessible from anywhere in the world. They inform us, enlighten us and entertain us.

They exist to serve every one of us. As Ray Culos, the chair of British Columbia's old Library Development Commission, said in 1973, the library is the last place in town where a person can get service without an immediate over-the-counter payment. Even better, Culos said, librarians aim to please.

Opposite: Vancouver's Carnegie library was built in 1903 at Hastings Street and Westminster, which later was renamed Main Street. *Philip Timms photo, Vancouver Public Library, Special Collections 3427*

Above: Libraries provide free, easy access to all British Columbians. *Vancouver Public Library*

Officially, this book marks the 100th anniversary of the British Columbia Library Association in 2011 as well as the British Columbia Library Trustees Association, which traces its roots to the start of the BCLA. It honours the ninetieth anniversary of the Public Library Services Branch in 2009. It is being published as the School of Library, Archival and Information Studies at the University of British Columbia completes fifty years, and regional library systems on Vancouver Island and in the Okanagan mark seventy-five years.

Two British Columbia libraries have been featured on Canadian postage stamps. The first one was Victoria's old Carnegie library, on a $5 stamp in 1996, part of a series on architecture. The second was a 52-cent stamp to mark the centenary of the University of British Columbia in 2008, and featured the Walter C. Koerner Library.

It is also a celebration of libraries, of librarians, and the service enjoyed throughout this province. British Columbia's libraries have a rich history, one we can learn from.

"We are not dealing with anything in libraries today that hasn't already been dealt with," says Jacqueline van Dyk,

the director of the Public Library Services Branch. "We can see that in our collective history. There has always been a commitment to the growth and development of libraries as a whole, based on the belief that libraries can do much more collectively than any one library could do on its own."

It's a simple concept. If we all pooled our books, magazines, newspapers, DVDs and CDs, making them freely available to everyone, we would all be able to access a much larger collection than any of us could afford, or have room to store on our own. Sharing is at the heart of libraries.

"We lend materials, that's what we're about," says Paul Whitney, the former city librarian of the Vancouver Public Library. "We're about providing access to intellectual content." But that is not all. "Sometimes the streets can be unfriendly. Sometimes people have difficult home lives and the public library is one of the places that you come and essentially be yourself without having to justify what you're doing or explain yourself."

In an age of easy library access, ebooks and huge bookstores, it should be remembered that our ancestors did not have the access to books that we enjoy today. The first libraries, established centuries ago, provided the educated class with places to read books and manuscripts. Later, as literacy rates grew, more people were allowed to look at these items on site, and then borrow them, first for a fee, and then at no cost. That became possible when taxpayers started supporting libraries in the fading years of the 19th

Modern libraries provide plenty of natural light and comfortable reading spaces.
Vancouver Public Library

century. Books were expensive and hard to find through the 1800s, and even as late as the 1950s, libraries reported that purchasing was limited by a paucity of books.

The strength of libraries results from the strength of the remarkable people who believed in them and fought against incredible odds to expand and improve them. This book tells of some of those people with vision and determination — including Ethelbert Olaf Stuart Scholefield, Helen Gordon Stewart, Edgar Stewart Robinson, John Ridington, Jeannette Sargent, William Kaye Lamb, Lois Bewley and Ray Culos.

Thanks to these people and others like them, libraries have developed a reputation for getting things done, no matter what the obstacle. British Columbia has led the country in library services, with innovations such as travelling libraries, regional libraries and a commitment to Internet service. Library development over the past eighty years has been guided by a series of ten provincial strategic plans, each one endorsing the theory of library co-operation through provincial initiatives. These plans have also inspired the rest of Canada.

A library is a place that welcomes anyone who wants to learn anything, find a fact about anything, listen to music, view a video, read a book or borrow a book. A library is a source of joy, a source of information, a place for your mind to grow.
Lois Bewley, librarianship professor

Our libraries have evolved into state-of-the-art facilities on the leading edge of technology. Librarians have become guides rather than gatekeepers, as they were in the early days, and they have helped us discover many technological advances — from classification systems and card catalogues, to microfiche and CD-ROMs, to the Internet and ebooks.

Libraries matter. More than 2.7 million British Columbians are members of public libraries, which circulate more items than their counterparts across Canada. These public libraries come in all shapes and sizes; some have several branches and cover a region or a large municipality, while the work of others is decidedly local in nature. All public libraries are supported by local and provincial taxation.

Even libraries that are separated by thousands of years are connected by a common goal: To provide us with information about where we've been as we move forward into the future. Libraries link people who live today with those who came before and those who are yet to be. They are places where ideas take flight.
Maureen Sawa, librarian and author

Libraries in colleges and universities receive operating funds from their institutions, and their collections support the courses taught, the programs offered and the research done. School libraries are provided by taxes or private school funds, and are geared toward students. There are dozens of special libraries, belonging to newspapers, research institutions, governments, corporations and industry associations, and not generally open to the public. Law and medical libraries are also found throughout the province.

All of these libraries stand for freedom — freedom of access, information and thought. They welcome people who are looking for reference information or something light to read. They are sanctuaries for people searching for a deeper understanding of themselves or needing a place to go. They provide a warm, welcoming environment, just as they have for decades.

Libraries help children learn to read and choose careers. They provide adult education. They help seniors keep up with the fast-paced world around them. Libraries can be an oasis of sanity and librarians might be the best friends that some of their patrons have. Libraries provide books and resources as well as reliability and stability, and can be crucial to the happiness and well-being of the people they serve.

More than anything, libraries bring people together for the common good. People who pool resources and share benefits can achieve more than they could on their own. That thinking helped inspire some of British Columbia's first libraries, and it remains just as valid today.

2

An Alternative
to Saloons

Simon Fraser, the fur trader and explorer, gave his name to one of the most important rivers in British Columbia — and gave us our first libraries as well. Fraser worked for the North-West Company, which maintained circulating libraries for its employees. When he arrived in New Caledonia, as the central part of British Columbia was known in the first decade of the 1800s, he brought books with him.

They were not the first books to arrive in what is now British Columbia. James Strange brought some on a 1786 fur-trading mission, and left them at Vancouver Island's Nootka Sound with John McKay, the surgeon from the ship *Experiment*.

Opposite: A drawing of New Westminster's library appeared in the 1892 B.C. directory. *New Westminster Public Library photo 1874*

Above: In 1899, the New Westminster library was established in a temporary home, sharing a building with the fire department. *New Westminster Public Library photo 3077*

Little is known about these books, although one of them was said to be James Atkinson's *Epitome of the Art of Navigation*, first published in 1753.

New Westminster's Frederick William Howay, a British Columbia historian as well as an advocate for libraries, discounted those books, and gave credit for the first formal libraries to the North-West Company. Daniel William Harmon of the North-West Company stated in 1813, "If I were deprived of these silent companions many a gloomy hour would pass over me."

The Hudson's Bay Company, a rival fur-trading organization, also provided books to help its employees get through the long winters at Fort Victoria and other outposts. Hubert Howe Bancroft's *History of British Columbia*, published in 1890, refers to a circulating library the company had in 1833: "The officers subscribed, sent the order for books and periodicals to the company's agent in London; the books were sent out and as everyone had subscribed, they were sent to all forts throughout the length and breadth of the land. The Hudson's Bay Company, by their ships, sent out the *Times* and other leading papers for circulation. This was the first circulating library on the Pacific slope."

> I have always imagined Paradise as a kind of library.
> *Jorge Luis Borges, author*

The first books and periodicals came from England or the eastern United States, usually around Cape Horn or across the isthmus of Panama although sometimes overland from eastern Canada. These collections were a priority for the many immigrants. For example, Richard Blanshard, the first governor of Vancouver Island, brought a small library with him when he came from England in 1849.

The discovery of gold on the Fraser River inspired the first large-scale settlement in the colonies of Vancouver Island and British Columbia in 1858, with most new arrivals

coming from San Francisco, the largest city on North America's Pacific Coast. Over the next quarter of a century San Francisco provided British Columbia with its strongest ties to the outside world.

Several newcomers brought books with them. It was a small collection of books from England, however, that eventually formed the basis of the first municipal library in British Columbia. The books brought by the military men of the Royal Engineers in 1858 found their way into New Westminster's public library. Attempts were made to start other libraries as well, especially in Victoria, then the largest city in the two colonies, and in November 1858 W.F. Herre opened a reading room and library on Yates Street near Wharf.

Although the stock was limited, the *Victoria Gazette* said Herre's commercial enterprise filled "a much needed want of the town." The YMCA opened a reading room in Victoria in 1859. The *British Colonist* newspaper said it would provide a "healthy check against dissipation which has made fearful sacrifices in countries like ours where a large portion of the young men were deprived of the society of home." To the same end, the Dashaway Association — an offshoot of a temperance organization in San Francisco — set up a library and gymnasium in Victoria in 1860.

A small library opened in Fort Hope, the gateway to the Fraser Canyon, in 1859. Small reading rooms were soon available in several communities, promoted by business and religious leaders who wanted men to spend their free time doing something other than drinking alcohol. The owners of mines and mills apparently believed that having little libraries would increase the chances of their employees showing up for work on time — and sober as well.

"The little company town had always had a fine book collection," Edgar Stewart Robinson, a long-time Vancouver librarian, said many years later. "The mill company, sensing that a satisfied and happy employee is an asset to business, had early made provision for reading for its help." The Church of England helped open a library in the Cariboo in

Adrian Raeside

the 1860s to try to provide suitable recreation to gold miners, and churches throughout British Columbia offered books to anyone who wanted to read.

Wealthier British Columbians built their own libraries. Early arrivals such as Dr. William Fraser Tolmie, Sir James Douglas and Archibald McKinley were noted for their book collections. There were also reading rooms, which had newspapers and magazines, and commercial libraries, often part of stationery or dry goods stores, with a variety of recent books. In 1862, for example, Mike Cohen opened a coffee shop and lodging saloon in the El Dorado Building on Yates Street in Victoria. He promised that a "good cup of coffee and a good bed" would greet the stranger "as long as water runs and grass grows." He said English and American newspapers "arrived by every steamer from San Francisco," and in addition, a library was attached to the saloon.

How little our libraries cost us as compared with our liquor cellars.
John Lubbock, 1st Baron Avebury

The next year, Joseph Corin opened a for-profit library in his book and stationery store in Victoria, which he sold the next year to David Spencer. That little business was the start of the Spencer chain of department stores, which was bought by the Eaton family many years later.

The earliest patrons were usually male, but women were not forgotten. In Victoria, Christopher Loat promised a major change to the Exchange News Room when he bought it from Henry Frederick Heisterman in 1863. "The ladies of Victoria will be enabled to participate in the advantages of the institution," Loat said. "To attain that, immediate arrangements will be made for obtaining all the new literary works of the United Kingdom, Europe and America."

In 1866, financial troubles caused by the end of the Cariboo gold rush forced the colonies of Vancouver Island and British Columbia to merge. By that time, Mechanics' Institutes had been formed in communities such as Victoria, Nanaimo, New Westminster and Vancouver. They were designed to provide circulating libraries, reading rooms for periodicals and evening lectures to workingmen, modeled after the Mechanics' Institutes that were popular in Great Britain and in Canadian cities such as Halifax, Montreal and Toronto. Access was by a small subscription. The idea of a free library was years away.

Nanaimo started a literary institute in 1862 and it was a huge success for several decades; within five years of its creation, it had its own building on land provided by the Vancouver Coal Mining Company. In the Cariboo, Williams Creek's literary institute opened in 1864, with a library that was later moved to Barkerville.

Many southern Interior communities did not get libraries or reading rooms until the closing years of the 19th century. In Nelson, for instance, the first reading room was opened in 1890 by tobacconist and news agent Gilbert Stanley. Competition came in 1895 with the opening of the Nelson Public Reading and Amusement Rooms in the Victoria Hotel.

When many people come together, they inevitably recognize the need to start a library in order to share their books.
Basil Stuart-Stubbs, librarian

What was popular in the 1860s? In fiction in England it was the age of Charles Dickens, George Eliot, Charles Kingsley and Anthony Trollope; in America, Nathaniel Hawthorne, Oliver Wendell Holmes and Mark Twain were popular. In non-fiction the great names in England were Matthew Arnold, John Ruskin, Charles Darwin and John Stuart Mill; in America Ralph Waldo Emerson and Henry David Thoreau. The poets were Lord Alfred Tennyson, Robert Browning, Algernon Charles Swinburne, Walt Whitman and Henry Wadsworth Longfellow.

In the 19th century, novels became the most popular form of writing. Fresh ideas and realism took the place of sentimentality. Detective and mystery novels were popular during the Victorian era, with authors such as Wilkie Collins and Sir Arthur Conan Doyle, who gave the world *The Adventures of Sherlock Holmes*.

Fort Hope

Rev. Alexander David Pringle, sponsored by the Society for the Propagation of the Gospel, arrived in British Columbia in 1859 and was assigned to Fort Hope. Almost immediately he started a campaign for a reading room and library that would be "for the perusal of newspapers, the advantages of a permanent and circulating library, the delivery of lectures, and the promotion of social and friendly intercourse."

Pringle declared himself the honorary secretary and said he needed $400 to buy a house and lot. He suggested a subscription of $5 for the first month and $1 for subsequent months. "The project of a reading room in connexion with a circulating library is one which cannot fail to be beneficial to those for whose use it is intended," he wrote in September 1859. "The honorary secretary earnestly asks the assistance of that large class of persons who are benefitted directly or indirectly by the connexion of the two colonies of British Columbia and Vancouver Island for their kind help in any direction they may think fit."

When assistance did not materialize, Pringle bought the building himself. He still asked for financial aid, but offered to treat the money as a loan and pay ten per cent interest. His reading room and library was established in November 1859, making it the first of its kind in the colony. It did not make money, but at least it kept some of Fort Hope's men out of the bars.

New Westminster

Credit for the first formal library in British Columbia is usually given to a company of the Royal Engineers, a small military force that sailed from England on the ship *Thames City* in 1858 under the command of Col. Richard Clement Moody. They carried a "valuable library of excellent works" among their supplies. The books were chosen, legend has it, by Sir Edward Bulwer-Lytton, a politician and writer, with the possible help of Charles Dickens.

The corps was disbanded in 1863 and many members remained in the new colony. The library was handed over to those men.

In November 1864, a meeting was held in the New Westminster home of Dr. W.H. McNaughton-Jones to consider establishing a public library. Twenty-four men appointed to an organizing committee called a public meeting the following month to discuss plans for a "British Columbia Institute to embrace a library reading room, Mechanics' Institute and museum." Membership fees were to be $1 a month or $5 a year, with a life membership offered for $50. The Royal Engineers agreed to donate their books

and all members of the Royal Engineers' Circulating Library were offered free membership for life.

The new library opened on February 1, 1865, with between 400 and 500 books. It was quickly transformed into a public library, opening in the Mint Building on Columbia Street on August 15, 1865. The *British Columbian*, published by future premier John Robson, reported that on the first day, "the desks were rather bare in consequence of the non-arrival of eastern papers and magazines etc. A supply may be expected, however, by the next steamer." Major financial support came from the colonial government and memberships were sought through newspaper advertisements.

Frederick Seymour, the governor of the colony of British Columbia, presented the library with a collection of photograph albums and books. "The institution is now well lighted, and is gradually assuming a more inviting aspect," the *British Columbian* said a week after it opened.

The first librarian, William Edward Wynne Williams, served for just a few months. George Ramsey succeeded him in January 1866 but was forced to leave when he was found guilty of stealing gold samples from a case in the library. He was sentenced to six months in jail.

Next came John B. Harris who, with an assistant, kept the library open from 10 a.m. to 10 p.m. six days a week, and from 2 to 9 p.m. on Sundays. He also maintained subscriptions to many newspapers, including the *Sacramento Union* and the *Boston Journal*. Soon, however, the good times were over. The government of the combined colony of British Columbia cut the library's grant, the assistant was let go, and Harris chose to resign rather than accept a drop in salary.

William Epps Cormack was next. He was famous for having been, in 1822, the first person to walk across the island of Newfoundland, and his name lives on with the Cormack Trail. His term did not last long. The colonial government withdrew its last funding in April 1868 and the library was closed. Cormack died soon after.

The library reopened three months later on a subscription basis, and for the next thirty-two years it received no government support. The reading room remained open all that time and space was made available to the local Mechanics' Institute, which had its own book collection but was in no better financial shape than the library. The Mechanics' Institute relied on a government subsidy, then the support of local citizens, but finally closed. The *Herald* mourned the loss. "In a town which pays from $60,000 to $80,000 a year over the bars of saloons, a literary institute, always fairly well managed, and which could be 'run' in good style for $1,000 a year, has been forced to close its doors."

The public library, relying on subscriptions, moved from one financial crisis to the next. There is no accurate record

New Westminster library was on the second floor of city hall until the Carnegie library opened in 1905. *New Westminster Public Library photo 210*

of the people who served as librarians. By January 1890, the *Columbian* newspaper said residents had turned against the library and used "vigorous language against those who are responsible for this grave-stone of buried usefulness." The library building, it said, was "mouldering in decay while all around fine modern buildings are springing up to grace the city."

Hope was raised when the dominion government gave the Mint Building, which still housed the library, to the city on the condition that a new library be built there. The city set aside $20,000 for the work, tore down the Mint Building and held a competition for plans for a new one. Architect George William Grant was awarded the contract for a three-storey stone and brick building with shops on the first floor and the library and reading room on the second level. It would be a handsome building with stained glass windows depicting Handel and Shakespeare.

"Our public library will not only be a credit to this city, but to British Columbia," the *Columbian* said in an editorial. It warned that the building, while beautiful, would need books, staff and an "enlightened supervising committee." Useless volumes needed to be weeded from the collection and a catalogue compiled to show what was available. "So little seems to be really known about the contents of the old shack which formerly did duty as a city lounging room."

The building was completed in 1891 and the retail space was rented. As the city had pledged its support, the library no longer relied on subscriptions. The city's promise did not mean much; only the reading room, with newspapers and periodicals, was open to the public. The library had just 600 books; five commissioners appointed by council asked repeatedly for $4,000 to $5,000 to buy 5,000 new books. In November the commissioners hired a librarian, former private school proprietor Julian Peacock. He was paid $45 a month, raised to $50 when he agreed to be janitor for the Board of Trade office in the same building. There was still no money for books; Peacock's job was basically to look after the reading room and keep it clean.

In February 1892, city council approved a list of about 1,000 books that would cost less than $800, freight from London included. The free lending library was opened on June 29, 1892, and the *Columbian* reported that it was "unequalled in any other part of the province." By the end of the first year, 1,271 books had been borrowed and there were 613 borrowers, about three-quarters of them men. The library suffered for years, however, because of a lack of funding. It received no money for new books in 1893 or 1894, and circulation dropped because, commissioners said, anyone interested had already read everything. There was an improvement in 1896, when the library spent about $2,500 on books.

On September 10, 1898, the library and most of its contents were lost in the great New Westminster fire. A book given to the city by Queen Victoria in 1866 was one of the

New Westminster's great fire of 1898 destroyed the public library and the Holy Trinity Cathedral. *C.E. Bloomfield photo, City of Vancouver Archives, P1033*

few items saved. After the fire Peacock returned to England, leaving the library commissioners without a library or a librarian at a time when much of the city, including city hall, had to be rebuilt.

The commissioners sought money from council and even resigned briefly in April 1899 to press their case. Council finally found space for the library in a building also used by the fire department, which still used horse-drawn engines. The smell from the stables, it was said, curbed the enthusiasm for reading.

A new city hall was built on the old library site, and in November 1901 the library moved to the second floor. Books were still in short supply; the ones that had been on loan when the fire destroyed the old library had survived, but the library could not afford to buy books to replace the ones that had been lost. The library could not resume lending books until the next year, and even then, the circulating library was open just six hours every week. The reading room, for periodicals, was open twelve hours a day.

There were other problems between council members and the library commissioners. Councillors wanted the library to have a smoking and checkers room, saying it would be popular with men in the evenings. The commissioners worried that a bad example would be set, but finally agreed to the room on a temporary basis. Temporary lasted until 1937.

In time, city hall needed the library space, so there was pressure to move the books and the reading room to a new location. That's when Andrew Carnegie came to the rescue.

Nanaimo

A library under the auspices of St. Paul's Anglican Church, the St. Paul's Literary Institute and Society, opened in 1862. The group, which included notables such as industrialist Robert Dunsmuir, held its first meeting on November 22, 1862. A year later the name was changed to the Nanaimo Literary Institute. The society ordered periodicals from W.F. Herre in Victoria, including *Orcadian, Punch, Illustrated London News, Pacific Review, London Art Journal, Scottish American, Bells Life* and *Chambers' Edinburgh Journal*. It also spent $5 on a can of oil and three lamps.

Residents could use the library if they paid a $1 initial fee plus 50 cents a month. Members who took books were supposed to put their names on a slate kept in the room. A list of all members in good standing was posted in the reading room, which was open from 10 a.m. to 10 p.m. every day except Sundays. Smoking was not allowed at the tables.

Members chose the librarians in annual elections. The first librarian was Thomas C. Parry, who quit after a testy exchange with one of the members, David Gordon, at a committee meeting.

"Mr. Parry librarian attended the present meeting as requested, and was called upon to give a reason for neglecting the duties of his office," the institute's minutes say. "He complained of the difficulties he met with in the performance of his duties, of the way in which members strewed the papers over the room and carried them away contrary to orders. He grumbled and found fault with the arrangements and constitution of the society. He also threw reflections up on the committee which were far from being gentlemanly or courteous.

"A suitable reply was returned by Mr. Gordon. The chairman enquired of Mr. Parry if it was his intention to continue as librarian, an answer in the negative was given, after which he retired." Gordon and another man were named to serve as joint librarians for the rest of Parry's term.

The library's first home was a building supplied by the Vancouver Coal Mining Company; mine manager Charles S. Nicol was the first president. In 1863 the institute took space in a new hall being built by David Gordon and Jacob Blessing, both members in good standing. The next year, the institute obtained from the coal company a lot on Bastion Street at Skinner. Plans were drawn up for a building twenty-five feet wide and fifty feet deep with three windows along the front. The contract went to Gordon and Blessing, and Vancouver Island Governor Arthur Kennedy laid the cornerstone on November 15, 1864.

The building — the first purpose-built library building in the colony — had a lecture hall, reading and committee rooms and a library. It had about 450 books, nearly all donated by directors of the coal company and private gentlemen, that were split into two collections, a circulating one and one to be used in the reading room.

In 1864 the institute had seventy-six members, including many of the most prominent men in Nanaimo. It did not have female members but women were allowed to use the library, unlike children, who were barred. Subscription fees paid for the periodical collection, the most important service, while many books were acquired by donation. Old periodicals were sold through auction, and more money was raised through concerts.

The institute wrote to the colonial secretary in 1867 asking for a share of the grant voted for public libraries. It was turned down even though $500 had already been given to reading institutes in New Westminster and the Cariboo. Cato, the nom de plume for one of Nanaimo's members, argued in Victoria's *Daily Colonist* that once again New Westminster was being favoured.

"In the estimates sent down by the executive and voted by the legislative council last winter, was an item of $1,500 for literary and Mechanics' Institutes, etc.," Cato wrote. "During the year now nearly closed the Nanaimo Literary Institute and Reading Room have twice respectfully applied for a portion of the grant. Their first application, perhaps, never reached its destination, as it elicited no reply. The other has been replied to by an expression of regret that the financial condition of the colony does not warrant any assistance to the Nanaimo institute from public funds!

"Yet the governor has actually handed over to the New Westminster Reading Room this year a grant of $250, and another, the amount of which has not been allowed to transpire! If all other things were equal, this would be gross partiality. But its injustice is enhanced when the circumstances of the two are contrasted. The building occupied at New Westminster was erected by the government, for other purposes, out of the public funds, and has been placed, free of charge, at the disposal of well-paid officials and hangers-on of the executive. Who does not see the inequitableness of such a course?"

A few years later Nanaimo's literary institute was closed. In 1887 its building was taken over by the city, which expanded it and used it as a city hall. The building, a key piece of British Columbia's library history, was demolished in 1972.

Victoria

A Mechanics' Institute reading room and library was opened on December 16, 1864, with about 500 books. This had not been an overnight accomplishment: the opening followed three years to talk about the need for a library.

On November 18, 1864, the *Daily Colonist* published a letter from Edward Graham Alston, a lawyer who had been in Victoria since 1859, who pointed to Nanaimo's institute as a reason to try something similar in Victoria. Alston said $500 to $600 should be raised to rent a room, pay an attendant to light the fire and buy paper, periodicals and lighting. He said he thought books and periodicals would be donated, and proposed admittance of $1 a month.

One week later, in Huskinson's Royal Exchange Building on Government Street between Broughton and Courtney, the Mechanics' Institute and the Young Men's Literary Institute merged to form the Mechanics' Literary Institute. The first officers were Capt. D.M. Lang, Gilbert M. Sproat, Thomas Trounce and Alston. One of the keenest supporters was Joseph Corin, who had operated a commercial lending library for a year.

The institute rented two rooms in the Hibben-Carswell building on Yates Street, and stocked it with copies of the leading American and colonial papers as well as those from other countries. Colonial Governor Arthur Kennedy donated his used copies of the *London Gazette* with the condition that they be properly filed and returned if requested. Kennedy also expressed concern that Victoria did not have a library or a free school, but did have "eighty-five public houses."

In December 1865 the institute moved into the Moore's building on Yates Street. Thomas F. Swannick was the secretary for a few months. He was succeeded by Edmund T. Coleman, an artist who had written an illustrated book, *Scenes from the Snowfields, Being Views of an Ascent of Mount Blanc.* (In 1868, Coleman took part in the first successful ascent of Mount Baker in Washington state.)

The library moved to the Occidental Building, at Fort and Government streets, in 1869, and Capt. John Richardson Stuart, the librarian, compiled a catalogue of its holdings. In 1871, the institute moved to the Turner Building on the northeast corner of Fort and Government streets and John Quantock Hewlings was named librarian. He was paid $60 a month, but the institute was in bad financial shape; to keep it going the members had to raise money through events such as picnics.

In the 1880s the library moved to Roderick Finlayson's Philharmonic Building, on Fort Street between Douglas and Blanshard streets. It boasted that it had 5,000 books, and memberships were available for just $1 a month, $5 for six months, $10 for a year, or $50 lifetime. More money was raised through concerts and theatrical events.

The institute was an alternative to the saloon and a refuge for those with no place to go. It helped bring the fine arts to Victoria with displays of artwork, photographs and curios that drew hundreds of people. It was a vital part of the community, but it ran into severe financial problems in the 1880s when the opening of a new theatre reduced attendance at its fundraising events. It had trouble coping with competitors such as the Yates Street Circulating Library, which charged just 50 cents a month and promised to bring in any book requested. By the spring of 1886, the institute had only fifty or sixty members and closure was inevitable. That fall the members offered the books to the city to form the basis of a public library. The city accepted.

Borrowers returned the books they had, and the entire collection was put in storage above the fire hall. Joshua Davies conducted an auction to get rid of other assets, including a curtain, scenery, eighteen benches, 340 chairs and miscellaneous items from the theatre, as well as desks, chairs, a bookstand and a table from the reading room. After the proceeds were counted the institute was $450 in debt.

City council members wanted to pay off the debt and use the books to start a free, or partially free, library with operating costs not to exceed $1,200 a year. The expenditure would require the approval of voters, so a plebiscite was set for January 5, 1887. "The young people and for that matter the old, will have some place where they can spend a pleasant evening other than the usual and seductive haunts," the *Daily Colonist* said. "There in the presence of books and literature the nobler side of their lives will be formed and a foundation made for a successful and honourable manhood.

The first home of Victoria's Mechanics' Institute library was on the top floor of the Hibben and Carswell Building on Yates Street. *First Victoria Directory, 1860*

"That such an institution breathing such an influence is much needed in this city goes without saying, and we do hope that the bylaw will be carried today in the interest of the higher culture of the rising generation." The *Colonist* concluded: "We refuse to believe, however, that anybody will be found to cast his ballot against the bylaw, and against the best interests of the youth of this city."

Despite those strong words, the bylaw was defeated. Returning officer William King Bull counted 191 votes in favour and 218 against. Bull was a keen supporter of the proposal and had been involved in the Mechanics' Institute from the start. He took comfort in the fact that the books would be available "for the use and enjoyment of the citizens in that future when new and appreciative tastes have been created," and predicted that someday, "some liberal-minded

citizen" would provide money for a building to house a free public library.

In the meantime the city had to worry about the institute's $450 debt. Mayor James Fell, who had been the institute's president for several years, said he would be personally liable for the debt and would, if needed, take up a subscription to preserve the books. Fell's guarantee meant the city would not have to sell the books, worth an estimated $5,000, to pay what was owed.

For the next year and a half the books stayed in storage and the debts were left unpaid. From time to time Hewlings, the former librarian, and others who were owed money asked council for money. They were turned down. Supporters such as former school superintendent John Jessop, the institute's last president, also appeared before

In the 1890s, Victoria's library was housed on the second floor of city hall, to the right at the top of the stairs. Image A-02817 courtesy of Royal BC Museum, BC Archives

council to stress the need for a free public library.

In July 1888, the city put the library before the voters again, along with several other spending-related questions. The bylaw's wording was almost identical to the one turned down eighteen months earlier. Victoria's voters rejected improvements at Beacon Hill Park, an addition to city hall, an addition to the cemetery, new apparatus for the fire hall and a retaining wall at James Bay, but said yes to a sewer project, a waterworks extension — and the library. This time, Bull counted 232 votes in favour and 153 against. Council quickly paid off the debt and started planning for a library that would offer free access to all.

The plans were given a boost when Thomas Dixon Galpin, a partner in the Cassels and Company publishing house of London, England, donated 392 books to complement the old selection from the Mechanics' Institute. The books donated by Galpin, who had invested heavily in downtown Victoria and had two daughters in British Columbia, were prominently displayed when Victoria's Free Library opened on the top floor of the YMCA building on Broad Street, next to Trounce Alley, on the evening of May 10, 1889. The latest newspapers from the West Coast were also available.

Victoria Mayor John Grant was the first person to borrow a book; he selected *The Life and Speeches of Hon. George Brown*. The borrowers list was divided into ladies and gentlemen. Susan Robson, the wife of Premier John Robson, was the first woman to register with the new librarian, James Herrick McGregor. By the end of the year, the library had 1,000 members and lent 120 books on busy days.

"The present rooms are centrally located, easy of access, and well supplied with movable furniture; the reading room, although somewhat insufficient as to size, is being furnished with many of the leading periodicals," library board members Lawrence Goodacre and Louis Vigelius said in a report to council. The library's 1889 budget was $2,563, pocket change in the city's total budget of $451,000. About $550 was paid in rent, but that was a temporary cost. A new wing at city hall would house offices for the mayor and other officials, as well as a "commodious library and reading room, free of rent" on the second floor. The library moved to city hall in 1891.

To become a member a person had to apply with an endorsement by one responsible person. A card would be issued and the new member could start borrowing books. "In the case of absolute strangers, a small deposit will be required to insure the library against loss," the *Colonist* reported.

McGregor stepped down in 1895 and Henry Goward was chosen over about sixty applicants as the new librarian. Goward retired in 1905, the same year the library moved to a new Carnegie building.

Vancouver

There was not much at Vancouver in January 1869, when the New London Mechanics' Institute was opened by Capt. James A. Raymur so his employees at Stamp's Mill, at the foot of Dunlevy Avenue, would have a place to read. Two months later the mill was renamed Hastings Mill, and the reading room became the Hastings Literary Institute.

The library was closed in 1886, the same year Vancouver was incorporated and the first train arrived from the east. The books went into storage until the next year when Rev. Henry G. Fiennes-Clinton retrieved them to provide men with an alternative to the saloons along the waterfront. With the help of other leading citizens, Fiennes-Clinton opened a reading room and library in December 1887 above Thomas Dunn's hardware store, in the heart of the business district at 144 Cordova Street West.

James Edwin Machin, left, at the stairs leading to the library in the YMCA Building on West Hastings Street in the late 1890s. *Bailey Bros. photo, City of Vancouver Archives, Bu P118*

Starting with 400 to 500 books from the Hastings Literary Institute — collected by Fiennes-Clinton, Francis Lovett Carter-Cotton and R.H. Alexander, the manager of the Hastings Mill — the library grew through donations and a monthly subscription of 50 cents. All members of the

George Pollay, Vancouver's first librarian, arrived with his wife within hours of the great fire of 1886. He died in 1912 in Atlin. His library, the building on Cordova Street West, was demolished in 1925.

literary institute who were in good standing on June 1, 1887, were made life members of the new library. George Pollay was named librarian.

The library was not as popular as expected, and the monthly fee was blamed for the lack of interest. In January 1888 city council approved a request for $150 — the first civic library grant in B.C. Within a few years, the grant was increased to $2,000, and the library's bylaws were amended so women were welcomed.

Pollay left in 1890, and the job went to a recent arrival, lawyer James Edwin Machin. He was paid $65 a month and kept the library open from 9 a.m. to 10 p.m. six days a week with help from his wife Eliza and daughter Elsie. On Sunday afternoons the Machins opened the reading room

James Edwin Machin, Vancouver's head librarian until 1910. *Vancouver Public Library, Special Collections, VPL 976*

for four hours. Vancouver had many unemployed men and the library offered a refuge on cold, wet days, so the reading room was often filled.

In 1893, two council members joined the library board and the annual grant was raised to $3,600. That June the library was moved to 151 Hastings Street West, between Abbott and Cambie, later the home of the Astor Hotel. It had about 2,200 volumes and patrons were welcome to play chess or checkers in the reading room.

Machin found that fiction was the most popular but the arts and sciences were also well-read. "Thousand of persons in this city are keenly alive in the necessity of improving their mental faculties to enable them to compete the race for a living in these hard times," he said in his 1894 annual report. Among the periodicals offered were *Sketch*, *Boy's Own Paper*, *Scientific American*, *Knights of Labour*, *Cosmopolitan*, *Munsey's Canadian Magazine* and *Poultry Monthly*. In 1895 the library had subscriptions to twenty-nine monthlies and twenty-five weeklies as well as daily newspapers.

When large shipments arrived from England the Machins would close the library until the books were processed. Books were arranged on the shelves by date of acquisition rather than by topic. Patrons were not allowed to look for books; they wrote their requests on slips of paper, and one of the Machins would get the volume for them. Elsie Machin, later Beeman, said years later that the bookshelves were closed to the public because "bookworms had no conscience."

She said that at first, books were checked in and out from a large upended packing case with a small desk on top. "It was suggested that we have an indicator to show if a book was in or out. So a weird contraption arrived with rows of small holes, each having a number beside it, and it was my dreadful task to push pegs an inch long into the hole when the book was in," she said. "Being of the very cheapest construction, many pegs were either too big or too small and refused to go or fell out even when the book was in. One sad day the indicator departed."

Beeman said that during the smallpox scare of 1892 her parents continued to deal out books, surrounded by jars of disinfectant. "I don't remember that we ever contracted any infectious disease though borrowers were careless about returning books after illness," she said.

By 1901, the second-floor space on Hastings was simply too small so the library board started looking for a new location. The call for help went to Andrew Carnegie.

North Vancouver

The first library in North Vancouver resulted from a meeting in 1868 at Moody's Mills, later known as Moodyville, on the east side of Lower Lonsdale. Forty-six men pledged $5 apiece and promised to pay 50 cents a

month. Josias Charles Hughes and Ben H. Wilson were named the interim president and secretary, with George Deitz, Philander Wheeler Swett and J. Humphries asked to secure a building. Hughes, W.O. Allen and George W. Haynes were appointed to draft a constitution.

Sewell Prescott Moody, who ran the mill at Moodyville with Deitz and Hugh Nelson, provided a building, and Deitz donated the library's first books on February 1, 1869. They included *The Bible*, *Comstock's Philosophy*, *Comstock's Mineralogy*, *North West Coast* by Swain and *Signers of the Declaration of Independence*. Moody was given $100 and a list of requests, and asked to buy the books on his next visit to San Francisco. John T. Scott of New Westminster

presented a chess and checkers board, and more books were provided by Miss Watson of Victoria and Capt. Gilpin of the barque *Virgil*, which was at Moodyville to load lumber.

The masters and officers of vessels loading at the mill had free use of the reading room and library. The room was also at the disposal of preachers of the Gospel, regardless of denomination. By August 1869, the society had sixty-five members. Financially, the organization had its ups and downs. In some years, it reduced its membership fees, but in others it sold newspapers and magazines to cover the bills. The government provided a grant of $125 a year for several years. The last meeting recorded in the minute book took place in 1884.

Cordova Street looking east from Abbott in 1890, with the public library on the right side, above a hardware store.
Bailey Bros. photo, Vancouver Public Library VPL 19824

The Cariboo

The first library serving the Cariboo gold rush was founded in May 1864 after miners and traders on Williams Creek petitioned the government for a site for a reading room. A lot was provided in Cameronton and soon a library funded by subscriptions was open. John Bowron was in charge.

In April 1867, Bowron moved the library's 500 books, along with the Cameronton post office, to the old Parlour Saloon in Barkerville, and a month later to a new building. Colonial Governor Frederick Seymour donated books to the library, which had about 100 members. "We would recommend the citizens of this town to come forward at once with their subscriptions, as it is an institution which well deserves the support of the community," said the *Cariboo Sentinel*.

Bowron's building was destroyed in the great Barkerville fire in 1868, although about one-third of the books were saved. The library recovered, with help from people such as gold commissioner and judge Chartres Brew, and had 750 books two years later.

Benefit concerts enabled Bowron and other members to offer the best of music, books and the arts to the men working the gold fields, although there were frequent closings, reorganizations and pleas in the *Sentinel* for support. The library, known sometimes as the Cariboo Literary Institute, closed for good in late 1874.

Another source of books in Barkerville was Ben Lichtenstein's Occidental Cigar Store and Circulating Library, which had "the largest stock of novels ever imported on the creek." Two churches had libraries as well. Florence Wilson, who arrived in Victoria on the "bride ship" *Tynemouth* in 1862 and set up a stationery store there, took seventy books to the Cariboo in 1864. She has been given credit as the first librarian in the region, although it appears that she found a more profitable proposition: The business she lost in the 1868 fire was a saloon.

Other libraries

Rev. R. Reece of St. Peter's Anglican Church in Cowichan started a reading room in his home on Trunk Road in the 1870s. Later, a home on Janes Road was used as the

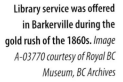

Library service was offered in Barkerville during the gold rush of the 1860s. *Image A-03770 courtesy of Royal BC Museum, BC Archives*

Cowichan Valley Lending Library. By 1877 there was a library board and service continued for many years.

In Kamloops in 1885, Henry Colbourn Maunoir Ridley opened a reading room that lasted only a year before closing because subscriptions were not paid and books were stolen. In 1891 the Canadian Pacific Railway opened a reading room and library with 200 books which became, in 1898, the basis of a library opened by the Kamloops Musical and Athletic Association. In 1909, after a public meeting was held, a library opened in the old courthouse with sixty books. The railway donated 130 books and 100 more were ordered from Toronto. The library closed in 1914 with the start of the First World War.

In Nelson, a library association was incorporated on April 7, 1899. It was in a couple of temporary locations before moving into a small building on Victoria Street, near Stanley Street, in May 1900. The building belonged to Harold Selous, a future mayor and an ardent supporter of the library.

In Rossland, the Sons of St. George obtained room in the fire hall in 1902. It was a tough deal; the fraternity had to furnish the free library, and all furniture, fixtures, books and literature would become the property of the municipality when the lease expired in five years.

Early public libraries faced a lot of competition as merchants started lending books in their stores. It was a good deal for the tobacco dealers, dry goods shops or grocery stores; the merchants knew that the books would keep their customers coming back. These private libraries continued well into the twentieth century.

School libraries, where they existed, were minimal. In the first half-century of British Columbia, most schools had little more than a shelf with books in a classroom. John Jessop, a former teacher who became the province's second education superintendent in 1872, helped expand the school system dramatically, increasing the number of common schools to forty-five from fourteen, tripling the number of teachers, and opening the province's first high school in Victoria in 1876.

A law library was established in Victoria in 1869, with another in New Westminster in 1890. A third was opened in Vancouver in 1893, followed by Nanaimo in 1894 and Nelson in 1897. In the twentieth century, the Vancouver law library became the main one for British Columbia. These libraries endured to become today's courthouse libraries.

In April 1891, the Legislature passed the Free Libraries Act, which established the public library as a legal entity, and allowed the creation of libraries supported through local taxes rather than user fees. The act, the second of its kind in Canada, did little to encourage the development of new libraries, but it set the stage for further legislation that promoted free libraries, allowed for government funding of libraries, and encouraged collaboration between libraries.

By the time the law was passed, three cities had free public libraries. The ones in Vancouver and Victoria were open, and a new building was going up in New Westminster. Of course, free access did not mean easy access. Patrons could use the reading rooms, where periodicals were kept, but could not browse the bookshelves for themselves. Borrowers looked for a book in a catalogue, and then presented the name and number at a wicket.

In 1892, the New Westminster *Columbian* published a summary of the procedure:

"Every ratepayer, upon application, is given a slip of paper upon which he puts the number of the book he requires and hands it to the librarian, who then gives the applicant a card with a number on it and the date on which the book was borrowed. If the borrower is a man, the number on the card is odd, if a woman even. Each time a book is returned and another borrowed, the date is entered on the card, so that the librarian can at once see whether a book has been returned. No book is lent without the presentation of the card each time.

"Persons who are not ratepayers must get a certificate from a ratepayer who is held responsible for the books lent on the strength of the certificate. The librarian's books have numbered lines so that at a glance he can tell how many books are out at a time. By means of the odd and even numbers he can tell how many borrowers are men and how many are women.

"Each department of literature is contained in a certain set of numbers, so that in a few minutes it may be ascertained just how many books of fiction, history or other branches are out. Every week a list of ratepayers, giving certificates, will be published in the *Columbian* to guard against any forgery, should anyone be mean enough to resort in such a way to taking advantage of the librarian."

The restrictions did not curb interest at British Columbia's free public libraries. In New Westminster, the wicket was at the top of the stairs in city hall, and sometimes on Saturday evenings the queue stretched down the stairs and onto Columbia Street. Readers wanted books and periodicals, and they wanted to use libraries. They were willing to put up with lineups and rules to do so.

3

THE PROVINCIAL LIBRARY

British Columbia's Legislative Library — known for many years as the Provincial Library — played a key role in the development of libraries throughout the province. It is older than the province it serves, set up in Victoria by the Legislative Assembly of Vancouver Island in 1863. Three years later, the colonies of Vancouver Island and British Columbia merged, and five years after that, in 1871, British Columbia became a province in Canada.

It took two attempts to start the library. The first came in September 1858, when the colonial House of Assembly voted to spend 250 pounds on a library for its use, with the money to come from the sale of licences. Nothing happened. More than

Opposite: The Legislative Library's 1915 building remains one of the most striking in the province. *Times Colonist*

Above: E.O.S. Scholefield, the Duke of Connaught and architect Francis Rattenbury at the laying of the cornerstone for the new provincial library in 1912. *Image H-00478 courtesy of Royal BC Museum, BC Archives*

a year later, the legislators decided to spend the money on a hospital instead, although they had trouble finding where the money had gone.

When the library was started in 1863, did not have a regular librarian or a proper location. Books were stacked in a small room adjacent to the Assembly Hall, and members of the Legislature helped themselves. The system was not perfect; without proper care, books were lost. The legislators eventually realized that a library cannot run itself, and in 1886 appointed William Atkins to serve as librarian when the house was in session. In 1889 and 1890 the job was filled by Nevil Edgar Graves, who was succeeded by Joseph Bridgman. By 1893, the library had a few hundred books, primarily parliamentary papers with only ten books of general interest. That year, Premier Theodore Davie hired R. Edward Gosnell to run the library and serve as Davie's private secretary.

Gosnell was born in Lake Beauport, Quebec, in 1860, and worked as a teacher and newspaper editor in Ontario for several years. In 1888 he came to British Columbia, accepting a job at the *News-Advertiser* in Vancouver. The newspaper's editor was Francis Lovett Carter-Cotton, an active supporter of libraries who later became the finance

R. Edward Gosnell helped create the Provincial Library in 1893 and the Provincial Archives in 1908. *Image I-51670 courtesy of Royal BC Museum, BC Archives*

minister and the first chancellor of the University of British Columbia.

In his first annual report, Gosnell said he had added 1,200 volumes and was trying to establish a "useful, up-to-date, standard reference library" with an emphasis on industries and natural resources, and also on British Columbian and Canadian affairs. A priority, he said, was to collect books about the history of the province and the "western country" as a whole. He obtained about 200 books through contributions and purchases and was looking for more. "Works relating to the early history of all parts of America are in great demand and steadily advancing in price, and it is with difficulty that they can be secured when offered for sale," he said. Driven by Gosnell's belief that it was important to preserve the story of the development of the province, the library also took responsibility for archival documents.

The library's role was made official in 1894 when legislation — "An Act to Establish and Maintain a Library for the Use of the Legislative Assembly, and to Constitute a Bureau of Statistics" — was passed. The library's primary purpose was to serve the members of the legislative assembly and government officials, not the public, but Gosnell still felt the need to remind patrons of their responsibilities.

"Members and others are requested not to remove papers from the files, and not to, in any instance, take books and magazines from the room without having the same entered in the register for that purpose, as well as their return," he wrote. "An observance of this request will avoid loss of books and papers that may be inadvertently mislaid, as well as misunderstandings that may arise regarding their return."

Years later, Gosnell said that when he became librarian he explored the halls and back rooms of the Legislature, searching through stacks of documents here and piles of books and reports there. He had to clean up the mess that resulted from years of neglect. Newspapers and books had been tossed into an outside passage, he said, where they piled up for years.

"One of my first jobs was to clean up this litter with a pitchfork and a wheelbarrow. It had grown hard, almost solid, from years of being trodden on; and what do you suppose I found at the bottom?" It was the original journals of the Vancouver Island legislature, written by Dr. John Sebastian Helmcken, the Speaker, as well as other official documents that had been lost for twenty years. "How they got under that heap of rubbish will always remain a mystery. They were, however, in excellent condition and are now in the archives, safe and sound."

Gosnell said the library had bound files of many of British Columbia's early newspapers, including the *British Colonist* from Victoria, the New Westminster *Columbian*, and the Vancouver *News-Advertiser*. "The room in which

Adrian Raeside

this flotsam and jetsam of official and other records rested, afterwards handed over to the library and archives, was a sight to behold. There was no arrangement of anything. When the shelves had been filled, everything was thrown on the floor," he said.

Gosnell donated to the library much of his personal collection of books and pamphlets, including the first two files of the *Cariboo Sentinel*, published in Barkerville in the 1860s. He also bought books from Victoria bookstores, including a collection about British Columbia and the West that T.N. Hibben and Co. had been unable to sell. Gosnell said he was able to set his own price for the books, although he did not say what that price was.

One of his prized acquisitions was the private library of Amor De Cosmos, the second premier and the founder of the *British Colonist* newspaper. De Cosmos, who died in 1897, had many books and pamphlets on Western Canada. When this collection was sold at auction by Joshua Davies, Gosnell snapped it up for $92 and made it part of the provincial collection. Gosnell later thanked Archer Martin, an avid collector who attended the auction but did not bid after learning that Gosnell was there on behalf of the Provincial Library.

Gosnell placed advertisements in newspapers in his quest to obtain old letters, newspapers, photographs, maps — anything, in fact, which could be part of B.C.'s documentary heritage. He obtained the records of colonial governors from Cary Castle, the residence of the lieutenant-governor, eighteen months before it burned to the ground in May 1899. The papers eventually went to the B.C. Archives.

Gosnell blamed a lack of space for his inability to organize the books properly, blamed the lack of organization for the dust on the books, and blamed the dust for the

deterioration of the books. Part of the problem was solved in 1897 when the library moved to larger quarters — two rooms in the new Legislative Buildings. Cataloguing began using file cards and the Dewey classification system, devised a few years earlier by Melvil Dewey. The cards were a vast improvement over catalogues in book form, because, as Gosnell said, they were neat, convenient and "capable of extension indefinitely." Under Dewey, the books were catalogued in two and, where necessary, three ways, according to author, subject and title.

Gosnell was not doing the tedious card indexing; he spent much of his time in his role as the provincial statistician, compiling and publishing his first *Year Book of British Columbia*. He printed 5,000 copies of the book and gave the profit to the library. The job of cataloguing the thousands of books in the Provincial Library was handed to Alma Russell, a Victoria native who had been trained at the Pratt Institute of Library Science in New York.

Russell was hired in August 1897, soon after she returned to Victoria, and went to work recording everything in the library. It was laborious work. Not only did Russell have to write every card by hand, she did not have catalogues from other libraries to guide her work. She had to devise subject headings and classifications as she went along.

"This was sometimes a difficult task, and one on which I should have been glad, very often, to have had the advice of some other librarian with more experience," she said later. Making matters worse, the library was overflowing with books so sorting was difficult. Russell did not have book carts, filing cases or even a typewriter when she tackled her assignment.

Gosnell vowed that the library would contain "not merely books, but those volumes which best anticipate the wants of those seeking information in various lines of study or research." He said knowledge had become so subdivided it was difficult to decide on the best works of reference. "It is questionable if the pabulum afforded by the majority of public libraries is really in the interest of the public, tending as it does, from the very multitude of books, to destroy the appreciation of literature as a whole."

Russell had an idea that would revolutionize library service. She suggested to Gosnell that the Provincial Library start a system of travelling libraries, similar to ones in Wisconsin, New York, Ohio and other states. At first Gosnell was hesitant, worrying that the government would not approve the work because of the expense involved, but soon became an enthusiastic supporter.

The travelling system involved, Gosnell said in a report to the assembly, "sending out boxes of books of special interest to agricultural communities and to mining camps, and to villages or other points where reading rooms have not been established." After books had been read in one community, they would be exchanged with books that had been sent to another.

"Where there are many isolated communities and not much literature in vogue, these libraries will be greatly appreciated," he said. "In the case of farmers it will enable them to have access to books of special value to them which they otherwise would not obtain, and in many cases could not afford to buy."

In an interview with Victoria's *Daily Colonist* in April 1898, Gosnell said travelling libraries would spread the library's benefits throughout the province. "The system is peculiarly applicable to British Columbia, where there are many remote settlements and mining camps to which the advantages of special literature suitable to their requirements will be very welcome and ought to be exceedingly useful as well," he said. The *Colonist* urged readers to donate books to complement the surplus books from the Provincial Library that would form the basis of the travelling boxes.

Russell went to work. She and Gosnell ordered hundreds of books, creating a special travelling libraries collection that was separate from the rest of the Provincial Library. Russell assembled sets of 100 books, and shipped them, along with book lists and cards for borrowers, around the province, with the first ones going to Duncan and Delta on June 24, 1898. The boxes were small but carried a wide variety, including John Bunyan's *The Pilgrim's Progress*, a book of Edgar Allan Poe's poetry, Margaret McNaughton's *Overland to the Cariboo*, and Gosnell's own *Year Book of British Columbia*. "The industrial needs were always taken into consideration, mining books being sent to mining localities, and agricultural to those in the farming and fruit belts," Russell said later.

The boxes were due back in the fall, but Gosnell was

Alma Russell, the first trained librarian in British Columbia, was hired at the Provincial Library in 1897 and retired in 1933. *Image I-67731 courtesy of Royal BC Museum, BC Archives*

Alma Russell was born in Douglastown, New Brunswick, raised in Victoria and educated in New York, but spent most of her life in the stacks in the Provincial Library in Victoria. She specialized in historical research, lecturing and cataloguing. She created and established a system of cataloguing in the archives that won praise from international authorities, including Sir Henry Miers, who surveyed museums throughout the British Empire. She also served as president of the British Columbia Library Association and the British Columbia Historical Association. She pushed herself too hard at times; twice she took extended leaves of absence to restore her health. Russell retired in 1933 and died in Victoria 30 years later. She is remembered with the Alma Russell Islands in Barkley Sound.

not around to see them return. In August the government changed, with Charles Augustus Semlin taking over from John Herbert Turner, who had been premier for three years. Semlin dismissed Gosnell, who blamed the firing on a suspicion that he had been involved in political activity. He denied the charge. "I was summarily chucked out of office," Gosnell said in 1925. He added that the circumstances had been long forgotten by everyone, except the "victim of the tragedy."

Gosnell had been effective. In less than five years he had established the Provincial Library, laid the groundwork for the provincial archives, started travelling libraries, and published an important reference book. He had also hired Ethelbert Olaf Stuart Scholefield, who became his successor. Scholefield was named acting librarian in September 1898 and received the permanent appointment the following year, even though he had no training in librarianship and was barely out of his teens.

Like Gosnell, Scholefield expanded the collection as much as possible and soon the library was pushing the limits of its 1897 space. Within four years the library had 1,250 bound files of newspapers, including copies of all those published in British Columbia. They were consulted regularly when the house was in session, but a lack of space meant they were scattered throughout several rooms, which delayed access. The library's classification system was also in danger of collapsing because it was difficult to keep the collection organized.

In his report for 1901, Scholefield said nearly 6,000 cards had been prepared for the library catalogue. The library had 15,000 books in its collection, so a lot of work was yet to be done. Still, the cards made it easier for members of the public, who were allowed to use the reading room when the Legislative Assembly was not in session.

The travelling library system was growing. Within a year of the first boxes being shipped, seventeen were in circulation. In 1899, books went to Abbotsford, Armstrong, Central Park, Chilliwack, Cobble Hill, Cumberland, East Kensington, Ganges Harbour, Hazelmere, Ladner, Langley, Saanichton, Shoal Bay, Sidney, Tynehead, Upper Sumas, and Whitewater. The Provincial Library received applications from many other communities.

In 1902, there were thirty-five travelling libraries, and each one held at least 100 volumes divided into a variety of classes: Ethics, social science, natural science, useful arts, literature, description and travel, fiction, juvenile literature, biography, history and reference. Each shipment had a list of the included books, and all books were marked so their ownership would not be in doubt.

Applications for travelling libraries were only considered from communities that were not part of an incorporated city, and they had to be signed by at least twenty-five people aged twenty-one or older. Applicants paid transportation charges, provided a space for the books, and appointed a custodian. They had to send $6 to cover the cost of the case

Stumped the librarian

E.O.S. Scholefield, the provincial librarian, usually preserves his savoir faire. But he was nearly knocked all of a heap a couple of days ago by a lady tourist from the other side. The following colloquy took place:

"Please, sire, is this the parliament buildings?"

"Yes madam, the legislative chamber — "

"Oh my! I'm so glad! And please show me which is the House of Commons and which is the House of Lords. I've come all the way from Portland to see where the lords sit."

Mr. Scholefield was hard put to it. Finally he explained that there wasn't a real live lord nearer than Saanich..

Victoria Daily Times, July 24, 1906

and the crate, and agree that they would not lend books to anyone younger than fifteen, or lend more than one book to a person at a time. Every borrower had to promise in writing to cover the cost of damage or fines.

Scholefield said libraries were sent to localities "widely divergent in interests and tastes," some primarily made up of farmers and others of miners. "It is not an easy task to prepare libraries that may be acceptable to each and all," he said. That said, he vowed that the libraries would be as suitable as possible.

In time, the staff gained a better sense of what worked, as Scholefield told a reporter from Victoria's *Daily Colonist* in 1903. "It had been somewhat difficult to know what would suit the tastes of the widely diversified classes to whom libraries were sent. In some cases where it was thought that something light and amusing would be required, it turned out that the community had felt quite affronted, and demanded intellectual pabulum of much more solid and substantial kind; a demand cheerfully and promptly granted. In other cases fiction was in request."

The books were sent to lighthouses, Women's Institutes, literary societies and community reading rooms. For several years, the boxes were shipped for free on Canadian Pacific lines, which eased the burden on the patrons. Every time the libraries were returned to Victoria, Russell checked the books, repaired them if needed, and sent them out again. She said later that only two communities lost their borrowing privileges. The books sent there had been damaged intentionally, she said, by people who had wanted to "get even with the government" in some way.

In May 1906, the *Daily Colonist* reported that fifty-six communities "from Cape Scott to Cranbrook" were involved, and two years later there were sixty-five travelling libraries.

The Provincial Library had 35,000 volumes, an increase of 20,000 in seven years, with another 2,500 books and 1,000 pamphlets being added each year. It was continuing to acquire everything it could on the early history of British Columbia and the Pacific Northwest, and gathered materials produced by governments in British Columbia and elsewhere. The *Daily Colonist* also said the Provincial Library compared favourably with other libraries in Canada, and was growing into "an institution of special usefulness of which the province may be justly proud."

Scholefield asked Sir Henry Maunde Thompson, librarian of the British Museum library in London, for a copy of the museum's catalogue of printed books. Sir Henry replied with a brief history of the catalogue and a promise to send a copy. When it arrived, as the *Colonist* reported, "it took a dray to fetch it the Provincial Library." The cart had to carry fifty fat quarto volumes, packed in a heavy case, which scientifically classified the titles of books on every conceivable phase of human thought and activity.

In 1908 Scholefield acquired two books he had been seeking for a decade. One was *Relacion del viage hecho por las goletas Sutil y Mexicana en el año de 1792 para reconocer el estrecho de Fuca*, published in Madrid in 1802, which told the story of Spanish exploration in the Pacific Northwest.

R. Edward Gosnell died in 1931 in Vancouver. Legend has it that Gosnell Station, a railway point on the Canadian National line close to the junction of the Albreda and North Thompson Rivers, was named after him. The community was settled when the Canadian Northern Pacific Railway was built in 1913. A Japanese-Canadian internment camp was there in the Second World War, followed by a Gosnell post office from 1960 to 1964.

The other was *Voyages from Asia to America, for completing the discoveries of the north west coast of America. To which is prefixed, a summary of the voyages made by the Russians on the frozen sea, in search of the north east passage*, published in 1761. Today, these books are in the B.C. Archives.

In the decade after he was fired from the librarian's job, Gosnell worked in a variety of jobs, including a stint as editor of the *Daily Colonist*. In 1908 the government rehired him, and asked him to set up the provincial archives. His budget was specifically for an exhibition that would celebrate the centennial of Simon Fraser's 1808 trip through British Columbia, but that did not deter Gosnell. He travelled to Seattle and to the Interior to collect historical documents, and set up a plan to organize the archives in the basement of the Legislative Buildings. He arranged for documents in London, England, to be copied, and he wrote historical articles to bring publicity to the archives.

The Simon Fraser exhibition proved popular, entertaining crowds in Vancouver and Victoria as well as in New Westminster. In 1909, however, the government eliminated the archives budget and Gosnell's work was suspended. When money was found for the archives in 1910, Gosnell was fired — and once again, Scholefield was his replacement. Effective July 1, 1910, Scholefield became archivist as well as librarian. The archival collection was already housed in the library, and included books and pamphlets, maps, charts, engravings, portraits and manuscripts relating to the early history and development of British North America.

Scholefield searched for books and other documents in antiquarian shops in Europe and the eastern United States, and collected documents from individuals, businesses and organizations throughout the province and around the world. In 1913 he obtained papers from Russian sources, along with the log of the ship *Ruby*, which sailed from Bristol in 1794 and engaged in the fur trade with the Queen Charlotte Islands. That year he added about 4,000 manuscripts, maps, charts, photographs, medals and other items of interest to the collection.

Alma Russell continued her work to catalogue everything in the library and archives collections. In 1908 she started another project that has given lasting benefits to the province. "As so many questions were asked by the members during debates which required exhaustive and frantic searches through files of newspapers, I decided to make an index, on cards, of the local papers, of such matters as I thought might be called for during the sessions," she said. After being stopped because of a staff shortage, the work was resumed in 1915, and continued until the arrival of computerized databases more than three-quarters of a century later. Russell's finding aid has grown into a massive newspaper index that is a valuable record of British Columbia's history.

Space was once again a problem. The library had one room devoted to books and another to newspapers, but much of its material was in storage elsewhere in the building, and effectively inaccessible. But relief was coming; a new building was going up on the south side of the Legislature Building. The Duke of Connaught, the Governor-General of Canada, had laid the cornerstone on September 28, 1912.

The Provincial Library and Archives moved to their new home, named the Connaught Building, in June 1915. The old library space became the Speaker's office. The *Victoria*

Daily Times noted that the new library building did not quite match the rest of the Legislature, but still offered praise. "The rotunda runs up through two storeys and is domed, with gallery openings on the second floor. It is octagonal in form, with columns in pairs at each side of the four openings, and the walls pencilled in marble. The veining of the marble is symmetrical in all four walls."

On one side of the rotunda was the reading room, and on the other, the reference room. Both were finished in mahogany and had high ceilings. The three-storey building had six levels of stacks, and the archives had a large room on the second floor, above the reference room.

Provincial library on the south side of the legislature, shown here in the 1920s, was named after the Duke of Connaught. Harold Fleming photo. *Image A-02828 courtesy of Royal BC Museum, BC Archives*

The *New York Nation* newspaper marvelled at the "large and rich collection of historical materials" at the Provincial Library. Scholefield had, the newspaper said, "unbounded enthusiasm, coupled with a fine sense of discrimination." The materials in Victoria were so important, the *Nation* said, "no one who is studying the history of the Pacific Northwest, exploratory or otherwise, can afford to pass them by."

The move to the new building meant thousands of books could come out of storage — and that Arthur Herbert Killam, an experienced librarian from Nova Scotia who had been hired in April 1912 to run the travelling libraries, could expand the service. Killam drew from about 12,000 books kept in the basement of the Provincial Library as he prepared boxes of fifty books each to send to individuals or societies.

Half the books sent out were fiction. "A good story is the best relief from the monotony and drudgery that are inseparable from life in new places," Maria Lawson wrote in the *Daily Colonist*. "Of the rest, ten books are for children and the remainder form a miscellaneous collection suited to the needs of serious readers."

By 1915 about 175 communities were receiving travelling libraries, and Lawson said Killam's resources were almost exhausted. Recipients included mines and other industrial establishments such as the pulp mill at Powell River, which had its own collection of books and magazines but supplemented it with books from Killam.

Lawson said no one shut away from the world need worry that books could not be delivered. They were being sent to locations that could not count as communities, and that did not have twenty-five readers — locations such as lighthouse stations. The station on Triangle Island had sent a request by wireless, so a box of books was quickly prepared and delivered to the *Estevan*, a boat on the coastal service, before her last trip of the season.

The arrival of travelling libraries was big news in small towns. "The new provincial library arrived this week, and is now on the shelves at the drug store," Quesnel's *Cariboo Observer* reported on July 7, 1917. But there was a catch. As the library's custodian, C.H. Allison, said, the library had just $10.65, but needed $20.15 to cover its bills. The Quesnel

The reading room in the Provincial Archives as it appeared in 1949. *Image A-09542 courtesy of Royal BC Museum, BC Archivess*

library had to place a deposit on the library, and had to pay for freight both ways and for incidentals such as glue. As a result, every user would have to pay an additional 50 cents.

At times, borrowers wanted books that were not in Killam's stock, but were upstairs, on the main shelves of the Provincial Library. The 1894 legislation that created the library specified that those books had to stay in the library, so the Legislature amended the act so selected items could be shipped out if the Legislative Assembly did not need them. That increased Killam's stock by about 20,000 books.

The library also served readers in Victoria. In 1917, Finance Minister John Hart announced that it would be open on Monday and Wednesday evenings and Saturday afternoons. "Business and professional men would be able to leave their offices at five o'clock to avail themselves of that learning which was the secret of the ultimate success of the modern industrial world, where thoroughness and efficiency were established as standards," the *Times* reported.

While service was being expanded on several fronts, Scholefield planned for the future as well. Soon after the end of the First World War, he asked members of the Great War Next-of-Kin Association to donate letters from the men of the Canadian Expeditionary Force to the archives. He wanted the letters, and permission to copy them, so the next generation could see the spirit of the fighting men during the "greatest epic of suffering since the dawn of history." These men, he said, had provided "a mass of heart-touching and spirit-raising literature which would live through the ages." Scholefield said the letters would be in fireproof facilities, and if families wished, the letters would remain private.

Scholefield died on Christmas Day 1919 at the age of forty-four. John Forsyth succeeded him as the provincial librarian and archivist. Forsyth said in his 1920 report that the Provincial Library had more than 100,000 volumes, received copies of all newspapers published in the province, and had started to index the local dailies. He said that reading tastes had changed since the end of the war, with less interest in literature, history, biography and travel, so there was a need to build up strong technical sections in libraries.

After several busy years, growth of the archives slowed in the 1920s because of a lack of funds. The institution was unable to buy new materials — although donations were still being accepted — and it stopped copying documents at Hudson Bay House and the Record Office in London as well as the Dominion Archives in Ottawa.

The archives received the early manuscript records of the lands department. Some of the pre-Confederation gems acquired in the early 1920s were 1848 correspondence between the Hudson's Bay Company and the Secretary

of State regarding the colonization of Vancouver Island, addresses in the House of Commons dating from 1848 and 1849, and original letters of Sir James Douglas and others.

Sir Leicester Harmsworth, a British businessman and politician, donated early materials such as the notice of the appointment of Richard Blanshard as the first governor of Vancouver Island and the original passenger lists of ships such as the *Harpooner* in 1849, the *Cowlitz* in 1850, the *Norman Morison* in 1850 and the *Tory* in 1851.

John Forsyth, who succeeded E.O.S. Scholefield as provincial librarian and archivist in 1920, came to Victoria from Glasgow in 1913, and worked for the government for a decade. He resigned in 1926 to open an antiquarian bookstore in Victoria. He moved the business to Parksville in 1948, and died in Nanaimo in 1954.

Forsyth retired in 1926, after six years. He was succeeded by John Hosie, who served as librarian and archivist for eight years and was also a member of the Public Library Commission. In 1930 Hosie said that the collection in the archives, which had been acquired "for a song," was worth about $500,000. It would take two and a half years, he said, to catalogue everything.

In 1934, William Kaye Lamb was placed in charge of the library and archives. When he resigned in 1940 to become the head librarian at the University of British Columbia, the two jobs were split. Charles Keith Morison became the librarian and superintendent of the Public Library Commission, and Willard Ireland became the archivist until he entered the military.

In 1946, after Ireland returned, he was given responsibility for both the Provincial Library and the Provincial Archives, allowing Morison to devote his time to the expansion of the public library system. Ireland retired in 1974, the same year that the Provincial Library became known as the Legislative Library.

By then the archives had been moved to the provincial museum precinct, so the government replaced Ireland with two people — J.G. Mitchell as the legislative librarian and Allan Turner as the provincial archivist. The roles have remained apart ever since.

4

ANDREW CARNEGIE'S
THREE GIFTS

Andrew Carnegie never visited British Columbia, but he had a great influence on its public libraries. By providing money for library buildings in Vancouver, New Westminster and Victoria, he established the importance of libraries in a province that was still quite young.

In all three cities, Carnegie helped move libraries from crowded, second-floor spaces to buildings erected specifically to serve their patrons. The libraries built with Carnegie's money served for more than half a century. Two of the buildings are still standing, and one of them is again providing library service as home to the Carnegie Centre, a beacon of hope in Vancouver's Downtown Eastside.

Opposite: Vancouver's Carnegie Library under construction in 1902. *City of Vancouver Archives, CVA 1376-27*

Above: Two field guns from the South African (Boer) War were placed in front of the New Westminster Public Library soon after it opened in 1905. *Philip Timms, Vancouver Public Library, VPL 3473*

Carnegie was born in Dunfermline, Scotland, on November 25, 1835, the first son of William Carnegie, a linen weaver, and his wife Margaret, a daughter of shoemaker Thomas Morrison. Both William Carnegie and Thomas Morrison were active in the push for political and social reform. In 1848, William and Margaret Carnegie moved to Allegheny, Pennsylvania. The next year, when Andrew was thirteen, he began working as a bobbin boy in a cotton factory and later as a Western Union messenger boy and a telegraph operator. When he moved to Pittsburgh he began borrowing a book from a free library every Saturday, and said later that the experience inspired his love of libraries.

Andrew Carnegie in the early 1900s. *Dave Obee collection*

Carnegie rose to become superintendent of the Western Division of the Pennsylvania Railroad and invested in a company that manufactured railway sleeping cars and built bridges, locomotives and rails. In 1865, he established the Keystone Bridge Company, and in 1873, a steel factory. The steel business prospered, and when Carnegie sold it to John Pierpoint Morgan in 1901, the Carnegie Corporation was valued at more than $400 million.

After the sale he devoted his life to giving away his fortune, in keeping with a theory he expressed in his 1889 book *The Gospel of Wealth*. Carnegie said the rich were merely "trustees" of wealth, and had a moral obligation to distribute that wealth to promote the welfare and happiness of the common man. As his book said, "the man who dies thus rich dies disgraced." Carnegie created several endowed trusts or institutions bearing his name. He provided organs to churches, helped establish colleges, schools and non-profit organizations and associations, and provided money for library buildings.

Andrew Carnegie died in 1919. In 1935, to mark the 100th anniversary of his birth, November 24–30 was declared Andrew Carnegie Week in much of the English-speaking world. It was estimated that more than 50 million people were using Carnegie libraries at that time.

His first public library gift, in 1881, was to his native Dunfermline. In the years that followed, he gave library gifts to 2,508 other communities in the English-speaking world, including 125 in Canada. In British Columbia, three offers from Carnegie were accepted in 1901 and 1902. His money was to be spent on buildings, not library collections, and Carnegie would not provide funds unless the recipient municipality agreed to provide an annual amount equal to ten per cent of his donation to cover salaries, maintenance and book purchases.

Some municipalities balked at that requirement and rejected his offers. In some cases, his money was turned down because of his reputation as a tough businessman. Many labour leaders condemned Carnegie because of his role in the Homestead strike in Pennsylvania in 1892, which escalated into a battle between strikers and private security agents.

James Bertram, Carnegie's chief aide, administered the library program, issued guidelines for buildings, and even influenced their designs. Many Carnegie buildings had a

There is not such a cradle of democracy upon the earth as the Free Public Library, this republic of letters, where neither rank nor office, nor weight receives the slightest consideration.
Andrew Carnegie, philanthropist

A crowd gathers for the cornerstone ceremony at the new Vancouver library in March 1902. *W.M. Bruce photo, Vancouver Public Library, VPL 3422*

standardized style, were made of stone or bricks, and had low-pitched, hipped roofs. Carnegie libraries were built as temples of knowledge, and usually became focal points in their communities. Their influence on library architecture lasted until the 1950s, when more utilitarian designs became popular.

By the time he died in 1919, about $350 million of Carnegie's fortune had been given away. Through trusts and institutions, his legacy continues to provide benefits — almost a century after his death.

Vancouver

Vancouver was the first B.C. community to approach Carnegie for money to erect a library building. Urged by lawyer Alfred Allayne Jones, city council sent a request in February 1901 for money to erect a library building. The answer came quickly. "If the city of Vancouver will furnish a suitable site and agree to spend $5,000 a year to maintain a library, I shall be glad to give $50,000 towards the erection of a building," Carnegie said in a letter on March 6. By March 25, council accepted the offer.

That prompted wrangling about a location. An early

contender was the corner of Pender and Hamilton, adjacent to Victory Square, but aldermen from the east end argued against a site that far west. Another suggestion was the city hall site on Westminster, now Main, just south of a market on Hastings. There was talk of a library replacing a tennis court at the northwest corner of Georgia and Granville, even farther west than Victory Square. Then another contender appeared: The southwest corner of Hastings and Westminster, the site of the market on the north side of city hall.

In August the matter went to a plebiscite, with voters asked to pick between Pender and Hastings. The location on the east side, Hastings, won even though the library had more borrowers from the west end. More people from the east end voted, and that is what mattered.

Architect George William Grant, who had been responsible for the New Westminster library a decade earlier, came up with plans for the new library. Prisoners working on a chain gang dug the foundation with Eliza Machin, the wife of librarian James Edwin Machin, providing them with cocoa and buns. In those years, the Masonic Lodge held official ceremonies to mark the start of new public buildings, and the library certainly qualified. Its cornerstone was laid under Masonic auspices on March 19, 1902.

The foundation and base were of granite from Indian Arm, opposite Croker Island, and the remainder of the building was of Gabriola Island sandstone. The library had a beautiful fireplace of Carrara marble, imported from Italy. Legend has it that the fireplace was supposed to have gone into the Legislature Buildings in Victoria, but did not fit the plans so it went to the library instead.

Grant's plans were not always followed; brick partitions were installed where the plans called for glass ones, for example; the brick would make it impossible to watch patrons. The design caused problems for years. Machin's daughter Elsie Beeman said later that her father had not been consulted, so Vancouver got a building that was "a fine plan on paper, but a most inconvenient one from a working standpoint." Much money was spent on alterations to make the library more practical.

The building had been designed with expansion in mind, and the library did not need the top floor yet. Council allowed the Vancouver Art, Historical and Scientific Society to open a museum there. The library's reading room, just inside the main door, was opened on October 26, 1903, with newspapers and periodicals ready for the patrons. The lending library had about 10,000 volumes; 4,000 fiction books were the first made available.

The circulation desk in Vancouver's Carnegie library building in 1920. *Vancouver Public Library, Special Collections, VPL 10440*

Carnegie library, shown here in 1904, was built on the north side of Vancouver's city hall. *Philip Timms photo, Vancouver Public Library, VPL 3433*

From the start, staff members had to deal with people sleeping in the building. The board recommended that the library be developed as a social meeting place to help those who were lonely or unemployed. It also approved the playing of chess and checkers, activities that had been banned in the old library.

In 1905, the library board approved expenditures of $7,000, including $2,000 for books. Among other things, the members agreed to get rid of the drinking water tank and install a pipe from the water main instead.

Victoria

Victoria was the second city to ask Carnegie for money. His offer of $50,000 was received in March 1902, but it took three months for council to say yes. The problem was that the book budget had to be approved by voters. As Mayor

Charles Hayward noted, the Carnegie deal would require $5,000 a year for books and maintenance, but the city could spend no more than $1,600 a year. In June, the $5,000 annual expenditure was approved in a plebiscite, but a bylaw to provide $15,000 for the purchase of a site was turned down. That meant the library would have to be built on land already owned by the city.

The choices were narrowed down to lots on the northwestern end of the Inner Harbour causeway, where Government and Wharf streets meet; at Yates and Blanshard streets; and at Pandora and Chambers, which had been purchased for use as a water reservoir. The city had land in the James Bay district, including a former gravel pit close to Beacon Hill Park, but it was too far from downtown.

The cost of developing the Yates site was estimated at $700 more than the Government site. Stephen Jones, the

Victoria's Carnegie Library, shown here in about 1913, has been a landmark on Yates Street for more than a century. Image D-04000 courtesy of Royal BC Museum, BC Archives

proprietor of the Dominion Hotel on the south side of Yates at Blanshard, offered to cover the difference so the library would be built across from his hotel.

His strategy worked. In April 1903, voters chose the Yates site, which had previously been home to a brewery, a grocery store and a second-hand store. The *Colonist*, which had lobbied for the Government Street location, said after the vote that the exact location was not as important as the fact that a library would be built. "There is a very strong desire on the part of the people to see the last of the grimy hole which at present is the only temple of polite literature available to the general public in Victoria," it said, referring to the library on the second floor of city hall.

Architects Thomas Hooper and Charles Elwood Watkins designed the building. The plans called for the building to use sandstone from Saturna Island. In April 1904, after a

delay because the foundations had to be dug deeper than planned, the cornerstone was laid by William W. Northcott, the city building inspector, in the presence of contractor George Snider and some friends.

While the building was going up, council chose a new librarian, Dr. J. Griffith Hands. He had no experience running a library, but he beat 45 other applicants. The *Colonist* noted that Hands was "considered in every sense an excellent man for the place, being splendidly recommended." Hands was prominent in Victoria's Dickens club, an organization inspired by the work of Charles Dickens. A native of Gloucestershire, England, Hands worked as a teacher in England before moving to Collingwood, Ontario, where he was a teacher and journalist. He arrived in British Columbia in 1870 and taught school for a several years before going to Detroit to be trained as a medical doctor.

Hands went to work in the old library at city hall while construction continued. There was a delay while council members debated whether to use steel or wooden stacks; in the end, they went with wood. By the time the building was finished, the library was behind schedule and over its budget, thanks to the shelving and the foundations.

Council named Alderman Thornton Fell, Canon Arthur Beanlands and provincial librarian Ethelbert Olaf Stuart Scholefield to the library board, and they tackled the next problem. "For years the city of Victoria maintained what purported to be a free public library, but today, when we examine the stock of books in that institution, we find that fully fifty per cent of the volumes are completely worn out and only fit for the rubbish heap," Scholefield wrote.

The new library could hold 15,000 books, but the old one had only 5,000, including the ones Scholefield wanted to discard. He called for donations to stock the shelves, and delayed the opening of the library until new books could be obtained. "The citizens must possess their souls in patience for a little longer. We have got the building and we shall gradually get the books to put in it," Scholefield said.

The reading rooms — one for men, another for women — were finally opened on December 4, 1905, four months after the old library closed. Between fifty and seventy-five people registered as borrowers on the first day. Some patrons were angry about new restrictions, but were told that the rules were needed because at least 300 books had gone missing from the old library. The library board vowed, somewhat optimistically, that no books would be taken from the new building without being duly noted by the librarian.

At first, the library used only the ground floor of the new building. In the first few months the upper floor was the site of flower shows. In 1910 the reading room was moved upstairs and a room devoted to chess and checkers was opened. The games were removed in 1923 to make more room for books.

New Westminster

New Westminster asked for Carnegie money in early 1902, and Mayor William Holland Keary received an offer of $15,000 with the standard condition: The city would need to provide $1,500 in annual support. Council members agreed to the deal on April 21, 1902.

The grant to New Westminster was much smaller than the ones given to Vancouver and Victoria, but the population of New Westminster was much smaller. With 6,499 residents, it was similar in size to Nanaimo, Nelson and Rossland.

The site chosen for the library was the block bounded by McKenzie, Carnarvon, Lorne and Agnes streets, where city hall had stood before the great fire. On August 25, 1902, the contract was awarded to former mayor Henry Hoy. Alderman W.E. Vanstone said it was a good deal because the grant would cover the cost of excavation, architect fees, the building itself, fixtures, heating and lighting.

A chain gang from the penitentiary prepared the site. By early September, Hoy reported good progress, with arrangements made for all materials that would be needed. The walls went up before the cornerstone was in place; Hoy had to leave a corner open to allow members of the Masonic Lodge to complete their ceremony on October 1. The cornerstone included a time capsule with a handwritten history of the library as well as coins inside a copper box.

The library contract turned into a potential disaster for Hoy, because strikes delayed the completion of the building. He lost about $1,500, although Carnegie reimbursed him. Carnegie also provided an additional $1,000 to the city to furnish the library.

New Westminster had a wonderful new building but only about 2,000 books, so the library did not open. Then members of council and the library board started squabbling; in 1904 the trustees hired someone to rearrange and renumber the books, but council deemed the work an extravagance and ordered it stopped. Two of the five commissioners resigned in protest, so council appointed two new ones, including Agnes Hill, the first woman to serve as a library trustee in British Columbia.

Members of the Masonic Lodge laid the cornerstone for the New Westminster Carnegie library in October 1902. *New Westminster Public Library photo 2979*

In January 1905, council disbanded the commission and assumed direct control of the library. Susan Gilley, the widow of local builder George Gilley, was hired as librarian, starting work on March 1 and opening the library three days later, on March 4.

"The front entrance admits the public to a spacious and comfortable hall, floored with mosaic linoleum, and the first impression is one of lights and cleanliness," the *Columbian* newspaper reported. "Behind the glass wickets the neat tiers of books on their steel stacks all aid in producing the effect of comfort and order." The library had a general reading room as well as a sitting room and a smoking room, and offered, the newspaper said, "unlimited inducements for a quiet half-hour's leisure time." The reading room was open twelve hours a day on weekdays and six hours on Sundays.

Light came from a glass cupola. There was another benefit at night. "The electric lights give an illumination in that part of the city that does a great deal towards improving the location in which the Carnegie library is situated," the *Columbian* said.

In the first few years, council did not try to meet its commitment to spend $1,500 a year. Not until 1910 did council again appoint a committee to run the library, and allocate the amount of money required by the deal with Carnegie.

Nelson

In 1906, Carnegie offered between $7,000 and $20,000 to the West Kootenay city of Nelson, with his usual ten per cent requirement. His offer was made after a request from the local Women's Council, and was presented to council by John Laing Stocks, the manager of a local mine.

Stocks said $7,000 would be enough to buy the Hall block in downtown Nelson and convert it for use as a library. Any amount up to $20,000 should be considered, he said. At the time, Nelson's population was almost the same as that of New Westminster, which had been given $15,000.

Nelson council balked at the thought of a minimum of $700 a year on books and maintenance. Some council members noted that while the city's existing library cost about $80 a month to run — $960 a year — it would not be fair to bind future councils to a set amount. Then the *Daily News* mounted a campaign against Carnegie, challenging the way he had made his money. "The *Daily News* is absolutely and unqualifiedly opposed to the city's acceptance of any financial assistance from Andrew Carnegie for any public purpose on any conditions whatever," the newspaper said in an editorial.

"Objection is taken on the grounds that the establishment of any public institution here to be known by the name of 'Carnegie' is calculated to create entirely false ideals in the minds of all classes of the community, but more particularly in the minds of the young. In addition, because of Mr. Carnegie's well-known avowed enmity to, and contempt for Canada and Canadian institutions, it is most undesirable that Nelson should be inflicted with a monument to the false and vicious economic principles crystalized in the life work of Andrew Carnegie." The newspaper did not expand on its claim that Carnegie, who provided money for more than 100 libraries in Canada, had contempt for this country.

Rev. E.H. Shanks defended Carnegie. "Either you were grossly misinformed or were guilty of having an axe to grind. Certainly your sentiments are not to the best interests of your constituents," Shanks said in a letter to the *Daily News*. The newspaper fought back, saying that Shanks had a "want of observation of current affairs," and restating the belief that the offer should be "unhesitatingly condemned." Stocks, in turn, accused the *Daily News* of making an "unprovoked and uncalled-for" attack, but the editors would not be swayed.

Council members, worried about the financial obligation, let the Carnegie offer die. A month after the offer was made, council awarded the library a $600 grant, up from the $450 given the previous year but still short of the $960 it cost each year to keep the library open. The library charged borrowers an annual fee, although reading in the premises was free to everyone. Before approving the grant, one of the aldermen suggested that the library be closed for a month to gauge interest.

The three Carnegie libraries saw many changes as the years went by. One of the most important ones came in 1911 and 1912, when all three hired librarians with experience, training, or both. That brought a notable shift in attitude at the same time that the B.C. Library Association was being formed. Almost overnight, libraries starting reflecting professional ideals.

In Vancouver, librarian James Edwin Machin fell from a streetcar in October 1909, suffering head and shoulder injuries. He resigned the following January, saying he could not continue. He was succeeded on a temporary basis by Alfred E. Goodman, a member of city council and the library board.

Bernard McEvoy, another board member, challenged Goodman's appointment, saying the librarian should be a specialist, just as the city engineer should be a specialist. McEvoy noted the existence of library training schools in the United States, and said the job should be advertised in Vancouver, Toronto and London, England. Other board members disagreed, so Goodman was appointed, with Machin's wife Eliza as his assistant. Goodman quit within a year, and in January 1911, Robert W. Douglas, an experienced librarian from Toronto, was hired in his place.

In New Westminster, Susan Gilley resigned in 1912, and Annie O'Meara, from London, Ontario, was hired as her replacement. O'Meara was the first librarian in New Westminster who had been trained in the field and had experience at another library. In Victoria, Dr. J. Griffiths Hands retired in 1912 and the library board promoted his assistant, Helen Gordon Stewart, to succeed him.

In 1908, Vancouver librarian James Edwin Machin reported with regret that most of the books being read were lightweight, while the classics, "with their tremendous human tragedies and lasting criticism of life," were left unread.

The libraries opened their shelves so patrons could browse for themselves, and brought in catalogues that made it easier to find books. It was a welcome change. Years later, Robert Connell, a local minister who was chairman of the library board — and later became the first leader of the Co-operative Commonwealth Federation in B.C. — reminisced in the *Victoria Daily Times* about what it had been like to get a book when Hands was in charge.

Patrons would walk to the counter, choose from a printed catalogue of 5,000 books, fill in a slip and pass it to Hands. If the book was on the shelves, the patron could take it. The librarian relied on a system of green and red tags to keep track of which volumes were available. "I filled in my slip one day with the name 'Charles Keene Layard' and gave it to the Doctor," said Connell. "In a few minutes he handed me my book, and without scrutinizing it I walked off. As soon as I went along the street I noticed that I had got the life of Charles Kean, the actor, instead of Charles Keene, the artist of *Punch*, so back I went. I explained the error to Dr. Hands, but he resolutely shook his head.

" 'A book taken out can under no circumstances be exchanged the same day,' was his reply ... and the mistake was his! But rule three said: 'Only one volume may be taken out on one card and only once a day.' "

The catalogue itself was a work of art. "Sport" was under "Travel," but "Sports and Games" came under "Education." Connell admitted that no catalogue could be perfect, and it was a challenge to establish order in Victoria's spacious new library. Then Helen Gordon Stewart arrived. "The new order was definitely established and the public library began to be what it is today, a source of pleasure, profit and pride to the citizens of Victoria," Connell said.

Much of the order was made possible by Melvil Dewey, who in 1876 had established a decimal system for classifying books so patrons could browse for themselves, rather than having to ask for titles. Machin opened the stacks in Vancouver in 1909, and the following year the Dewey system was introduced there. Vancouver's lead was followed in Victoria by Stewart and in New Westminster by O'Meara, who also introduced a card catalogue.

Another major change was the introduction of sections for children, with Vancouver opening its children's room in 1913. "Here the kiddies gather — half past three is the children's hour — especially on Friday, when there are no lessons to prepare, and on Saturday this place is thronged," the *Vancouver Sun* reported. The room featured well-illustrated books and child-sized tables and chairs. The section had stuffed birds native to the region, along with leaves and plants to help children learn about them.

"The children, with the curiosity that has made the world's progress, examine them. This childish trait, so valuable when rightly directed, is catered to in this room," the *Sun* said. "A globe is placed on the table and childish fingers trace where they have been or the countries they have heard discussed."

Victoria had added a department in 1907 with about seventy volumes for teenagers. There was also talk of a Canadiana department, with works of Canadian literature and history — but Victoria's children's room, opened on July 8, 1913, made the biggest difference.

Cases filled with books loved by boys and girls were supplemented by pictures around the walls with scenes from popular stories. "The children's librarian hears the needs of her readers and advises and suggests," Connell wrote later. "There are many homes where knowledge of books and especially books for the young is small, and the children's librarian has to be mother and father to the young minds as they turn towards the wonderland of books.

"The children's library goes beyond the immediate needs of the little ones in the room. Into the public schools of the city its books go and have gone for some time now as adjuncts to the ordinary work of the classroom. To implant in children a love of books with a sense of values is to give them the very crown of education, citizenship in the democracy of books."

While the Victoria library had a taxpayer-approved budget of $5,000 a year, it spent $7,000 in 1910, and by the end of 1911 had $1,600 in unpaid bills, including those for heat and light. Carnegie's $5,000 requirement was clearly not enough; salaries alone in 1911 were $4,100.

Victoria's taxpayers were told that the library would be in jeopardy unless they agreed to pay much more than $5,000 a year. Staff would need to be reduced, the library board said, the classification and reorganization resulting from the adoption of the Dewey system would be rendered useless, and there would be no money for alterations or improvements. Service might need to be sharply curtailed, and in the worst case, the library would have to be closed. If that happened, the building — valued at about $275,000 in 1911 — would be handed back to Carnegie.

Council went to the voters for the first time on May 22, 1911, asking that the library's annual grant be increased $10,000 from $5,000 immediately, with the potential of a $25,000 grant in the future. The proposal was endorsed by more than half of those who voted, but fell short of the sixty per cent required to pass. That prompted 1,100 people to sign a petition seeking another plebiscite, which was held on November 17. But half of the 1,100 library supporters stayed away from the polls; only 521 people voted in favour of the spending, while 554 voted against it. The proposal was defeated.

The flaw in the system — the need for voters to approve the book budget — was obvious. A resolution passed by the Union of B.C. Municipalities meeting in Victoria that year recommended that councils have the power to allocate library budgets.

At the time, board chairman E.O.S. Scholefield was the president of the Pacific Northwest Library Association and a member of the council of the American Library Association, yet his request for funding had been turned down twice in one year in his own city. The second failed vote prompted Scholefield and Alderman W.H. Langley to resign from the library board, leaving William Marchant as its only member. To make matters worse, Helen Gordon Stewart resigned as librarian.

She said the library had 3,000 active members and about 6,000 books, although the collection was in sorry shape. Of 200 books on natural science, 100 were so old they were useless. All the books on physics and chemistry were published before 1870. There was one prehistoric book on geometry, the *Colonist* said, in which "the triangles are threatening to become circles through sheer senile decay."

The crisis continued for weeks. In December Scholefield worried that Mayor Alfred J. Morley had not read his letter of resignation, so he wrote a second one. On January 11, 1912, the library went to a plebiscite for the third time in eight months, with voters asked to let council devote a portion of tax revenue to the library. The proposal was once again endorsed by a majority, but once again fell short of the sixty per cent required for approval.

The Legislature intervened with a bill enabling the city to set the library's budget without getting the approval of taxpayers. That ended the crisis and Stewart withdrew her resignation. One of her first moves was to have a telephone installed in the library, but she had much more in mind.

In 1913, Stewart started British Columbia's first systematic training course in librarianship. Applicants had to be high school graduates, although a university background was preferred. The courses lasted eleven months, with eight months in the Victoria library and three more in at least two other libraries, such as the ones in Seattle and Portland. Two hours a week were allowed for individual study, and the remaining time for the practical application of theories.

Students were paid $10 a month for the first three months, $20 a month for the second three months, and $30 a month for the remainder of their instruction. There was no guarantee of a job at the end of the course, although successful students would certainly be considered. "It will require hard work and self denial to fit oneself for the position of assistant librarian, but when that position is gained employment is sure," the *Colonist* said.

> In 1913 the Victoria library saw a sudden surge in book donations — all from France. Librarian Helen Gordon Stewart was baffled at first, but then Jeanne Berton, a French woman living in Victoria, explained that she had written to Yvonne Sarcey, a prominent French writer. In her letter she said that people in Victoria would welcome books from France, and Sarcey wrote about the request in the French periodical *Les Annales*.

The training had been designed to provide staff for the Victoria library, but it helped fill demand elsewhere. Several people who trained in Victoria went on to notable careers, including Madge Wolfenden at the Provincial Library. Graduates also sought further training. Clara van Sant, the first student to be enrolled, went on to the library course at Albany, N.Y. Doris Holmes and Hero Calvert went to Brooklyn, N.Y., to attend the Pratt Institute classes in library work. Margaret Clay, who had been in charge of Victoria's children's library, went to Pittsburgh for a year of training.

"Miss Stewart is training some of the young women of Victoria in a profession which is well paid, highly respected, and in which one is never told that the age limit has been reached, and it is time to give place to a younger generation," the *Colonist* said.

The Victoria library also worked with the Provincial Library in developing a librarianship course at Victoria's Provincial Normal School, where teachers were trained. The

Reading room in the Victoria Public Library in 1916. *Sherri Robinson collection*

twelve lectures, shared by Stewart, Scholefield and Margaret Clay, included sessions on books for children and the operation of a school library.

In New Westminster, Annie O'Meara resigned after 18 months and returned to Ontario. Despite her short time there, her influence had been remarkable, because she had brought the library into the modern age. Her successor was her assistant, Mabel Macmillan. Macmillan resigned in 1921 after a dispute with council about the purchase of books. The

next librarian, Pearl Hale, quit in 1923 to get married. Like most women of her times, her career ended on her wedding day. For years, only single women were allowed to work at libraries.

Julia Carson Stockett, who later became head of the reference division at Vancouver Public Library, said that in the early 1900s, most libraries were run by "some widow, high school girl or woman with time on her hands." That was because, she said, the pay was usually not enough to attract men, and library work was considered women's work. "As salaries went up, men generally stepped in, not always because of special education or ability," Stockett said.

For many years, female librarians were fired if they did not resign when they were married. As a result, some of the most influential librarians in the province were women who remained single, or did not marry until late in their careers.

Women could not vote in provincial elections — and in Vancouver, they could not get a library card without a reference from a man. Married women who owned property needed to have their husbands sign library cards for them. In February 1912, members of the Political Equality League, made up of men as well as women, objected, but the all-male library board would not budge. Women, the board members said, rarely lived up to their obligations at the library. Besides, there was enough freedom in the existing regulations to allow "any worthy person" to get books.

Samuel Tilden Dare, the New Westminster librarian from 1923 to 1936, was born in New York state in 1881. A machinist by trade, he served in the Boer War and the First World War, and came to British Columbia to serve as librarian in the penitentiary. He died at Vancouver's Shaughnessy Hospital in August 1951. His interests went beyond libraries; in 1932 he backed a local inventor who obtained a patent for a beverage dispenser for motorcycles.

That fall, the Victoria library eliminated its separate reading rooms for women and men. The reason, as noted in the *Colonist*, was financial; since the two rooms both needed the latest newspapers and magazines, the library was wasting money on duplicate copies. A few women's magazines were left in the old women's reading room, which could still be used by women and girls "if they needed a rest," as the *Colonist* said. "Any woman who really wants to read will find room and opportunity to do so upstairs." The discrimination did not end completely, however; a table in the reading room was reserved for the exclusive use of women.

The newspaper reminded mothers to keep their "pretty little ones" in check. Most of the children were good as gold, but "a few of their elders do not remember that a library is a place where quiet must be maintained. In such cases, the noise made by children is most annoying to students. The mother who can go on with her own reading sometimes forgets that other people cannot study where children are playing, much less crying," the *Colonist* said. Men did not escape the gender-specific rules. The Victoria library posted a notice to remind them to remove their hats while on the premises.

In February 1915, Annie B. Jamieson, assistant principal of King Edward High School, became the first woman elected to the Vancouver library board. Mary Ellen Smith, who later became the first female in the Legislature, endorsed Jamieson in the election. One of the unsuccessful candidates was a relative unknown: John Ridington, who was soon to become one of the most powerful figures in the library community.

Victoria chose its first female library commissioner, Mary Graves, in 1920. Her selection was not the dramatic step forward for women's rights that it might have been elsewhere; the library was being run by the strong-willed Helen Gordon Stewart, who would defer to no man.

In Vancouver, Eliza Machin made a difference in the lives of many people. She continued as assistant librarian after the retirement and death of her husband, until her own ill health forced her to resign as well. Since 1893 she had provided free Christmas dinners in the library for homeless men. At first the dinner drew twenty-five to fifty men, but by 1901, the dinner attracted 130 men who feasted on turkey, roast beef and plum pudding. The $78.60 cost was covered by donors, and merchants lent tables, plates and fixtures. Each man had to bring his own knife and fork.

After dinner the men enjoyed a concert that lasted until about 11 p.m. Edwin Machin and his daughter Elsie, along with Connie Lucas and George Wood, presented the concert accompanied by H.K. Evenson, a local music teacher, playing a piano provided by the Dyke, Evans and Callaghan music store on Hastings. Music dealer Walter Boult provided a phonograph for the amusement of the crowd. "We were very tired but happy, because we could see that many had been able to realize 'Merry Christmas' was not a mockery," Elsie Machin recalled years afterwards.

Eliza Machin served as Vancouver's assistant librarian from 1890 to 1916. *Vancouver Public Library, Special Collections, VPL 978*

In 1910, about 600 homeless men attended the dinner in the Carnegie library. "Undaunted by the long line of men hungry for Christmas fare which faced her yesterday afternoon, Mrs. Machin extended her hand in welcome to them all, and she, and those who assisted her, did everything in their power to make the guests feel that they were once again close to the old-fashioned Christmas celebrations they had known in some of the years gone by," the *Daily Province* newspaper reported. As they left the library, the newspaper said, many of the men must have felt that the world had a brighter outlook.

The *Vancouver World* said Machin had "a desire to aid the wrecks of humanity who have fallen beneath the pall of adversity," and was a friend to the "friendless, penniless, homeless, aimless men who congregate about the library for its cheer and warmth." The *World* also said that Machin, with the help of friends, sent gifts every Christmas to the children of poor families, never letting them know that she was the person responsible. "She is indeed one who practises by the Golden Rule and not by the Rule of Gold," the newspaper said.

In 1917, with the First World War raging, soldiers made use of local libraries. Those stationed in Victoria wanted to read newspapers from their home cities as well as journals from all over the world. They could borrow books without a sponsor. Late that year, the library reported a steadily increasing demand for literature from veterans who had returned home. Stewart cut red tape so all returned men could receive a card within minutes.

The Victoria library provided books for veterans from all over Vancouver Island, and noted that the reading interests of the men ranged from cookbooks to George Bernard Shaw. Every three months Stewart sent 200 to 300 books, including fiction, travel and many technical matters, to a convalescent home at Qualicum Beach. Veterans who asked for a special book would get it by mail and could keep it for one month.

The Spanish flu epidemic reached British Columbia near the war's end in November 1918. In an attempt to stop the spread of the disease, most public places — including public libraries — were closed. The provincial cabinet had ordered on October 8 that all "places of assembly" had to be shut. The order applied to cathedrals, chapels, missions, schools, colleges, universities, theatres, circuses, dances, lectures, drills, gymnasiums, swimming pools, skating rinks, fairs, auctions, social clubs and fraternal organizations, along with public libraries and many other potential disease-spreading locations.

In October 1918, Helen Gordon Stewart opened a temporary branch of the Victoria Public Library in an unusual location — the Home Products Fair. Stewart's booth had books on about 200 subjects, including many that were connected with the fair. The making of paint, soap and candy were all explained in the books on the little library's shelves. The booth also had a reading room with the latest magazines and newspapers.

Readers were not forgotten. "The health officer does not fear the dissemination of the disease by the circulation of books, but only as a result of the collection of crowds," the *Victoria Daily Times* reported. The Victoria library provided reference service by telephone five days a week. Patrons urgently in need of a book could request it by telephone and pick it up at the library.

The restrictions were lifted on November 19, although health authorities still warned against unreasonable crowding in theatres, churches, stores, cars and anywhere else where people gathered. Still, British Columbians were allowed to go back to their normal lives — including visits to libraries — for the first time in five weeks.

Even in the cities with Carnegie libraries, private lending libraries were thriving. These libraries charged fees to borrowers and could afford to buy recent books. In Victoria, for example, the Booklovers' Library boasted about 500 books. The library, operated by Millicent Perkins and Jean Clarke, was in the Hibben Block, but moved to the Campbell Block at 1029 Douglas in 1913. A Chinese library was at 552 Cormorant Street, with books, magazines and Chinese and English newspapers. In some communities, women's institutes helped run libraries, and there were also libraries in one-industry communities organized by companies or unions. In Kimberley, for example, the miners' union built a reading room at the Sullivan mine in 1912, with books as well as newspapers and periodicals in English, Finnish and Italian.

Helen Gordon Stewart left the Victoria library in 1924 to further her education. She was succeeded by Margaret Jean Clay, a daughter of Rev. W. Leslie Clay, who had served on the library board. Margaret Clay had been one of the first students in Stewart's librarianship training program.

Clay argued for libraries in schools, just as Stewart had. In 1926, for example, she pressed her case to the Shawnigan Lake Women's Institute. "The classrooms of most schools are complete in all but the essential — books other than textbooks," she said. "Given a school furnished with good books, chosen by an expert, bearing on the subjects the scholars are studying, you will have intelligent students."

In 1924, the Vancouver library got a new librarian: Edgar Stewart Robinson, only twenty-seven years old. Robinson — known as Robbie — served as Vancouver's head librarian for thirty-three years, until his death in 1957. He was painfully shy but pushed himself to become a public speaker and a powerful advocate of libraries, eager to ensure that they were seen as a priority.

Robinson was born in Michigan in 1896 and came to Canada with his parents as a boy. He worked as a page at the Calgary Public Library when it opened in 1912, then attended the University of Alberta and the University of Toronto. He returned to the Calgary library before going to library school at the University of Washington.

Claiming that he was "about thirty" when he became Vancouver's head librarian, Robinson quickly dropped the name Carnegie, making the name of the institution simply Vancouver Public Library. He had many concerns about the library building, describing the massive staircase — once considered a key feature — as a "monstrosity." The building's brick walls were impregnable, he said, so the public and the staff had not been able to make changes.

Robinson said Vancouver needed a new central library for its reference, circulation and administrative departments, as well as a system of branch libraries. He argued that the library should serve all of Greater Vancouver, and noted that it was already welcoming non-residents into its reference and reading rooms. "Shorter working hours and more speedy methods of production have left men and women with longer hours of leisure than ever before," he wrote. "The most important problem facing the social world today is that of meeting this long daily period of leisure with something worthwhile to do."

He stated his vision in an essay published in the *Daily Province*, complete with an artist's conception of what a new library might look like. "British Columbia looks to Vancouver for leadership," he wrote. "This city is expected to set the pace. As Vancouver does, so does British Columbia." Robinson wanted a building that would offer more than books; it would be a community gathering place with a lecture hall to seat 500 people and rooms devoted to art and music. Books in high demand would be readily available, but many others would be in high-density storage and would be retrieved by attendants.

Robinson believed that branch libraries would be able to provide books using buildings in less costly areas of the city, and save the residents a trip downtown. He said each branch should have separate rooms for children and adults, with the main entrance between them.

❧

Vancouver's first branch outlets were simply shelves in neighbourhood stores, a far cry from the full-service branches that were needed. In February 1927, the library opened its first real branch, on Fourth Avenue in Kitsilano. It was the first library branch in British Columbia, and for many years the only one. More than 3,000 new patrons used Kitsilano, and one-tenth of the people who had used the Carnegie library downtown shifted their borrowing to the branch.

Teachers told Sarah Fisher, who was in charge of the branch, that they had noted a change in the attitude of their students since the branch opened. Parents were also happy, as were neighbourhood shopkeepers who had seen an increase in traffic. One day, only one fiction book was left, and as soon as the books were returned they were quickly checked out again. The most popular book in 1927? *Revolt in the Desert* by T.E. Lawrence.

Robinson also believed that schools should have librarians, but was not able to convince the Vancouver school board when it was deciding on staff for the new Templeton Junior High School. The trustees were worried about the cost. Robinson's offered to provide help with cataloguing was declined.

"No opportunity should be lost of strengthening the relations of school and library," he said. "It is not sufficient that children form the book habit. The library habit is also important, and without the teacher to link the two, much of the library's efforts will be nullified." The public library should have, he said, a department with books selected for school use.

In 1928 the public library circulated a total of 700,000 books. It had 38,000 borrowers, 55,000 circulating volumes and 25,000 more on reference shelves. In June 1929, the central library expanded to the south, into the old city hall building, and moved the reading room and the children's room there. The structure, built in 1890, had served as a market, theatre and public hall before being used as city hall.

In Victoria, the library board announced in 1929 that it was looking for someone to buy the Carnegie building, which was no longer large enough. The board repeated the call in 1930, saying the library was simply too congested. There were no takers.

5

ONE VAST CIRCULATING LIBRARY

E thelbert Olaf Stuart Scholefield, British Columbia's provincial librarian and a driving force in the development of libraries, recognized that progress would come in a variety of ways. One of the most important tools, he believed, would be a provincial association that would bring librarians together for the good of all. It took almost a decade before he got his wish.

Victoria's *Daily Colonist* newspaper first reported in 1902 that Scholefield had proposed an association to promote the establishment and welfare of public libraries and reading rooms. "There is plenty of scope for such an institution," the newspaper said. "Facilities for reading and research outside of the two largest cities are almost nil.

Opposite: Prince Rupert library, shown here in about 1942, was one of the province's first public libraries. *City of Vancouver Archives, CVA 586-858*

Above: The front desk of the Victoria Public Library in 1916. *Sherri Robinson collection*

Cooperation and organization would certainly increase them to the advantage of everybody."

In 1909 Scholefield and librarians from Oregon and Washington organized the Pacific Northwest Library Association to work on behalf of libraries throughout the region. Scholefield quickly assumed a leadership role, and was elected president when the association held its 1911 meeting in Victoria. He told the convention that Premier Richard McBride had asked him to draft new legislation to replace the 1891 public library act, which had not done enough to promote library development.

The legislation had made it next to impossible for small communities to start public libraries. As the *Colonist* reported, the law "applies only to cities, and not adequately to these." Libraries were allowed in incorporated municipalities if 100 people signed petitions in favour and councils passed enabling bylaws and established boards to run them. "The British Columbia statutes contain absolutely no machinery for the formation or stimulation of public reading centres," the *Colonist* said.

Scholefield recognized that while the Pacific Northwest association helped librarians exchange ideas, an association that was exclusive to British Columbia would have more

Dr. Henry Esson Young, the Minister of Education, was the first honourary president of the B.C. Library Association in 1911. *Image A-02547 courtesy of Royal BC Museum, BC Archives*

influence with the provincial government. At the close of the PNLA conference he called a meeting in his office in the Legislative Buildings. There, in September 1911, ten passionate librarians and trustees agreed to form an organization to improve libraries and library service throughout the province. It was the start of the British Columbia Library Association.

Robert W. Douglas from the Vancouver Public Library was elected president. The secretary was Rev. Charles W. Whyte, and the treasurer was Helen Gordon Stewart from the Victoria Public Library. Other executive members included Dr. J. Griffith Hands, Victoria's head librarian, Alma Russell from the Provincial Library and Bernard McEvoy, a library trustee from Vancouver. Dr. Henry Esson Young, the minister of education, was named honourary president. The association went to work quickly, and was not shy about its goals; its letterhead proudly stated: "Our aim: A modern public library in every community in B.C."

The *Victoria Daily Times* said the association would help establish libraries in outlying districts. "The first thing they have taken in hand is the formation of a proper and adequate Library Act, which will give the proper facilities for the organizing of library boards everywhere," the newspaper said. Less than two months later, Scholefield and Whyte attended a meeting of the Union of B.C. Municipalities to press for new library legislation.

In December 1911, association members met at Russell's home in Victoria to review a draft act, based on a law in Ontario, which would allow a free library to be created in any municipality that desired one. The act, they said, would allow for libraries and branch libraries, as well as evening classes for artisans, mechanics and working men in any subjects that would promote a knowledge of the manufacturing and mechanical arts.

They wanted the province to provide each library with up to $300 for books and $50 for magazines. Municipalities would supply premises and a librarian, and would levy a sum for library purposes as part of their annual assessment. They said no more than 55 per cent of a book budget should be spent on fiction. Whyte said keen interest in the idea was reflected in letters he had received from Trail, Prince Rupert, Salmon Arm, Fernie, Grand Forks, Point Grey and Burnaby.

The association submitted the proposal to the provincial government, but the government did nothing with it. The economy was booming, people were flooding in, new construction was changing the look of the cities, and there was a sense of opportunity. It was difficult, apparently, to convince the government to make a library bill one of its priorities.

Undaunted, Scholefield continued to promote libraries as often as he could. In 1913, he told Vancouver's Progress Club that there would be a strong demand for new public libraries modelled after the Vancouver and Victoria ones. The following year the association assigned Helen Gordon Stewart, John Hosie and Arthur Herbert Killam to revise the proposed bill to ensure it was in line with recent legislation. They did their best, but again could not convince the government to move.

The association tried again in 1917, convinced there was a need to close the huge gaps in library service. Small districts could not afford libraries with many technical books, and travelling libraries served only unorganized areas. The dream was to give all small towns and hamlets the same access to books that was found in the cities, and at a reasonable cost.

Victoria's *Colonist* envisioned "one vast circulating library" that would make all resources available everywhere. "All that cataloguing and indexing would be done by expert library workers in the larger centres, and it is believed that the scheme would be very simple to work, and in the course of a very short time would become a great asset in the educational and business affairs of the province."

The association wanted legislation that would address the needs of unorganized districts by extending the travelling library system, and would also help partially organized districts and fully organized municipalities. It proposed a public library commission with three unpaid members appointed by the lieutenant governor in council. The government would direct policies, oversee library activities and provide a salary for a library organizer. Above all, the association wanted more sharing of resources. "For practical purposes the mainspring of the present draft is the possibility of co-ordination," the *Colonist* said.

One idea was that a district could impose a small tax for library purposes, and then draw on the resources of Victoria, Vancouver or any other library that had the books required. If public libraries could borrow from each other, more of the 150,000 books they held would get into the hands of the 400,000 people in the province.

The association proposed a system of library districts, with the economic centre as the library centre and branches in smaller communities. As an example, the Victoria library could provide about 200 books to Ladysmith, where a local board would provide a home for the books, arrange for their care and circulation, and compensate Victoria. The books would be exchanged at regular intervals. This would give Ladysmith access to Victoria's 32,000 books for a small amount of money.

During the First World War, the British Columbia Library Association sought to establish library service in provincial military camps and start reading rooms for all men in service. E.O.S. Scholefield said there should be service for the special needs of hospitals, as well as prisons and reformatories. Arthur Herbert Killam was put in charge of a committee to determine how to provide service to military camps.

Helen Gordon Stewart, elected the association's president in 1917, expressed disappointment that the association had not been able to provide service to the camp at Vernon. Libraries were, however, providing discarded books to tuberculosis wards in hospitals, and had "brightened many a moment for the stricken patients," said Vancouver librarian Winnie Davenport. Scholefield posted a notice in the Provincial Library asking patrons to donate for the benefit of hospital patients.

The Victoria library was already lending books to people from Esquimalt, Oak Bay and Saanich in exchange for financial support from those municipalities. Helen Gordon Stewart was optimistic that the concept could work on a wider basis, and went to Shawnigan Lake, Ladysmith, Alberni, Parksville and other Vancouver Island communities as well as towns on the mainland to build support.

She did not have much success, even in Victoria. When she explained the idea to Victoria council, she learned that the aldermen preferred things the way they were. They did not believe that Victoria had an obligation to help smaller communities, and thought the existing library act suited Victoria.

"The library in Victoria is simply a city department under city jurisdiction," Alderman William Frank Fullerton told Stewart. "It should remain so." He said the proposed bill was an attempt by the provincial government to encroach on municipal territory, and he warned that it could be a sign of worse things to come — "I see inspectors and secretaries." He conceded, however, that combining the operation of libraries with schools might make sense.

Stewart, who as head of the library association was leading the campaign for new legislation, argued that without the act it would be impossible to do important educational work in rural areas.

Less than a week later, Education Minister J.D. MacLean introduced the new library act, based on the association's

Library staff members on the front steps
of Victoria's Carnegie building in 1916.
Sherri Robinson collection

proposal, in the Legislature. The act established the Public Library Commission, encouraged the creation of volunteer-run public library associations if ten or more people wanted them, and extended the travelling library system. It allowed larger centres to impose library taxes and allowed libraries to lend outside their town limits, something that had not been possible under the previous law.

The major benefit was the potential to co-ordinate library services. At the time, B.C.'s school, provincial, university, public and travelling libraries were operating independently, and there was no policy to prevent overlapping, nor was there a recognized method for the dissemination of books.

"An Act to Provide for the Establishment of Public Libraries" received royal assent on March 29, 1919, four days after MacLean introduced it. The act won praise from the *Colonist* in Victoria, which said the war had changed reading habits — and something more important. "There is a wider appreciation today of the desirability of more intelligent citizenship, in large part created through the enfranchisement of women and their desire to inform themselves," the newspaper said.

"The knowledge that libraries have to offer will aid in solving the problems of reconstruction, it will widen the vision of citizenship, and nothing will tend more to quiet irrational unrest, which is largely the result of ignorance of the past which implies an inability to judge of the present and of the needs of the future. The methods about to be adopted to enlarge the circle of the reading public of British Columbia cannot fail to accomplish good. In what is being done in this direction the public owe a debt of gratitude to Miss Helen Stewart, the city librarian, who has been assiduous in her advocacy of the new library law."

On June 13 Stewart was named to the Public Library Commission along with Malcolm Bruce Jackson, who represented Victoria in the Legislature, and Garnett Gladwin Sedgewick of Vancouver, an associate professor of English at the University of British Columbia. The positions were part-time and unpaid. Jackson was named chairman, and Stewart served as interim secretary until Arthur Herbert Killam was given the role. Killam's travelling libraries were shifted to the commission from the Provincial Library, and Killam's office in the basement of the library became the commission's headquarters.

Along with operating the travelling libraries, the commission was supposed to help set up public libraries and distribute grants to libraries on behalf of the government. Its role was also to co-operate with public library associations, public library boards and librarians on matters pertaining to the organization, maintenance and administration of

libraries under the act. It was not, however, given money to hire a professional organizer.

The commission saw quick results because both Nanaimo and Duncan wanted to get books from the Victoria library. In August 1919, Nanaimo became the first community to create a public library association under the new act, and Victoria sent 600 books to Nanaimo to help get it started. The Nanaimo library obtained ground-floor space in the Athletic Club on Chapel Street in January 1920, and moved four years later to the New Ladysmith Lumber Co.'s old building at Wallace and Fraser.

The Victoria library also sent books to Duncan, Alberni and Sidney. They were to be exchanged four times a year, and people could send requests at any time. Victoria charged $65 for each 100 books borrowed. The small centres gained because they could get fresh books on a regular basis, and Victoria gained because it could get more money to replenish its stock.

The theory was that Vancouver and a city in the Interior could also become distribution centres. Residents of Kamloops were already talking about borrowing books from the Vancouver library until a municipal library could be started in Kamloops. The greatest success in 1920 was in Nelson, where the city took over the community's library. It became the fourth municipal library in British Columbia, after New Westminster, Vancouver and Victoria.

Travelling libraries were supplemented in the 1920s by a service that used mail to put high-quality books — basically just about anything other than fiction — directly into the hands of readers. After a limited trial it was expanded to the entire province in 1926. The service, named Open Shelf, drew from 7,000 books donated by the Provincial Library and 20,000 more that could be borrowed from it when needed. It was designed to serve anyone who could not use a public library. Books could be borrowed for six weeks, with a renewal for four more weeks if no other books had been requested. The borrower paid return postage.

The new spirit of co-operation was not universally appreciated. Victoria council members became increasingly concerned about the number of books being borrowed by non-residents. Victoria was getting a total of $950 a month from Esquimalt, Saanich and Oak Bay, but council maintained that it was not enough. Alderman George Sangster said many people who frequented the library were "loafers" and it would be impossible to get a day's work out of them. "You just ought to see them," he said.

Under pressure from Victoria, Oak Bay agreed to pay more, but when Saanich and Esquimalt held out, Victoria cut off library privileges for residents of those two municipalities. The reading room, reference library and games department were watched to ensure that Saanich and Esquimalt residents did not slip in, although exceptions were

A selection of Open Shelf books sent from Victoria
one day in the 1920s:

Art of Florence

Ibsen's Plays

Life of Schumann

General Introduction to Psychoanalysis

Handbook of Nature Study

The Normans of European History

A Half-Century of Conflict

Montcalm and Wolfe

Inge's Outspoken Essays

Goldberg's Havelock Ellis

Your Heart and How to Take Care of It

Bees and Beekeeping

Successful Teaching in Rural Schools

High School Debate Book

Rural Education

Education and the Good Life

Man's Judgment of Death

Adventures of Missionary Explorers

Men and Missions

made for people from the naval college, military hospitals and the Provincial Normal School, where teachers were trained.

George I. Warren, the president of the Associated Boards of Trade of Vancouver Island, argued in 1921 for more spending on libraries. "Nanaimo relies on the Daughters of the Empire for the operation of its library. Duncan has a fiction library only. Cumberland has just started a library, and has started well. Port Alberni spends $55 per year on school books, but nothing for its older students, while Ladysmith has nothing at all." The state of Washington, meanwhile, had twenty-three libraries in towns with 5,000 people or less. Warren said Victoria provided almost $19,000 a year to its library, which was patronized by fifty per cent of the population. Nanaimo's library, used by only nine per cent of the population, did not get a city grant and had revenue of just $730 a year. Duncan's library received a $10 annual

grant from North Cowichan, and collected $166.50 in other revenue.

In the year ending March 31, 1923, the Public Library Commission had a budget of less than $9,000. It spent $3,600.40 for books and periodicals, and provided $884.85 in grants to libraries in Cassidy, Cumberland, Enderby, Fernie, Hollyburn, Nanaimo, Nelson, Penticton, Prince Rupert and Sidney. It spent $917.69 on freight — to railway companies, trucking companies and the Grand Trunk Pacific steamship company.

In its first few years the commission helped create a couple dozen local library associations, bringing basic service on a volunteer basis to their communities. These organizations were described as "a fair substitute for a public library in an unorganized district, a municipality with a small population or a city which is unable for various reasons to establish a municipal library." They covered their costs by charging patrons small fees.

The commission saw these associations as an interim step toward public libraries supported by municipal taxes rather than user fees, but most of the associations struggled to stay alive. One notable exception was in Nanaimo, where the library became the fifth municipal public library in B.C., open to all citizens for free. In 1922 another municipal public library was started in Prince Rupert, bringing the total to six.

The Public Library Commission was started with great enthusiasm, but soon ran into difficulty because the government did not appoint new members when the terms of the three commissioners expired. By 1923 the commission was dormant, and Killam worked alone for three years. The notion of encouraging library development had to wait, and the new public library associations got little support from Victoria.

Some of the associations, including the ones at Corbin, Fernie and Port Alberni, went out of business soon after they began. "Little isolated libraries rarely succeed," the commission noted, and called for co-operation and interchange, particularly in rural and pioneer communities. The call for libraries to work together was repeated countless times over the years.

Some of the surviving associations were small. Ganges, for example, had twenty-two members in 1927, while Invermere had twenty-four, Kaslo twenty-five and Enderby twenty-nine. The largest was Cumberland, with 325 members. Penticton had 275, Revelstoke 246 and North Vancouver 261. Adult annual fees ranged from $1 in several places to a high of $5 in Duncan. Several small associations limped through the 1920s only to fail during the Depression.

A temporary failure was in Kamloops, where a library bylaw was defeated in 1923. But five years later, several residents formed a library association and asked for space in the three-year-old federal building at Third and Seymour. The library opened in April 1929 and rapidly became known as the most successful association in the province, with circulation numbers that suggested there would have been support for a municipal library after all.

When the Public Library Commission was revived, its members once again called for an end to user fees. "In very few cases has any effort been made to serve the general public," they said in their 1927 report. "This is a serious omission and the Public Library Commission has this year advised all parties concerned that henceforth it will not issue travelling libraries to these associations unless the books are made available to the general public."

Travelling libraries were being sent to community groups in the theory that people in rural areas should have the same opportunities for intellectual development as people in towns. As the commission said: "In such a province as British Columbia, where most of the territory is unorganized, and the rural population is something less than one to the square mile, it is impossible for the people in the country to give themselves adequate library service; and therefore it devolves upon the provincial government to supply those people with books.

"Travelling libraries have been, and probably will continue to be for some time, the only method of service," stated the report. In 1927, it loaned 386 libraries, averaging about ninety volumes each. There were no accurate statistics on the number of borrowers or total circulation, because the system relied on unpaid volunteers — and they were not asked to keep elaborate records.

Schools used travelling libraries to supplement their meagre selections of books. In the early 1900s the provincial government offered up to 50 cents per student for books, to a maximum of $50 per school, provided the local board matched the funds. An amendment to the Public Schools Act in 1919 required school librarians to ensure that books had stout paper covers and were kept under lock and key when not on loan.

A 1925 survey of the school system by Harold Putnam and George Weir recommended that libraries become an important part of the school system rather than simply a place to store books. At the time, few teachers had any training in library studies.

Killam's collection was crucial to schools. By 1919, when the commission was started, about twenty-five travelling libraries were being specially prepared for schools, with books suitable for children's general reading and for supplementary reading. During the 1926-27 school year, the commission supplied books to forty-three one-room schools, but many other applicants were turned down because the commission did not have enough books.

"Very many of the teachers are keenly alive to the value of books other than texts, and it is a pity that some adequate provision is not made in this regard. Teachers and trustees need guidance in choosing the best books, buying at the lowest rates, taking care of the books in their possession, and using them to the best advantage," the commission's report noted.

The slow progress under the new act did not discourage B.C.'s library community. They remained convinced that libraries were essential. As Alma Russell, of the Provincial Library, noted in 1925: Even though people could access knowledge in many other ways — the press, radio, movies, correspondence courses, university extension opportunities, lectures, service clubs and museums — libraries were still relevant.

David Wilson, a former school inspector, established the Department of Education's Text Book branch in 1908. The branch supplied schools with reference works, and helped get books from suppliers in Vancouver to schools throughout the province. Wilson retired in 1920 and died in 1935. He is buried in Royal Oak Burial Park in Saanich.

6

University of
British Columbia Library

J ohn Ridington had worked as a teacher and a journalist, but his passion was
books. In 1914, he leapt at the chance to catalogue and arrange the 20,000 books
that would form the basis of the library at the new University of British
Columbia. He became one of the most important librarians in the history of the
province, even though he did not have a university degree or any training on how to
run a library.

Ridington was born in England in 1868 and came to Canada in 1889. He taught
school in rural Manitoba and owned the *Carberry News* until a competitor forced
him out of business. After working for the *Winnipeg Free Press*, he brought his

Opposite: Concourse in the University of British
Columbia library in September 1925. *University of
British Columbia Archives, 1.1/1880*

Above: John Ridington, the first librarian at the
University of British Columbia, in the 1930s.
Vancouver Sun

family to Vancouver in 1912 to pursue business opportunities, but it was the chance to set up a library that appealed to him.

> A university is a group of buildings gathered around a library.
>
> *Shelby Foote, novelist*

The post-secondary institution was created after the legislature passed "An Act to Establish and Incorporate a University for the Province of British Columbia" in 1908. A university has at its heart a strong library, and Ridington set a high standard. The institution he helped to shape would become the second-largest research library in Canada.

UBC was the second post-secondary institution in British Columbia, after Victoria College, which came to life in a two-room building on the grounds of Victoria High School in 1903. Its library began with a half-dozen books in the principal's office and expanded as the college grew. The

In 1915, the University of British Columbia made its home in what became known as the Fairview shacks. The library was in the large white building in the centre.
University of British Columbia Archives, 11.1/12-4

college was affiliated with McGill University in Montreal, but was closed in 1915 with the opening of UBC, which also began as an affiliate of McGill.

Point Grey was selected as the site of UBC in 1910, but the outbreak of the First World War halted the work. In 1915 the university opened in temporary housing, the Fairview Shacks at 10th Avenue and Laurel Street, adjacent to Vancouver General Hospital.

The first purchases for the UBC library were made by James Thayer Gerould of the University of Minnesota, who went to Europe regularly to buy books for his own institution and the University of Missouri. UBC's first president, Dr. Frank Fairchild Wesbrook, had been the dean of medicine at the University of Minnesota before coming to British Columbia, and was aware of Gerould's skill at getting good books at a reasonable price.

On a trip to Europe in the summer of 1914, Gerould spent $18,000 in England and $4,000 in France on behalf of UBC. His selections included James George Frazer's *The Golden Bough*, which cost several pounds, and a set of *Blackwood's Magazine*, with 194 volumes from 1817 to 1914, which cost about 30 cents a volume. In France, he bought 4,000 volumes from the Turquem Librarie in Paris.

Gerould's plan to buy books in Germany was stopped by the outbreak of the Great War. He was briefly detained in Leipzig on suspicion of being a spy. A key piece of evidence against him was a set of plans he was carrying, but he was released when it became clear that the plans were innocent; they were for the UBC campus.

It took Gerould another ten days to get out of Germany, having to prove repeatedly that he was American and therefore not involved in the war. Despite this, he promised UBC that its library would eventually have books from Germany.

The first two shipments arrived in Canada from England in October 1914 and were placed in a temporary home at McGill University in Montreal. The UBC Library was also boosted by several private donations, including a gift from Reginald W. Brock, the first dean of Applied Science at UBC. Chancellor Francis Lovett Carter-Cotton donated a complete file of the Vancouver newspaper he edited, the *News-Advertiser*. Wesbrook also obtained a set of the publications of the Carnegie Institution for Science in Washington, D.C.

By June 1915, the library was in its temporary quarters, the new northwest wing of the Vancouver General Hospital, and Ridington was sorting and cataloguing the books. "For some months Mr. Ridington has practically lived among the books," the *Vancouver Sun* reported. "It is no small undertaking he is engaged in."

Ridington and his two assistants classified the books under the Library of Congress system, developed by the largest library in the United States and recommended to Ridington by leading librarians from throughout North America. There was, potentially, a strong financial incentive to use the system, because the Library of Congress had published a set of catalogue cards listing all of its books. Ridington's goal was to obtain a copy for UBC so new ones would not have to be prepared in Vancouver.

The UBC collection started with a wide range of books, some more than 200 years old and others recently published. It included philosophy, economics, classics, history, literature, psychology, botany and travel. The library also had sets of magazines and publications research societies. As Ridington and his helpers worked, faculty members went through the books to compile lists of volumes in each subject area to prepare for the fall term.

In 1916, Ridington was formally appointed as the librarian, and took summer courses at New York State University in Albany to learn more about how to run a library. He also visited several large libraries to try to build a network that would share books and expertise.

"A remarkably good skeleton brigade of books has been

collected and it will be brought up to full strength by and by," the *Province* reported in 1917. "Almost every department of 'humane' literature is represented; inhuman books, of which there are so many today, being left outside. It is manifest that there is no attempt here to collect volumes that are for just 'passing the time.' The atmosphere of the library is not only calm and classical but it is scientific.

"In this mine of knowledge there is a good thick vein of history, displaying unusual value to the ton; a considerable pocket of religion; borings reveal a very satisfactory amount of philosophy; in one gallery of the mine philology displays all sorts of colours. French literature has a rich lead by itself; English literature shows a good quality of ore in somewhat prolific quantity. It is the only sort of mine that can be 'salted' without any ethical transgression. It is being salted all the time by fresh ore being put into it.

One of the assistants hired by John Ridington was Dorothy Jefferd, who stayed with the university for four decades. When she left in 1957, the library had almost half a million volumes — and the *Vancouver Sun* said Jefferd had "catalogued them all and read many of them." She died in 1971.

"The library is open to receive books that are worth having. A handsome book-plate label is pasted into all donated books of this character that will keep the memory of the giver green in future years. In the department of natural science, our new university has probably a much larger selection than Oxford and Cambridge had when they started."

Ridington's passion for books and libraries came through in his speeches. He told the annual convention of the Pacific Northwest Library Association in 1919, when he was its president, that libraries held the key to preventing future warfare because they could uphold ideals, create sympathies and disseminate knowledge.

The Provincial Library in Victoria gave duplicate books from its historical collection to the university. "This will not impair the usefulness of the Provincial Library," wrote librarian John Forsyth. "They will be of great service to the students attending the university."

In Victoria, the college was reopened in 1920 as an affiliate of UBC. The following year it moved to one of the

The main library at the University of British Columbia in 1925. *University of British Columbia Archives, 1.1/1021*

most impressive campuses in the nation: Craigdarroch Castle, the four-storey mansion that coal baron Robert Dunsmuir had commissioned in 1887. The library occupied an upper room in the castle and was administered by staff members. The Victoria Public Library helped with cataloguing and lent books to the college library as needed.

The UBC Library was also, finally, on the move. The reference room in the old library was so short of space that some students were sitting on the floor. In 1925, after almost a decade in temporary quarters, a new library was opened on the Point Grey campus, one of the first permanent buildings there. The library's new home, the central portion of today's Irving K. Barber Learning Centre, had room for 135,000 volumes and study space for 350 students. At the time it had 55,000 books valued at $200,000.

Ridington's interest in libraries went well beyond the walls and windows of the university. In 1929 he argued that the public library system, "the people's university," needed to be expanded. He said that the greatest minds and their greatest thoughts are available to all through books, and that a public library was every bit as important as fire protection, police, water systems and light.

In 1930 Ridington was given a leave of absence so he could chair a national library commission on behalf of the Carnegie Corporation. He worked with George H. Locke, Toronto's head librarian, and Mary J. Black, who ran the public library in Fort William, Ontario, and had been the first woman president of the Ontario Library Association.

Ridington attacked his assignment with zeal. He visited every province, interviewed eight of the nine premiers as well as ministers of education and every influential person in libraries. The commission recommended increased service at all types of libraries, from university and legislative ones to public and school facilities, in all areas of Canada.

In a report to the B.C. Library Association, Ridington said conditions were worst in Halifax, where books were out of date, the staff untrained and the finances precarious. He recommended a rural library system using bookmobiles similar to one that was being tried in the Fraser Valley. Ridington said travelling libraries were popular in rural Ontario, but of the 500 there, only twenty-five functioned properly. There were no rural library services in Manitoba, and Winnipeg had fewer books than it did ten years earlier. Saskatchewan, on the other hand, had offered to match, dollar for dollar, any funds provided by the Carnegie Corporation.

In a profile of Ridington published in 1932, the *Daily Province* newspaper described him as a "kindly, bespectacled, philosophical man" who sat defiantly in the librarian's office at the university. Students reported that he ruled the library with an iron fist. By that time, the university's library had 80,000 books, served about 2,000

The Vancouver School of Decorative and Applied Arts came into being in the 1920s with a library that contained books and periodicals. The school was on the top floor of the Vancouver School Board building at Hamilton and Dunsmuir in Vancouver.

people and made 100,000 loans a year. Ridington told the *Province* reporter that he had dabbled in art, read many books and written a few, and travelled extensively. He said he played a rotten game of golf and a fair game of bridge, and hinted that he was a fine judge of whiskey.

Ridington joined the Public Library Commission in 1934, filling the vacancy created by the death of provincial librarian John Hosie. As one of three commissioners, he helped guide libraries through the end of the Depression and watched over the establishment of three regional library systems.

In the fall of 1935, one of Ridington's dreams came true when the library obtained a copy of the Library of Congress Depository Catalogue. The catalogue, worth $53,000, was donated to the UBC Library by the Carnegie Corporation. The UBC set was the third in Canada — others were at McGill and the University of Toronto — and one of only eighteen outside the United States. Ridington had been trying to get the catalogue for almost twenty years.

The Library of Congress cards were shipped to Vancouver via the Panama Canal in thirty-six cases weighing a total of nearly four tons. Each of the 1.5 million cards represented one book in the Congressional Library at Washington. The cards were sorted in special filing cases, with about 1,600 steel drawers, which the university had built at a cost of $6,000.

The cabinets were placed in the library's Main Concourse, two flights of stairs above the main lobby. The catalogue made it easier for the university to catalogue its own collection, saving it hundreds of dollars a year, and also made it easier for patrons to find books. The cards included bibliographic data on almost every book in existence. Each one had the name of the author, the title, the name of the publisher and the date of the book's publication. Processing the cards would occupy staff for three years, and two file clerks were assigned to handle the 24,000 cards to be added each year.

Ridington was not shy about expressing his views on libraries and literacy — or virtually any other topic. He was

Victoria's Craigdarroch Castle, home of Victoria College from 1921 to 1946. *Times Colonist*

known as an effective public speaker, and gave talks on a wide variety of topics to audiences throughout the province. Speaking to the Vancouver Institute in 1936, he attacked the education system, the complacency of the educated minority, UBC, correspondence schools and travelling Chataqua circuits, which were popular summer entertainment diversions at the time.

"How many garages are there in Vancouver?" Ridington asked. "To succeed, every one of them must have at least one man, and a working man, with no qualms about dirty hands or broken fingernails, who knows more about electricity and internal combustion engines than anybody did thirty years ago except professors of science.

"Who taught them? They taught themselves, with what help they could get from textbooks, from night schools and from correspondence courses." He said that $100,000 a year in Vancouver, and $70 million a year in North America, went to correspondence courses, yet less than one per cent of that went to teaching expenses. The rest was divided between salesmen and promoters. "This situation is a reproach to our educational system."

Chataqua circuits had been designed as educational tools, he said, but they had become big business and had degenerated into "a combination of circus and vaudeville." He argued that education was the insurance policy of democracy, "yet the only material that can be shaped by real education is the grown-up personality. All that can be done with youth is to get it started toward self-education. Wherever there have been signs of a desire to go on with education in mature life, it has not been among the majority of college graduates."

He praised Alberta's university extension program and accused UBC of inaction. "Almost everywhere — Vancouver is an exception, I am sorry to say — the library is recognized as an essential institution in community life, a pervasive influence for information, inspiration and recreation. The necessary finances are voted with no more reluctance than are those for the maintenance of other civic services.

"The librarian of today desires, as men desire salvation, to make the use of books possible to everybody; not only for scholars and leisurely book users, but for that formidable, democratic everybody so detested and feared by lovers of privilege. To achieve this and to make it easy, the whole library idea has been made over in the last fifty years."

Ridington said few libraries could compare to the "starved" Vancouver Public Library in its rate of non-fiction reading. Excluding children's books, forty-eight of every 100 books borrowed were non-fiction. Only about twenty-three per cent of the library's book budget went to fiction, which was much less expensive that non-fiction.

He criticized Vancouver city council for fighting a proposed provincial library law that would have required a minimum contribution to libraries of 50 cents per person at a time when Vancouver was spending only 29 cents. "Those we elected to run our city do not believe that information and inspiration derived from books have any part or lot in civic welfare," he said. "Of course, they mask their indifference or hostility under the pretence of consideration for the afflicted taxpayer."

In March 1939, Ridington warned the Vancouver Institute that a major international conflict seemed almost certain. He said "the menace of propaganda" was partially to blame for the tension in the world. The disciplining of public opinion "leads to a warped and artificial enthusiasm,"

he said, and moves people to applaud through merely being told what to do and think. His point was obvious: Libraries would help to keep minds open.

Ridington retired from the library in 1940 at the age of seventy-two. The *Sun* noted that he had seen the library grow from humble wooden huts containing just 800 books — an inheritance from the old college under McGill University — to 125,000 volumes at the Point Grey campus. It was the fifth largest university library in Canada, and second in Western Canada to the University of Alberta.

For the next five years, Ridington wrote editorials for the *Vancouver News-Herald*. In 1946, the Canadian Library Association, which Ridington had worked towards for years, came into being. Ridington, however, had died in Vancouver in April 1945.

He left a tremendous legacy. He led a national commission and served on the provincial Public Library Commission for six years. He was twice elected president of the Pacific Northwest Library Association, and was named an honourary life member the year he retired from the library. He had also been president of the British Columbia Library Association.

More than anything, his legacy was the main library building on the Point Grey campus of the University of British Columbia — a library he built from scratch into one of the finest in Canada.

> Whatever the costs of our libraries, the price is cheap compared to that of an ignorant nation.
> *Walter Cronkite, broadcaster*

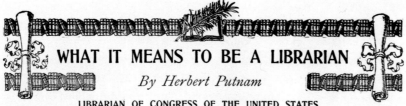

WHAT IT MEANS TO BE A LIBRARIAN

By Herbert Putnam

LIBRARIAN OF CONGRESS OF THE UNITED STATES

ONE of the leading library training-schools has recently issued a statement concerning the career of its alumni. Of ninety-nine graduates reporting, all but one are regularly employed in library work; the majority found employment within three months, and seven-tenths within six months. The lowest salary reported was four hundred and sixteen dollars per annum; the highest, two thousand; the average, six hundred and eighty-six dollars: for an average of forty-two hours and a half of service a week, with an average vacation of four weeks and five days. Of the ninety-nine persons, ninety-four were women. The above statistics might hold fairly for the graduates of the leading library schools. They would be, perhaps, over-favorable for the profession at large except as the salaries paid to a few librarians in high administrative positions be taken into account.

There are no accurate statistics of the total number of persons engaged in library work in the United States to-day. As there are over eight thousand libraries, an average of two employees to each library would indicate at least sixteen thousand such persons. Probably three-fifths of these are women.

HERBERT PUTNAM

Library Work is Well Adapted to Women

LIBRARY work is a form of educational service. And in the qualifications which it demands, in its privileges and in its compensations, it has many analogies with teaching. It deals with material that is agreeable and with persons in a relation that is agreeable. It is in most of its departments an occupation for which women are well adapted, and in certain of its departments an occupation for which women seem peculiarly constituted.

The analogy with teaching holds. In a small library, as in an elementary school, a woman may be preferred. A village library is more or less a social centre; its constituency is chiefly of women and children, and a woman in charge may have better understanding of their needs, may meet them more sympathetically, and endure with better patience the constant repetition of questions which women and children ask. The larger library is more nearly like a university. The work is highly differentiated, and the personal characteristics of the employees are relatively of less importance than the thoroughness of their bibliographic knowledge. In the work not touching the public, employees may be of great value in spite of personal characteristics which are perverse. If in the smaller libraries a woman may bring qualifications which are to be preferred, in the larger ones there is no position from which her sex need exclude her. In the purely executive positions, however, the prejudice is still in favor of men. And if in the others women do not, as a rule, yet receive a compensation equal to that of men it may be because they do not as a . . .

of prints and photographs (since the modern library includes these, besides printed books), of manuscripts and of documents; very likely a department of patents, and certainly a department handling the current magazines and newspapers, and one especially for young people.

Work of the Order Department

THE Order Department conducts all the correspondence with dealers. To it the book is an article of commerce. Its employees must be informed as to prices, editions and sources. As to current publications, the questions are easily answered, but at least one-half of the books purchased by a large library are books out of print, which turn up only occasionally in second-hand catalogues or at auction sales. The proper price may be determined only by long experience, thorough bibliographic knowledge and careful comparison. In the Order Department ordinary commercial experience, especially in the book trade, is of service, for there are trade usages to be understood, invoices to be handled and accounts to be kept. But in a large library there is needed in the control of the work a wide bibliographic knowledge also; and as perhaps fifty per cent. of the books bought are in foreign languages, linguistic knowledge is a necessity beyond that required in the ordinary book trade.

Before the book reaches the reader the invoice is checked up (and perhaps identified in the volume by a memorandum on the reverse of the title-page), the book is entered in the "accession book," a record of each volume in the order received—author, title, volume, imprint, date, size, source and cost, at least, being given. The accession number is minuted on the reverse of the title-page, the title-page stamped with the name of the library; a book-plate inserted, with the name of the fund (or the donor, if the book be a gift), and the volume is ready for the Shelf Department. It must then be classified, find a proper location, and a number that shall fix it in its place on the shelves.

Cataloguing is Usually Quite Elaborate

THE process of cataloguing may be as elaborate as the information sought to be conveyed. The minimum is an entry under the author, followed by the title, imprint, size and date of publication. But no catalogue does complete service which does not group the books also under the subjects of which they treat, and this subject index presents difficulties which may be solved only by long experience and technical knowledge. And besides the main catalogues there are special catalogues, bulletins, bibliographies and reference lists in which the book may appear in a score of serviceable relations. There is no limit to cataloguing except that set by the resources of the library.

The registration of the readers is a matter of simple clerical record under the rules of . . .

A Library is Not a Literary Workshop

THE bulk of the miscellaneous library of to-day consists of history (in the broader sense) and of pure literature (belles-lettres). The history is not merely the ordinary civil and political history, but the history of the sciences, and of the arts, and of literature. And as regards the capacities of the library attendants in the handling of pure literature there is a distinction. It is not skill in literary composition nor skill in literary criticism that is needed. A library is not for the employees a literary workshop; it offers to them almost no opportunity for the exercise of purely literary accomplishments. What is serviceable to the library is a knowledge of the facts of history and of literature—of the literature of history and of the history of literature: the events of each. The tendencies are the study of the reader himself. Chronology, which may be contemptible to the philosopher, may be of the utmost use to the librarian: for his chief service is to locate, not to explain.

The following questions are taken from the entrance examination of a library school: "What was the Holy Roman Empire? For what ideas do the following men and women stand before the world: Robert Owen, Froebel, Demosthenes, Frances Willard, etc.? What is suggested to your mind by the following: Seleucidæ, Argon, Naseby, Weissmannism, The Gloucester, Brünnhilde, Filioque, Unearned Increment, Le Salon Carré, etc.? Who were the schoolmen? Which are the great periods in the history of English literature and the men most prominent in each? Who wrote—(and here various books were given by title)?"

A Thorough General Education is Needed

THESE questions indicate very fairly the kind of knowledge required of a library attendant in the ordinary course of his work: history, literature and general information. In addition, as a tool, he should have a knowledge of languages, of which French, German and Latin are the most serviceable.

The best general education for library work is therefore a thorough and systematic general education. Mere "love of books and reading" will never take the place of this. But there is such a thing as special training also, and there are library schools which provide this. There is, for instance, a school at Albany, there is one at Brooklyn (the Pratt Institute), at Philadelphia (the Drexel Institute), in Illinois (the University of Illinois, Champaign), at Washington (the Columbian University). The courses in these vary from one year to three. That at the University of Illinois is two years of library economy combined with two years of general university work, leading to a degree of Bachelor of Library Science. The course at Albany will yield a degree of B.L.S., and if combined with practical library work of M.L.S. or D.L.S. The entrance examinations for these schools are already severe, and the tendency is to advance the standards.

How to Obtain the Best Positions

FOR persons who cannot afford the time or the expense of the winter schools there are summer schools—at Albany, for instance, also at Amherst, Massachusetts, and Madison, Wisconsin, etc. These in a few weeks give a summary view of the chief departments of library economy.

As time goes on the best positions in library work, as in any other profession, will go to those who have had such special professional training in addition to a thorough general education. At present of the thou- . . .

7

Two Pioneers:
E.O.S. Scholefield and Helen Gordon Stewart

British Columbia has seen many keen librarians and library supporters, but there is no doubt about the two most influential ones: Ethelbert Olaf Stuart Scholefield and Helen Gordon Stewart.

Scholefield had a high school diploma; Stewart had been trained in library work, and eventually earned her doctorate. Scholefield was keenly interested in history, while Stewart looked to the future. Scholefield married and had four children, but Stewart remained single. Scholefield was forty-four when he died; Stewart was

Opposite: A feature article in *The Ladies' Home Journal*, February 1900, inspired Helen Gordon Stewart to become a librarian. *Dave Obee collection*

Above: Beech tree planted in memory of E.O.S. Scholefield beside the Legislative Library in 1920 was still paying tribute at the start of the 21st Century. *B.C. Legislative Library*

ninety-one. Both came from large families — Scholefield had nine brothers and sisters, and Stewart had eight. Both had ministers as fathers, although Scholefield's was Anglican and Stewart's was Presbyterian.

Most important of all, Scholefield helped bring Stewart to British Columbia. Working together and separately, they revolutionized library service in the province.

E.O.S. — as Ethelbert was known for most of his life — was born in 1875 in Ryde, on England's Isle of Wight. In 1887 his father, Rev. Stuart Clement Scholefield, brought the family to British Columbia, living briefly in New Westminster before settling in Esquimalt. E.O.S. attended St. Paul's parish school, then Victoria High School. On graduating he became a page in the Legislature.

In April 1894, provincial librarian R. Edward Gosnell hired eighteen-year-old Scholefield as his assistant at $25

E.O. S. Scholefield served as provincial librarian from 1898 to 1919. *Image B09788 courtesy of Royal BC Museum, BC Archives*

a month. When Gosnell was fired as librarian in late 1898, Scholefield, just twenty-three, was given the position on an interim basis for a few months before being formally appointed. Over the next two decades he worked for eight premiers, added about 100,000 books to the Provincial Library, acted as the driving force behind the Provincial Archives and led the fight for library development. In his spare time, he was the co-author of a four-volume history of British Columbia.

His accomplishments were especially remarkable considering that Scholefield had no formal training as a librarian, as an archivist or as a historian. He learned as he worked, and set a high standard for those who followed. At the time of his appointment, British Columbia had only one trained librarian: Alma Russell, who catalogued books at the Provincial Library and ran the travelling library service.

Scholefield attacked his job with enthusiasm, adding to the collection as quickly as he could and travelling extensively to acquire books and documents. In May 1905 he was appointed to the board of the new Carnegie library in Victoria. Two months later, Scholefield and Russell went to Portland, Oregon, for the American Library Association's annual conference. Scholefield gave a presentation on B.C.'s travelling libraries. Another speaker was Melvil Dewey, the creator of a cataloguing system that was being embraced throughout North America.

In 1907, Scholefield was honoured by both sides of the legislature before he went to New Westminster to marry Lillie May Corbould. After an extended honeymoon in the eastern United States, the Scholefields settled into a home on Pemberton Road in Victoria.

Scholefield built a collection of relics relating to Simon Fraser's trip along the Fraser River in 1808, and helped William Holland Keary, the mayor of New Westminster, celebrate the Fraser centennial in 1908. Gosnell, newly appointed as the provincial archivist, also helped mark the anniversary by helping create a Fraser exhibit at New Westminster's 1908 fair.

In 1909, Scholefield went to the University of Washington in Seattle for a three-day meeting with thirty-five librarians from Oregon and Washington. He was the only Canadian at the meeting, which was tied to the Alaska-Yukon-Pacific Exposition. The world's fair promoted the development of the Pacific Northwest.

On June 10, the group adopted a constitution and a set of bylaws, and the Pacific Northwest Library Association came into being as a body that would encourage a spirit of co-operation and an exchange of ideas. It was, and is, the only regional library association to cross an international boundary. The following year, Scholefield was elected the group's first vice-president. At his urging the group scheduled its next gathering in Victoria. That meeting, in September 1911, would help shape the future of libraries in British Columbia.

> Fiction is always read with avidity, but it seems a pity that the usefulness of a public library should be judged by the number of novels that it circulates.
> *Ethelbert Olaf Stuart Scholefield*

In the meantime, Scholefield became the provincial archivist in addition to his role as provincial librarian. The archives had been created in 1908 with Gosnell in charge, but once again Gosnell was fired and Scholefield was named as his replacement. Scholefield's heart had always been in historical documents, and he was enthusiastic about the role of the archives: To collect, arrange, catalogue and securely guard historical data relating to the early years of British Columbia.

"It is the intention to make the provincial department of archives the repository for all manuscripts relating in any way to the history of British Columbia," he said. It was important to get documentary testimony that would illuminate early history. "All history is, or rather should be, founded upon original sources and not upon what are termed 'secondary sources' which, in the past, have been responsible so often for the perpetuation of false impressions of men and events," he said.

Scholefield said rich sources of information on early B.C. were in libraries and archives such as the Hudson's Bay Company offices, the admiralty offices and the colonial offices in London, England, as well as the Archives of the Indies in Madrid, the archives of the Oregon State Historical Society, the universities of Washington and California and the national archives in St. Petersburg, Russia.

He promised that the Provincial Archives would soon become "the Mecca of the historians of Western Canada," and predicted that interest in history would rise. Scholefield organized the archives by creating four eras: The period of apocryphal voyages and explorations, dating from 1578 to 1774; the period of discovery, exploration and fur trade, 1774 to 1849; the colonial period, reaching to 1871, when the united colonies of Vancouver Island and British Columbia entered Confederation; and the modern period, from 1871 to 1910.

As a member of the Victoria library board, Scholefield hired Helen Gordon Stewart to serve as the assistant to Dr. J. Griffith Hands, the head librarian. Stewart was the second trained librarian in British Columbia, after Russell, and the first to come from outside the province.

Stewart was born in 1879, in Raleigh township near Chatham in Ontario's Kent County. Known as Nell to her family, she moved to Manitoba when her father Frank B. Stewart accepted a position in a church there. Hers was a family of high achievers; her brother David became a prominent tuberculosis doctor who helped change the way the disease was treated, and her sister Isabel moved to the United States where she became a leading nursing educator and co-wrote *A Short History of Nursing* in 1920.

Stewart lived in the small town of Carman before going to Winnipeg to attend Manitoba College. When illness forced her to quit her studies, she worked as a teacher and then in an office. One day, reading *The Ladies' Home Journal*, she saw an article that changed her life: "What it Means to be a Librarian," by Herbert Putnam of the Library of Congress. Putnam told of five librarianship courses in the United States, and Stewart decided to apply to three of them. She had never been inside a public library — Manitoba did not have any — but the courses were in keeping with her love of books.

She was accepted at all three schools, but chose a one-year course in librarianship run by the New York Public Library. She left Manitoba in 1908 and a year later, at the end of the course, she was hired as the assistant children's librarian at New York's new Hamilton Fish Park branch. More than 12,000 children were members of the branch, which lent more than 900 books every day.

In 1910 Stewart returned to Winnipeg and saw an advertisement placed by Scholefield on behalf of the Victoria Public Library, which was looking for an assistant librarian familiar with the Dewey and Cutter cataloguing systems. Stewart applied and was hired. She arrived in Victoria on October 15, 1910.

The library stacks were closed to patrons, which meant that staff members retrieved books as they were requested. They used a cumbersome system of coloured markers, developed in England by Alfred Cotgreave, to determine whether a book was on the shelves or on loan. The books were in no particular order. That changed when Stewart introduced the Dewey decimal system, with books sorted by topic. She also allowed patrons to find books for themselves.

Soon after Stewart arrived in Victoria, she wrote a lengthy essay in the *Daily Colonist* newspaper, saying that forty to fifty per cent of a library's collection should be fiction. She suggested that technology could help libraries provide better service. Reference questions could be answered, she said, by mail or by telephone, and typewritten lists "scattered here and there" would provide suggestions for patrons not sure of which book to borrow.

She argued for a children's room, a concept that had not yet caught on in Canada, saying that in New York City, reading enabled boys and girls to gain a broad, sure education. "By the time they left the public school and earned the right to be admitted to the shelves of grownups, they had read most of the works of Stevenson, Fenimore Cooper, Eliot, Thackeray, Dickens and Scott in fiction and history and travel and poetry and civics and science and art, suited to their years, that would make their elders stare if they were confronted with the list," she wrote.

On January 1, 1911, she wrote again in the *Colonist*, saying that a children's section should be a priority. "A children's library helps to equalize chances, helps to take away handicaps and allows everyone an even start. It stimulates healthy appetites and satisfies them; it suggests higher ambitions; it supplies standards."

A few weeks later, Stewart said schools and libraries needed to work together. "They need each other — must supplement, reinforce, complement each other — the one to guide, the other to open the way. There must be specialized care and freedom, and this with the one end always in view — the adequate education of the individual from infancy to death." Stewart's dream of a children's library had to wait, however — the Victoria library simply did not have enough money to start something new.

Stewart and Scholefield welcomed librarians from throughout the region to Victoria in September 1911 for the Pacific Northwest Library Association's conference. Scholefield was elected the organization's president. At the end of the conference, Stewart, Scholefield and eight other librarians founded the British Columbia Library Association. But their efforts on behalf of all libraries and readers in the province were put on hold because of a financial crisis. Both resigned when stingy voters would not provide more money to the Victoria library.

Rev. William Washington Bolton, who two decades earlier had taught Scholefield in Esquimalt, said in a letter to the *Colonist* that Stewart's departure would hurt the library. "She has been a great acquisition to that institution, and has won the regard of all book lovers by her intelligence and courtesy," he said. "The system she was introducing, which pertains in all up-to-date libraries, would have resulted in very great benefit to all frequenters of our local library, and it seems altogether too bad that we should have to lose so

Helen Gordon Stewart soon after she arrived in Victoria in 1910. *Victoria Public Library*

highly trained a public servant."

More money was found for the library, the crisis passed, and Stewart returned to work. Soon, new books were being ordered and the board members could resume their discussions about a children's room that would, they said, "undoubtedly prove a valuable adjunct to the institution."

Scholefield continued building the collection at the Provincial Archives. On a vacation to the United States in December 1911, he addressed the Oregon State Historical Society and met several prominent historians in California. His goal was to increase co-operation between the historical societies along the Pacific coast.

In May 1912, Stewart was named the head librarian, succeeding Dr. J. Griffith Hands on his retirement. Within weeks she started speaking to community groups about libraries, books and the value of reading. She had a way of getting attention; when she addressed the Young People's Society of the First Baptist Church, for example, she started by talking about the Middle Ages, when few men could read. "Why should they?" she asked. "There were plenty of other things to do — other people's heads to hack off, distressed maidens to rescue, enemies' crops to burn, wild boars to hunt, great feasts to eat — why should they bother with books, monkish things not seemly for full-blooded, lively men?" Now, however, there was time to read.

She also warned of the dangers of inveterate fiction reading. "Fiction fiends, as we often call them, are usually poor unfortunates who are not in the least acquainted with themselves, and who have grown up such strangers to the real world that they have to drug themselves to make them forget their loneliness. Some get drunk instead, or smoke opium, or use laudanum or cocaine. These demoralize the body more, and react a little more strongly upon other people, but after all, there is not much difference in result."

In August 1912, Scholefield again travelled to the Interior to collect information and material, noting — as archivists have noted countless times — that the trip should have been made a decade earlier, before irreplaceable items had been lost and many pioneers died.

In Kamloops he examined the sites of three Hudson's Bay Company forts, and had reference photographs taken for the archives. He then travelled to Ashcroft, Quesnel and Barkerville. It was hard to realize, Scholefield said, that fifty years earlier Barkerville had been "a thronging, bustling, wide-open town, with all the appurtenances to be expected in civilization where gold was plentiful." The prosperity had departed but the spirit of hope remained.

Scholefield collected photographs of the early 1860s and spent a morning in the Barkerville cemetery, recording inscriptions such as one written by chief justice Matthew Baillie Begbie on the grave stone of former judge Chartres Brew: "A man imperturable in courage and temper, endowed with a great and varied administrative capacity, a most ready wit, a most pure integrity and a most human heart."

Scholefield continued to the courthouse in Richfield, the first community on Williams Creek, which he described as rich in historical documents. He also visited other historic communities such as 150 Mile House, Fort George, Fort St. James and Fraser Lake.

Scholefield and R. Edward Gosnell, his former boss, worked together on *British Columbia: Sixty Years of Progress*, published in 1913. Scholefield also worked with Frederick William Howay, a keen historian and library board member in New Westminster, on *British Columbia From its Earliest Times to the Present*. For his work on the history and geography of the north Pacific coast and northwestern part of the continent, Scholefield was elected a fellow of the Royal Geographical Society. One of his sponsors was Sir Ernest Shackleton, the Antarctic explorer.

It is more or less commonly supposed that our province has no history worth speaking of, although as a matter of fact we have a history brimful of interest and fascinating in the extreme, for the exploits of the British and Spanish navigators on our seaboard, and the long and hazardous journeys of great explorers through our territory, the doing of the fur traders, the rush of the gold seekers in 1858 and the years immediately following, the landing of the Royal Engineers and the story of their pioneer work, the establishment of colonial government in the land, and our joining with the Dominion of Canada in 1871, and the long discussion which led up to that happy consummation are each and all themes of surpassing interest, and it is only meet and right that something be done at this happy juncture in our affairs to commemorate suitably these historic landmarks, as well as to honour those single-hearted and noble men who bore the heat and burden of the day.
Ethelbert Olaf Stuart Scholefield

Scholefield and Stewart spoke at dozens of public meetings, Scholefield exploring history and Stewart promoting libraries. Scholefield became a popular speaker in Vancouver and Victoria, and accepted more engagements than he could fill. His workload took a toll on his health and he needed to take time off to recuperate.

Stewart also worked tirelessly. She always welcomed ways to get attention for her cause. "If any organization wanted to know about the public library, I made it my business to accept the invitation to speak, and give them what they wanted," she said in a 1964 interview. "I went to the Women's Institutes and such. Usually it was just somebody to fill a program, but it seemed to me if they wanted it, it was publicity anyway."

Victoria's children's room opened in 1913, and while it increased the number of library patrons by 80 per cent, the library was still committed to serving adults. That December, in a letter to J.J. Shallcross, the president of the Board of Trade, Stewart said the library had about 12,000 books for adult circulation. Victoria's building boom that year had been reflected in library activity. Books on concrete, cement and construction were in high demand, along with books on electricity and illumination. Agricultural books, especially those on chickens, sheep and pigs, were popular, along with books on accounting, engineering and oil.

> The school gives the preliminary preparation for education; the library gives the means by which the individual completes and accomplishes his education, and in the doing of it, fills the cracks of his life with joy beyond comparison, gives him the lamp of Aladdin with its attentive genius, and renders him, if he will, invulnerable against the vicissitudes of life.
>
> *Helen Gordon Stewart*

The reference desk had seen increased interest in sociological and economic theory. "A larger percentage of people do not take socialism for granted, but hunt it down, pros and cons, and decide for themselves," Stewart said. Patrons were eager to discuss the advisability of government ownership, the pros and cons of women suffrage and the ideas raised by Karl Marx. Librarians were asked about topics such as immigration, liquor legislation and infant mortality.

Stewart launched a training program in the library to encourage more young people to become librarians. "For taking the trouble to establish and conduct this training school, Miss Stewart is entitled to the gratitude of the women of Victoria," columnist Maria Lawson wrote in the *Colonist*.

In 1914, Stewart addressed the British Columbia Teachers Institute in Vancouver, stressing the need for libraries in high schools. That summer she introduced a reference library for teachers from both regular and Sunday schools, and made plans for a branch library in the Victoria high school. Stewart's workload was too much; the following year she took a three-month leave of absence to restore her health. Her leave also helped the library, which was having trouble paying her $75 monthly salary.

In early 1916, with war raging in Europe, Stewart announced that she was quitting her job so she could help the war effort in Britain, and said she felt that she had nothing more to accomplish at the Victoria library. By that time, Stewart's staff included six assistant librarians and four general assistants, along with four students in training.

"Victoria needed Miss Stewart when she came, more than five years ago, and it needs her still," the *Colonist* said in an editorial. The library board members were reluctant to let her go, but finally agreed to an indefinite leave. Stewart said that if she could not find war work in England, she would get in touch with social movements for ideas that would help her on her return to Victoria.

In late May, Stewart went to New York, then sailed to Glasgow and made her way to London. She worked with Lady Julie Drummond, a philanthropist and humanitarian, who visited wounded soldiers and provided conveniences not otherwise available in hospitals. Later she worked for the French Wounded Emergency Fund, packing parcels to be shipped to convalescing soldiers. By September she was working in a rest station in Le Bourget, a major railway junction northwest of Paris, serving hot coffee, bread and soup and playing gramophone records for soldiers as they waited for trains. Many of the men had been in the battle of the Somme.

"We dole coffee and wind gramophones steadily," she said in a letter home. "We usually let the men choose their own records. Rather hard on the records, but they enjoy it so, and we chat away in the meantime. My hat, the amount of gramophone — all the way from American ragtime to grand opera. We grind out French things mostly, except that *Tipperary* and *God Save the King* sandwich in about every two, by special request."

Stewart provided basic first aid, dealing with, as she put it, "bashed thumbs, festered nails, blistered heels, cut lips, aching teeth, heads, stomachs." Serious wounds were referred to a nearby Red Cross train. She also described a church service she attended with scores of soldiers: "It was all so simple and straight from the shoulder, and they knew, those silent listeners, that probably their next mass would be on the other side of Jordan. They go back to the front tomorrow and to die, if necessary, for God and country."

After serving in Le Bourget for six months, Stewart went to Rambervillers, near Strasbourg in eastern France, and helped men whose feet had been frozen at Verdun. Then it was off to Scotland to visit a cousin. She returned to Canada in May 1917, and arrived in Victoria on June 9. Her first words at the dock: "Oh, it's good to be back." Within days she was back to her job as Victoria's head librarian.

Stewart gave lengthy interviews to both Victoria newspapers, and noted that she had spent two weeks doing research in the Bibliothèque Nationale. She stressed the need for everyone to get involved in the war effort, and urged readers to send whatever they could to the men at the front. She admitted that she had changed her mind about one thing. "When I left here I had a sort of sneaking contempt for the gramophone, but that is past," she told the *Daily Times*. "After seeing how these men, some of them so crippled that they would hobble out on their knees, would gather round to hear the music, I have changed my opinion."

Stewart was the special guest at a reception organized by Rev. Bolton and E.O.S. Scholefield. Her calendar was full in the weeks after her return as she spoke to groups to stress how impressed she had been with the strength of the French people in the face of war. Her audiences included the Women's Canadian Club, the Victoria Nurses Association, the University Women's Club, the Garden City Women's Institute and the Unitarian Church in Victoria as well as the Women's Institute in Duncan and the University Club in Seattle.

In September 1916, while Stewart was in France, Scholefield was elected president of the B.C. Library Association, and the next year Stewart succeeded him. The two were named to a committee to push for improved library legislation, and together promoted the idea that greater co-operation between libraries, with increased sharing of resources, would result in better public service. They also worked with Margaret Clay, the head of the children's department at the Victoria library, on a series of lectures on libraries at the Victoria Normal School, where teachers were trained.

Stewart broke an important barrier in November 1917 when she became the first woman to address Victoria's all-male Rotary Club. "It is indeed time that we should consider ourselves past the period when men and women must be divided," she said. "It is foolish to place man in one airtight compartment and women in another. We are all human, all living in one world, and the interests of us all are related."

She told Rotarians that a library should be an extension of a university, a recreational centre to rival movies, and a workshop and laboratory. A library should help the public choose the best books, she said, and she urged club members to use the library more often. "Why not make the Victoria Public Library a spoke in your famous Rotarian Wheel?" The club president told Stewart that if the members ever decided to admit women, her application would be one of the first to be considered. And with that, she received a standing ovation.

Scholefield, meanwhile, had a high profile as the head of the Provincial Library and the Provincial Archives. His stature was reflected in a variety of ways. In March 1918, for example, he handled the arrangements for the public funeral of former premier Harlan Brewster.

The war in Europe ended on November 11, 1918. "With peace comes reconstruction in all its complexity," Stewart told the *Daily Times*. "Labour problems and trade problems and government problems confront us, social adjustments and the rearrangement of ethical values — and the vital importance of the decisions which must be made give to some at least an almost fierce determination to get to the bottom of things."

She predicted a rising demand for information, and warned that B.C. was not ready to meet that demand. "Victoria and Vancouver make some attempt to give their residents free access to the bulk of the expressed thought of the time, and New Westminster does what it can, but elsewhere there is practically nothing. Two or three towns keep a meagre assortment of books, largely fiction, but not one makes any attempt at a well-equipped workshop of ideas."

Travelling libraries, she said, were only designed to remove the worst handicaps from the isolated and sparsely settled districts; they were not meant to serve towns and villages. And while schools were teaching children to read, most did not have access to public libraries. Stewart compared that to training a man for seven years to make shoes or machinery, and then turning him loose without leather or iron.

Stewart took charge of the B.C. Library Association's efforts to encourage new legislation, and consulted with local organizations and legislators to draft an acceptable bill. In March 1919, after years of lobbying by the association, the legislation was approved and Stewart was named to the new Public Library Commission.

By that time Scholefield was seriously ill. He had been diagnosed with pernicious anemia, a fatal disease at the time, and was given a life expectancy of one to three years. He was admitted to Victoria's St. Joseph's Hospital in December 1919, and died there on Christmas Day at forty-four years of age.

"He was known and admired for his accomplishments in the avocation to which he had devoted the greater part of his life," the *Daily Times* said the next day. "No public officer ever gave more faithful service to this province; indeed, Mr. Scholefield's premature death is due to the exhaustion of his vital forces upon the institution of which he was the head."

Scholefield was buried in Ross Bay Cemetery. In the spring of 1920, members of the new Victoria Library Club — formed by staff members from the public and provincial libraries — planted a copper beech tree in Scholefield's memory next to the Provincial Library. Premier John Oliver expressed the Legislative Assembly's appreciation of Scholefield's service.

March 1920: Premier John Oliver plants a beech
tree in honour of E.O.S. Scholefield, witnessed by
Helen Gordon Stewart, members of the Victoria
Library Association and others. *Image G-06259
courtesy of Royal BC Museum, BC Archives*

Stewart devoted herself to library commission work while maintaining her hectic pace at the Victoria library. In 1920 that prompted a clash with Victoria's library board, and Stewart threatened to resign unless she was allowed time to work on the provincial organization. "The loss of Miss Stewart's services would be a blow from which the library might never recover," the *Daily Times* observed. William J. Sargent, the Victoria alderman who was chairman of the library board, settled the dispute by saying it had all been a misunderstanding.

Stewart served on the Women's Canadian Club executive and the Esquimalt School Board. The Canadian Labour Party asked her to run for the Legislature, but she declined. In 1920 she was elected president of the Pacific Northwest Library Association.

In 1922, Stewart went to Prince Rupert for a week to lead a library campaign. Many prominent citizens were working on the project, and had collected about 1,750 books. She addressed a public meeting, met city council and spoke to community organizations to stress the need for a library. In 1923, after a Nanaimo bylaw failed to allocate money for a public library, Stewart went there to encourage the library association and lead the drive for the creation of a library. In both cases her efforts were successful.

In 1924, Stewart resigned from the Victoria library so she could tour Europe and further her education. Her accomplishments had been remarkable. The library had 19,000 members, representing forty-nine per cent of the population, and offered children's services, training for librarians and ease of access because of the Dewey decimal system. Stewart had been president of the Pacific Northwest Library Association and the B.C. Library Association, which she helped organize. She had helped draft a public library act and ran the commission created by the act. She had helped start twenty public library associations as well as public libraries in Prince Rupert, Nelson and Nanaimo.

"It can be said of Miss Stewart that she worked all her wakeful hours," the *Daily Times* said in an editorial. "The library has been both means of livelihood and absorbing hobby. But her duties there have not isolated her from the realm of community service."

Stewart went to Columbia University in New York City to work on a bachelor's degree, followed quickly by a master's and a PhD. She also worked as secretary to Geraldine Livingston Morgan Thompson, a social reformer in New York and New Jersey. In 1927 Stewart was appointed head of the Department of Sociology at Wells College in Aurora, Cayuga County, N.Y., and stayed there for two years.

With Scholefield dead and Stewart out of the country, library development in British Columbia slowed. Arthur Herbert Killam, the superintendent of the Public Library Commission, looked after travelling libraries and the Open Shelf books-by-mail program, but the commission did little to encourage expansion or development.

Leadership of the library community passed to people such as John Ridington at the University of British Columbia; Alma Russell, John Forsyth and John Hosie at the provincial library; Edgar Stewart Robinson at the Vancouver Public Library and Margaret Jean Clay at the Victoria Public Library. They were supported by hard-working library trustees such as Frederick William Howay and Hugh Norman Lidster.

Starting in late 1926, Norman Fergus Black led a revival of the Public Library Commission that saw a huge survey of service and resulted in an experimental library in the Fraser Valley, testing the viability of a library covering a wide geographic area, and the return of Helen Gordon Stewart to British Columbia.

The Carnegie Corporation had offered $100,000 to the demonstration as long as a suitable manager could be found. Stewart had the unanimous support of the commission members as well as Carnegie president Dr. Frederick Paul Keppel. Her selection made sense, even though she had never been to the Fraser Valley, because her PhD thesis had been on "Rural Library Services with Special Reference to British Columbia."

Stewart arrived in Victoria in February 1930 to discuss the project with the library commissioners. Then it was off to Vancouver on the midnight boat so she could set up an office and get to work. As always, she worked as many hours as she could, snacking on almonds and raisins so she could keep going. Her job was to convince Fraser Valley residents of the value of libraries in the midst of an unprecedented economic depression.

In her talks to community groups, Stewart stressed it would be impossible for a person to keep up with the flood of information being made available. Four hundred billion sheets of paper were leaving presses every year but she argued that a library would help its patrons find their way through the great chaos of printed material. Someday, she said, libraries might not have books, but they would still help patrons find what they were looking for.

In May 1930 she told the Women's Canadian Club in Victoria that a great effort was being made to supply reading material to people in the country. For years, she said, it was believed that a person outside a city would be satisfied with "his hoe or patent incubator," and would have no need of "stimulus of mind and spirit." Now that theory had been rejected and a great effort was being made to supply reading material to country dwellers.

In August, Stewart suggested the establishment of "reading diets," collections designed for circulation through hospitals. A study had found that one-third of hospitals did not have libraries and most of the libraries that did exist had only twenty-five to fifty books.

In 1931 she was elected, for the second time, president of the B.C. Library Association. She also remained heavily involved in the Pacific Northwest Library Association. In May 1933, she told a meeting of librarians that they needed to learn more about their communities and ensure they were doing all they could to serve their patrons. Reading, she said, had become more and more a universal language, no longer a specialized art. Under the old order, librarians had adopted a "benevolent paternalism," believing that merely placing the best books within reach of everyone would result in everyone reading the best books. That thinking changed because of the development of a great reading mass dominated by mob opinions.

Stewart worked eighteen hours a day, six and seven days a week, to make the Fraser Valley demonstration a success. "Choosing the books, actively acquainted with every detail, working with school teachers and leaders of communities, addressing large gatherings, driving miles to have an hour for the morrow, she is indefatigable in mind and body," Mary A. Barber wrote in the *Daily Province*. "There is just one little weakness … she is not the world's best motor driver, but she always gets there just the same, as she always gets anywhere she wants to go." Stewart had learned to drive only after getting the job in the Fraser Valley.

No dream is more generally held by all mankind than that of freedom, no tool more vital in its pursuit than knowledge, no source of knowledge more rich than libraries.
Helen Gordon Stewart

After the Fraser Valley library was accepted by taxpayers and converted to a union library — referring to a union of several jurisdictions — Stewart worked to establish similar systems in the Okanagan Valley, on Vancouver Island and in the West Kootenay. She spoke to elected officials, community organizations and the public, always arguing that they would be better served by pooling resources.

She continued to promote the regional concept even after she realized it was time for a change in career. On April 22, 1936, she was at the Sunset Inn in Qualicum Beach, explaining to taxpayers how they would benefit from a union library. Six days later, she left Victoria, bound for Baton Rouge, Louisiana, where she would be the interim associate director of the School of Library Science at Louisiana State University. On her way to Louisiana she stopped in San Diego to address the annual conference of the California Library Association, and in Richmond, Virginia, to attend an American Library Association meeting.

She had planned to return home in 1938, when her term in Louisiana was completed, but she was sidetracked by a telegram from South Carolina asking her to promote the benefits of library development throughout the state. Her work ended in 1939 when the legislature refused to support a library system. After the failure — one of the few in her career — Stewart returned to Vancouver Island with retirement in mind.

She bought a five-acre estate on Feltham Road, close to Mount Douglas in Saanich, and lived with her collie, Peter, in a single-room cottage with a large fireplace and curtains of rustic-coloured onion sacking. She planted tomatoes and cabbages, daisies and dahlias, as well as marketable crops of registered seeds and roots. Everything was carefully labelled, just as she would label books in a library. Asked why she wanted to be a farmer, Stewart said that like the mythological giant, Antaeus, contact with Mother Earth renewed her strength.

It must have worked. In October 1940, at the age of sixty, she again agreed to help the Carnegie Corporation launch a library service. This time, it was in the Caribbean, where the government of Trinidad and Tobago wanted a regional system similar to the one in the Fraser Valley and based on a 1933 survey by Dr. Ernest Savage of the Edinburgh Public Library. Carnegie offered $70,000 for the project, $30,000 of which was for a central service. The remainder was for operating expenses over four years.

Stewart established the library's administrative and financial headquarters in Port of Spain, with a main library there for the northern region and another in San Fernando for the southern and southwestern region. She introduced centralized book selection and processing, created a catalogue, started a bookmobile service, and trained staff following the methods she had developed three decades earlier in Victoria. Her goal was to provide initial training that could be a base for more formal education at proper schools.

Stewart faced many difficulties establishing the service during wartime. Her travel to Trinidad in 1940 was risky considering the dangers in shipping lanes. One shipment of books for the library was lost in the blitz in England, and two shipments from Canada were lost at sea through enemy action. In 1944 Stewart went to England for meetings with colonial officials in London that led to scholarships being offered to her trainees.

The Carnegie deal required Trinidad and Tobago to take over the service after four years, ensuring it would be developed and remain free to patrons. Stewart continued as director after the transfer to the government in January 1945. Her framework was so effective that decades later, some branches remained in locations she had picked, and most of the senior librarians were people she had trained. By 1948, when Stewart resigned, there were 25,000 books in the Trinidad and Tobago library and another 25,000 elsewhere in the system.

She returned to her home and garden in Saanich that July. She sold much of her property, then set about organizing family papers and putting together a family tree.

At sixty-eight years old, she could look back with pride on a career that saw tremendous strides in library development, and her contribution was recognized by a new generation of librarians.

In 1954, Stewart was named an honourary life member of the Pacific Northwest Library Association. In 1962, the B.C. Library Association announced that it had created an award, named for Stewart, that would honour its members who had made, or were making, extraordinary contributions to librarianship. The accolade was designed to mark outstandingly varied and important careers, "work of particularly fundamental significance and unique merit which brings honour to the entire profession." In announcing the award, the association's executive said it would only be given with careful discrimination, and was not meant to be an annual or regular award.

The first Helen Gordon Stewart Award went to Stewart herself.

In 1963, in a ceremony in the old Carnegie library in Victoria, where Stewart had been the chief librarian many years before, she was made an honourary life member of the Canadian Library Association. She was also made an honourary life member of the Fraser Valley Regional Library, which presented her with a scroll. A bursary in her name, initially worth $100 per year, was established at the School of Librarianship at the University of British Columbia.

Stewart sold her property in 1966 and moved to an apartment overlooking Juan de Fuca Strait in Victoria's James Bay district. In early 1971 she moved to Vancouver to live in a seniors' home. She died in Vancouver's St. Paul's Hospital on April 5 that year.

Stewart left $19,000 to her nieces and nephews, along with $2,000 to the bursary in her name at the UBC School of Librarianship, $3,000 to the university's department of nursing education in memory of her sister Isabel, and $3,000 to the library at the University of Victoria. The remainder went to the Victoria Foundation for use in charitable purposes.

But Helen Gordon Stewart's greatest contribution could not be measured in dollars. She carried the torch handed to her by E.O.S. Scholefield, and became the driving force behind the modern library system in British Columbia, giving hundreds of thousands of people access to books.

1786	Private library brought to Nootka Sound
1807	Simon Fraser brings books for the North-West Company
1813	Daniel William Harmon of the North-West Company stresses the value of books
1835	Andrew Carnegie born in Scotland
1843	Victoria selected as name of new fort
1846	Boundary set between Canada and United States
1849	Hudson's Bay Co. leases Vancouver Island
1851	James Douglas appointed governor of Vancouver Island
1854	First coal miners arrive at Nanaimo
1858	*British Colonist* newspaper started in Victoria
1858	Fraser gold rush brings thousands to New Caledonia and Vancouver Island
1858	James Douglas sworn in as governor of British Columbia
1858	Miners head for Fraser goldfields
1858	New Caledonia becomes the colony of British Columbia
1858	Royal Engineers bring books from England
1858	W.F. Herre opens a commercial library in Victoria
1859	New Westminster becomes capital of British Columbia
1859	Pig War erupts over San Juan Island
1863	Library, of sorts, started by the legislative assembly
1864	Esquimalt becomes chief naval site on Pacific
1864	Victoria's Mechanics Library opens
1865	Library opens in New Westminster
1866	Two colonies are merged into one, called British Columbia
1867	Queen declares dominion of Canada
1867	Queen knights James Douglas
1868	Fire sweeps through Barkerville
1868	Moodyville Mechanics Institute starts a library
1868	Victoria named capital of united colony
1869	New London Mechanics Institute opens at Hastings
1869	Law Society sets up a library in Victoria
1871	British Columbia becomes a province in Canada
1885	Canadian Pacific Railway completed
1885	Ottawa places head tax on Chinese
1886	Fire levels Vancouver
1886	Librarian named for legislature's collection of books
1887	Vancouver Public Library started
1888	Pioneer steamer Beaver sinks
1889	Victoria Mechanic's Institute library passes to the city
1890	Law Society opens library in New Westminster
1891	Free Libraries Act passed
1892	New Westminster's new library opens
1892	Theodore Davie becomes premier
1893	Eliza Machin provides a dinner for Vancouver's homeless
1893	Nakusp has small church and school libraries
1893	R. Edward Gosnell becomes provincial librarian
1893	Vancouver library moves to larger quarters
1893	Law society opens library in Vancouver
1894	Legislative Library Act passed
1894	Pioneer Judge Matthew Baillie Begbie dies
1897	Alma Russell, the first trained librarian in the province, joins the provincial library
1897	Klondike gold rush begins
1897	Legislative library moves to larger quarters in Parliament Buildings
1898	Ethelbert Olaf Stuart Scholefield becomes provincial librarian at the age of 23
1898	Nelson's first library opens
1898	New Westminster's new library is burned in the great fire
1898	Travelling libraries started
1899	Volunteers head off to war in South Africa
1901	Andrew Carnegie offers a library to Vancouver
1901	Queen Victoria dies
1902	Andrew Carnegie offers libraries to New Westminster and Victoria
1902	Rossland library and reading room opened
1903	Conservative Richard McBride becomes premier
1903	Vancouver's Carnegie library opens
1903	Victoria College opens
1905	Carnegie libraries open in New Westminster and Victoria
1906	Andrew Carnegie offers a library to Nelson, which says no thanks
1908	Provincial archives started

1909	Penticton public reading room opens
1910	E.O.S. Scholefield becomes archivist as well as librarian
1910	Helen Gordon Stewart arrives in Victoria
1911	British Columbia Library Association started
1911	Funding crisis at Victoria Public Library
1912	Duke of Connaught lays the cornerstone for new provincial library
1912	Gibsons library started
1912	New Westminster brings in the Dewey Decimal system
1912	Vancouver *Sun* starts publishing
1912	Powell River Company library started
1912	University of British Columbia holds first convocation – in Victoria
1913	Prince Rupert gets a reading room
1914-1918	First World War
1915	Connaught library opens at the legislature
1915	Kalamalka Women's Institute opens a library in Oyama
1915	University of British Columbia library starts with 20,000 books; John Ridington is librarian
1917	Prohibition starts in British Columbia
1918	Flu epidemic around the world
1918	Mary Ellen Smith becomes first female MLA
1919	Andrew Carnegie dies
1919	E.O.S. Scholefield dies
1919	Public Libraries Act creates Public Library Commission, with three members, reporting to Provincial Secretary
1919	Library associations formed in Corbin, Cowichan, Enderby, Nanaimo, Revelstoke and Sahltam
1919	Public Schools Act revised, and sets out duties of school librarians
1920	John Forsyth becomes provincial librarian and archivist
1920	Legislative library starts a reference department
1920	Library associations formed in Creston, East Collingwood, Fernie, Kaslo, Merritt, Nakusp, Penticton, Prince George, and Sidney
1920	Nelson municipal library formed
1920	Victoria College reopens after five-year break, moves to Craigdarroch Castle
1921	Library associations formed in Cassidy, Courtenay, Cumberland, Hollyburn, Kelowna and Port Alberni
1921	Teachers' professional library is established
1922	Books in print and raised type were sent to the School for the Deaf, the Dumb, and the Blind in Vancouver
1922	Prince Rupert public library opens
1922	Vanderhoof library opened by singles club
1923	Library referendum fails in Kamloops
1923	Nanaimo library wins taxpayer support
1923	Prince George appoints a librarian
1923	Public Library Commission appointments lapse
1924	Edgar Stuart Robinson becomes librarian at Vancouver at the age of 27
1924	Library associations formed in North Vancouver, Salmon Arm and Shawnigan Lake
1925	Library associations formed in Cranbrook and Invermere
1925	Trail library opened
1925	Putnam-Weir report confirms importance of school libraries
1925	UBC library moves to Point Grey campus
1926	John Hosie becomes provincial librarian and archivist
1926	Library associations formed in Ganges and Telkwa
1926	Quesnel community library started
1926	Vancouver School of Decorative and Applied Arts opens a library
1926	Public Library Commission revived

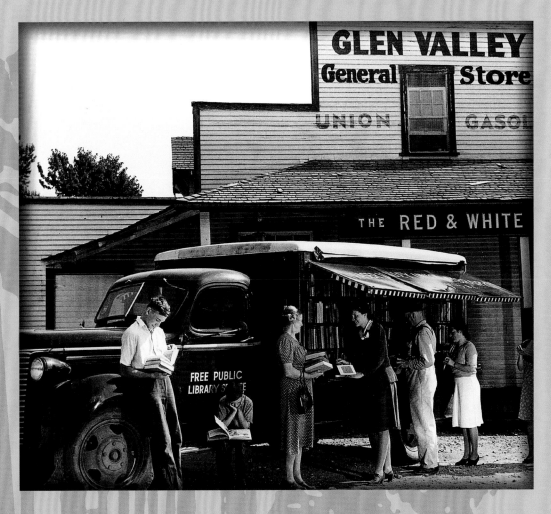

PART 2

1927 – 1959

8

LIBRARIES FOR
THE REGIONS

British Columbia's regional library systems — and regional systems around the world, for that matter — can trace their development to an overcrowded dining room in a house in Vancouver. There, in the home of Norman Fergus Black, the seeds were sown for the Fraser Valley Regional Library, the first of its kind in the world.

Black was one of three people appointed to the Public Library Commission after the provincial government decided to resume its efforts to establish library service in December 1926. The first commission, appointed in 1919, helped bring library service to several dozen communities, but its members were not replaced when their terms expired.

Opposite: Fraser Valley book van navigates one of the region's bumpy roads in the 1930s. *Bette Cannings*

Above: The Fraser Valley Public Library branch on Langley's Fraser Highway in the 1930s. *Langley Centennial Museum Photo Collection 925*

Norman Fergus Black in about 1912. *Dave Obee collection*

For three years it was a commission without commissioners. Superintendent Arthur Herbert Killam kept its work going as best he could. From his base in Victoria he was shipping hundreds of travelling libraries throughout the province and also looking after Open Shelf, the free mail-order service. His office also provided small grants to B.C.'s six municipal libraries and twenty-three public library associations, which were local organizations run by volunteers.

Besides the public libraries, books could be borrowed from school libraries, libraries run by businesses, and libraries that were simply shelves of donated books in mine or mill camps and settlements. Victoria had the Provincial Library and Victoria College, and Vancouver had the library at the University of British Columbia. But outside of Vancouver and Victoria, only thirty per cent of the urban population had access to libraries, and in rural areas, that number went down to five per cent.

It was time for another push. So Black and the other two new commissioners, Laura E. Jamieson of New Westminster and Christina Ross Frame of Victoria, met in January 1927 to consider ways to encourage library development. Their ideas included expanding service through travelling libraries, inter-library exchanges, delivering books by motor vehicle in regions such as the Fraser Valley and by railway in less-

accessible areas, more book lending by mail and express, and even the loan of sheet music and phonograph records.

Black set up an office on the fourth floor of the Dominion Bank Building in Vancouver, and the commissioners launched a survey of service so they could formulate policies and set priorities. "The immediate objective is to collect and to familiarize the public with definite information regarding not only public library associations and municipal libraries but any and all agencies contributing any form of library service in any part of British Columbia," Black said in a letter to newspapers. "The ultimate goal is the formulation of a provincial library which, with due regard to our financial conditions, will render existing libraries more efficient and will place a steady supply of good books within the reach of whoever in British Columbia desires such service."

The survey was the most ambitious project of its kind ever attempted in Canada. The commission enlisted about thirty people, including librarians, educators, businessmen and members of key community organizations. Almost every teacher in B.C. became involved, and a small volunteer army of correspondents — one estimate put the number at 2,300 — answered questionnaires on library services and needs. Black said later that he had been in contact with at least one person in every locality that had a post office.

A library expert, Clarence Brown Lester of Wisconsin, was hired to analyze the data and compile a report. The provincial government provided $896 to get the survey started, and the Carnegie Corporation donated $6,000 to complete it. Later, the province paid $850 to have the report printed.

In the fall of 1927, as the results started arriving, Black closed the commission's office and had the questionnaires shipped to his Vancouver home for tabulation. Every day the mail would bring "great bags of stuff," as his daughter Margaret Brunette said, and the replies eventually filled the family's dining room. Black used pins in a large map on the wall to keep track of communities and responses.

Black issued occasional bulletins with some of the ideas being considered. In January 1928, for example, he argued that every school should contain a public library branch. These libraries, he said, should have standard and reference books, and should exchange books with other libraries. Another idea was a library housed in a rail car, which the Canadian Pacific Railway could take to any hamlet needing service. The arrangement was similar to one in use in northern Ontario, where the CPR provided a car to the school system.

Black was considering putting books on rubber wheels as well. The cost to distribute a book by mail or freight was about 20 cents, but it would be about 8 cents through a book van. The commission sent out a questionnaire about the idea, and most of the people who responded expressed interest. Black said the plan could work year-round on the southeastern part of Vancouver Island and in the Fraser Valley, and in the Okanagan at least ten months a year. Vans became an integral part of the service introduced in these areas a few years later.

The commission's final report, prepared with Lester's help, was submitted to Provincial Secretary Samuel Lyness Howe on November 28, 1928, and was published in 1929. It laid out an ambitious plan to ensure that every area of the province would have library service. It recommended:

- Creating large self-supporting library districts in closely settled regions.
- Trying new ways of providing service to entire regions, using private funds — the Carnegie Corporation, in other words — to minimize the cost to the province.
- Improving travelling library service, including book trucks and railway library cars to serve sparsely settled areas and library boats to serve coastal settlements.
- Revising the 1919 library law to allow a permanent Public Library Commission that would encourage local library development.
- Setting up book distribution centres in B.C.'s north and east.
- Linking school libraries with public library services.

There was no doubt that the library commission was meeting a need. Many people who obtained books thanked the staff for their efforts. The ones using Open Shelf were the most grateful; in most cases, they had no other access to books. "Your books are literally a godsend to isolated people like myself," one recipient said. Another said "I also would like to receive books from your library, as I find it very lonesome away up here on a homestead after spending my life in the City of London."

By 1929, Arthur Herbert Killam had a staff of six people and the commission's budget was almost $19,000, including $6,000 for buying new books. The commission gave grants totalling more than $1,800 to libraries in Alberni, Armstrong and Spallumcheen, Courtenay, Cowichan, Cumberland, Ganges, Hollyburn, Nanaimo, Nelson, New Westminster, North Burnaby, North Vancouver, Ocean Falls, Penticton, Prince Rupert, Shawnigan, Sidney, Vancouver, Vernon and Victoria.

The commission also tried to improve the quality of service offered by school libraries. "Modern educational practice requires the wide and constant use of books for supplementary reading and study, but our schools

Norman Fergus Black came to British Columbia in 1920 after working as a teacher, principal and school inspector on the Prairies. He wrote several books, including *A History of Saskatchewan and the Old North West* and *English for the Non-English*, and he left a lasting legacy to libraries through his work on the survey of the late 1920s. He retired in 1941, then spent several years working with Japanese-Canadians who had been displaced from the coast. He was made an honorary life member of the Canadian Library Association in 1963, and died in Vancouver the following January.

provide very little of such material," it noted in its annual report. "Owing to lack of funds, the one-room, ungraded schools are almost entirely without such helps; and the commission, without any formal provision for the purpose, is endeavouring to give them some assistance." Collections were sent to fifty-eight schools, but many applications were refused because of a lack of books.

The priority for the commission, based on the survey, was a demonstration library in a region with a lot of people spread over a wide area, which would make it difficult to start ordinary municipal libraries. If municipalities could work together, the theory went, a region could have service to match that found in larger communities.

The Carnegie Corporation offered $100,000 to establish a five-year demonstration. This offer — to pay for books and labour, unlike the buildings-only grants of a quarter-century earlier — guaranteed a level of library service that had never been seen before. "This offer was gratefully accepted," the commission noted in its annual report.

The Fraser Valley, the Okanagan Valley and Vancouver Island were identified as potential areas for the demonstration, and all three expressed interest in getting the Carnegie money. In September 1929, Victoria's *Daily Colonist* reported that people in the Okanagan and Fraser valleys were getting excited about the possibility of library service, and said people on Vancouver Island needed to get on board as well.

The newspaper urged just about everyone — boards of trade, parent-teacher associations, school boards, churches, native sons' societies, and "any groups awake to community progress" — to impress the Public Library Commission that the Island was the best place for the demonstration. The newspaper noted that $100,000 spread over five years could do wonders. That $20,000 a year was almost seven times higher than the $3,000 being spent in total each year by the small volunteer-run libraries outside of Victoria and Nanaimo, and would give Island residents much better libraries with more books and better service.

"The people of the Island should visualize the possibility of not only getting books at a larger number of points but also more books, books more up to date, books of better quality and wider range and more frequently exchanged," the *Colonist* said. "The opportunity constitutes a real bonanza for anyone interested in reading."

The Carnegie idea was to start a demonstration library with municipalities providing space for branches and books, paid for with the Carnegie funds, to come from the commission. At the end of the demonstration, voters would decide whether the service was worth paying for. If it worked, the theory went, the demonstration would be an example to other areas and would inspire more regional libraries.

Dr. Frederick Paul Keppel, the president of the Carnegie Corporation, came to Victoria in December 1929 to meet government officials and confirm his willingness to help. At the Empress Hotel, he addressed a dinner that included among its guests Lieutenant-Governor Robert Randolph Bruce and Education Minister Joshua Hinchliffe. Keppel said he hoped the demonstration would be an illustration to other districts and other provinces. It would be, he said, a "departure from the stereotyped library forms from the viewpoint of its effectiveness."

A couple of days after Keppel's speech, the decision came: The Public Library Commission announced that it had decided on the most suitable region, a district which was geographically and economically a unit. With the commission's help and Carnegie's money, library service would be organized and developed in the Fraser Valley.

Fraser Valley

The decision thrilled the people of the Fraser Valley, but caused anger and resentment elsewhere. Charles J. Hurt, the president of Vernon's library association, said it would be impossible to find a district less in need of assistance than the Fraser Valley. Residents of the valley could visit libraries in New Westminster or Vancouver, and everyone could read daily newspapers the day they were published, he said. In the Okanagan, daily newspapers were one or two days late and no bookstores carried comprehensive stocks. Hurt said the public libraries in Armstrong, Vernon and Summerland were wonderfully patronized but offered only a small number of books.

"During the last year we have been visited by several

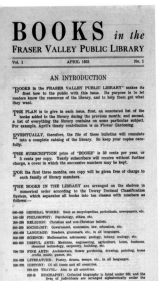

In the 1930s the Fraser Valley library published a booklist to help borrowers choose. *Fraser Valley Regional Library*

eminent messengers from the board who have delighted us with lectures descriptive of the wonderful intellectual treats in store for the lucky district to be selected as an experimental basis for this proposed gift of the gods," Hurt said in a letter to the *Daily Province* newspaper. "From the heights of intellectual anticipation we are plunged in the depths of dismal disappointment." He added that there would have been no complaint if another rural district had been selected — the objection was simply because more worthy districts had been "displaced by the milky monopolists of the Valley of the Fraser."

Hurt's blast did nothing to stop the demonstration. The commission hired Helen Gordon Stewart as the director-librarian in the Fraser Valley, and she returned to British Columbia from New York to take on the challenge. She said the demonstration was essential because people needed good reading material, because librarians had to find better ways of meeting their obligations to the public, and because people in rural areas did not have the same chance of mental stimulus as people in urban centres.

On February 17, 1930, the new library system started serving the Fraser Valley from Hope to Ladner with a truck. While it did not have branches yet, Stewart promised that books would be sent from a central station in Chilliwack in a bookmobile, the first of its kind in Canada. The one-ton truck had a specially built blue body and the words "Fraser Valley Public Library Commission" painted on its side in big letters. The vehicle could hold up to 1,200 books, with travel, biography, history and children's books on one side, and philosophy, the social sciences, science and arts and the practical on the other. The books were accessible when the sides were opened.

The vehicle was dubbed "Parnassus on Wheels." Stewart borrowed the title of Christopher Morley's 1917 book *Parnassus on Wheels*. The name Parnassus was a reference to the mountain that, in Greek mythology, was known as the home of poetry, music and learning. In the book, Morley wrote of Roger Mifflin, an itinerant bookseller who travelled through rural areas in a horse-drawn wagon named Parnassus selling books to farmers. "When you sell a man a book, you don't sell him just twelve ounces of paper and ink and glue," Mifflin says in the novel. "You sell him a whole new life."

The Fraser Valley's Parnassus followed scheduled routes through the valley, making circuits every two weeks and stopping at schools, community centres and, as they were opened, library branches. Children and settlers from isolated districts would meet the bus and exchange books.

Plans called for the system to have 15,000 books by the end of 1930 and 40,000 or 50,000 by the time the demonstration ended. Branches were planned for the major population centres, with the first ones scheduled for

THE ABBOTSFORD
PUBLIC LIBRARY

Requests the pleasure of your company at the

OPENING
CEREMONY

To take place on

Friday, August 29

At 4 p.m.

After that time books will be obtainable by all residents of Abbotsford, Sumas and Matsqui districts.

A number of horticultural books have been especially obtained for the free use of those attending the Flower Festival.

Left: Poster announces the opening of the Abbotsford library in 1930.
Bette Cannings

Below: Borrowers gathered at the book van to make their selections in the 1930s.
Bette Cannings

Bottom: Participants in a Depression-era spring festival take time out to celebrate the arrival of library service to the Fraser Valley. *Fraser Valley Regional Library*

Abbotsford, Mission, Cloverdale, Langley Prairie, Ladner and Haney. Smaller centres would be established at Hope, White Rock, Hazelmere and Agassiz. All 126 schools would have their own collections. Small community libraries, known as deposit stations, would be set up in places such as community halls, service stations and stores.

On August 6, 1930, the main library in Chilliwack opened to the public with several thousand books available. Branches opened in Mission on August 13, Abbotsford on August 29, Haney, Langley and Cloverdale in October and Ladner and White Rock in November. Parnassus carried books between the branches and to special book stops.

In February 1931, Stewart sent a progress report to Keppel at the Carnegie Corporation. "Every time we put a new book on the shelves, a new public arose to take it off, and we got no farther ahead," she said. The library owned 10,000 volumes at the end of 1930 and was struggling to meet demand. It had 1,000 books from the Public Library Commission and had borrowed others from the Provincial Library, the University of British Columbia library, and the public libraries in Vancouver, Victoria and New Westminster.

Stewart stressed that library service in the Fraser Valley

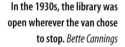

In the 1930s, the library was open wherever the van chose to stop. *Bette Cannings*

looked nothing like Carnegie libraries in large centres, noting that the branch in the community hall in Douglas, which had been built by volunteers, was "the ugliest little structure I have ever seen." She expressed concern about reading habits in the valley — "our circulation still shows a proportion of fiction which should pain the heart of a good librarian" — as well as satisfaction with the interest shown by the students in an isolated school. "Those infants are bottomless pits when it comes to books," she said.

In November 1932, Mary A. Barber of the *Daily Province* newspaper accompanied the bookmobile on its daily route. "It was pouring rain and the dusk of a Pacific Coast November day was crowding down on us," she wrote. "The two librarians on the library truck and their travelling guest, who had done nothing more (or less) than look and listen, were feeling just a little tired.

"It had been a full and happily interesting day, but a strenuous one, beginning at Chilliwack that morning before eight. Now, nearing five, after innumerable visits paid en route, we were at the other end of the Fraser Valley with two

stops to make to complete the day's schedule."

Barber described travelling through miles of virgin land, every so often glimpsing a settler building a home. Their last stop was at a school. "Our lethargy was shed as a cloak," she said. "Standing outside in the rain and crowding the narrow verandah and steps of the schoolhouse were men and women, boys and girls, faces alight with expectation. Radiating an enthusiasm that was contagious, they extended us a welcome that in spirit and warmth was everything the weather was not."

Barber said the truck followed roads that were little better than trails, and stopped at schoolhouses, corner grocery stores, gas stations and crossroads as it tried to meet the reading needs of 48,000 people in 1,600 square miles. Those people came to the bookmobile in a variety of ways — walking, cycling, wheeling baby carriages, riding horses, paddling in boats and driving in cars. And they were all happy to see it. "If we had been royal visitors we could not have been made more welcome," she wrote.

The youngest borrower was a four-year-old girl, and the oldest a man of eighty-five. One woman had walked several miles with a five-week-old baby. The bookmobile handled about 1,000 books during its four days on the road each week. The librarians processed ninety-nine books for every hour they were stopped. In fall and winter, when days were shorter, small gadget lights were clamped onto the sides of the truck to make it easier to see the titles. The librarians also relied on the lights from their patrons' cars.

By 1932, the system had 19,000 books and the truck was designed to keep them moving fluidly from place to place. The van was based in Chilliwack, the main receiving and distributing depot, and served six branches that were open fifteen to twenty-seven hours a week. Small sub-branches in Hope, White Rock and Port Coquitlam were open four to eight hours a week. Eight volunteer-run stations had 100 to 200 volumes. Altogether, twenty-two school libraries and fifty-five other points of call were visited every two weeks.

At every branch, deposit station or bus stop, a local committee was responsible for housing the books and paying incidental expenses. Some libraries were in purpose-built structures and others were in rooms in municipal halls. Deposit stations were usually on shelves in grocery stores or meat markets.

"The coming of the library service has meant the opening up of a new world for the people of the Fraser Valley, a world that holds a great revival of interest in the past as well as

Left: Like libraries, roads have changed dramatically since the 1930s. *Fraser Valley Regional Library*

Above: Book van drivers in the 1930s had to face tough conditions in winter. *Fraser Valley Regional Library*

a reawakening of interest in the new," Barber wrote in the *Province*. About sixty per cent of readers were interested in fiction, but the availability of non-fiction had sparked the creation of interest groups that discussed issues such as the five-year plans of the Soviet Union and travel in North America.

At the depth of the Depression, the $100,000 Carnegie funding for the Fraser Valley system ran out a year ahead of schedule; the library had been busier than expected. Now it would need taxpayer support to continue. Each jurisdiction in the valley would have the choice between taking part in the regional system, known as a union library, and withdrawing. A series of plebiscites was scheduled for the municipal elections in January 1934. More than 100 local committees were organized to help obtain favourable votes.

"It is pretty well understood that the cost of a public library service, as an indispensible feature of modern community progress, is a relatively small item of the total tax bill; a very small one indeed in comparison, for example, with that other educational cost of many years' standing and now accepted as a matter of course, the school tax."
Noel Booth, library board chairman and Langley reeve, 1935

John Willie Winson of Matsqui was one of the system's most ardent supporters. In the *Province* newspaper, he quoted a Langley woman who said that while her family was on relief, "poorer than we have ever been in our lives," they were happy because they could still get good books. Winson said the library had clearly demonstrated its value. "The country was book-hungry. Thousands of books have been bought in the four years now past, but always the van and the branch libraries are as the cupboard of a famous old lady, and the libraries never had 'bones' enough for the cupboard. Now there are 22,000 books, ever increasing — a thousand added since July."

He reminded readers that if they wanted a library, they had to support it. If they accepted the union library, the commission would hand over books and equipment valued at $50,000, and a board selected by the municipal councils and school districts would govern the library. If they rejected

the library, the books and equipment would be shipped elsewhere.

"These are hard times," Winson said. "No proposal is happily received if it involves expenditure, but even in these times picture shows are being patronized, radios are installed. This library service will cost about as much as radio service, or the price of one 'show' per year for the family." He said the library was the cheapest means of obtaining information and recreation.

In 1934, the Fraser Valley Union Library board members drafted a policy to deal with book donations. Although appreciated, many donations were simply not suitable. The classes of books that were "unsatisfactory or altogether unprofitable" included, in their words:

1. Sectarian or partisan books of the propagandist type.
2. Mediocre books or books with so little merit that it does not pay to handle them at public expense. Many volumes for children come into this class.
3. Books, especially non-fiction, so out of date as to be practically useless.
4. Poor editions — small print, cheap paper, narrow margins.
5. Incomplete or defective books.
6. Books in bad condition, which are not worth rebinding, or which cannot be rebound.

Editorials in local newspapers noted that no community could develop its own library for less money. "Everywhere there is a reaching out for a larger and more complete reading service, as one of the necessities of a community," the *Chilliwack Progress* said on January 11, 1934. The headline was straightforward: "Vote 'Yes.'"

On Saturday, January 13, the library was approved in a plebiscite. Twenty municipalities, cities and school districts voted in favour, with only Mission City and Delta opposed. "In times like these it is a healthy sign that the rural communities are willing to provide the sum required for the continued operation of the library," Stewart said.

On June 22, 1934, Lieutenant-Governor John William Fordham Johnson signed a proclamation bringing the new district into being. The deal was signed on behalf of the cities of Chilliwack and Port Coquitlam, the districts of Chilliwack, Kent, Langley, Maple Ridge, Matsqui, Mission, Pitt Meadows, Sumas and Surrey; and the rural school districts of Abbotsford, Barnston Island, Concord, Deroche, Dewdney, Hatzic Prairie, Hope, McConnell Creek and Popkum.

In September 1934, the library's base was moved to Abbotsford, a more central location, from Chilliwack. The next month, Stewart stepped aside so a new team could take over. Charles Keith Morison, who had been hired to drive the van, was named librarian and manager, and the physical assets of the demonstration library were formally transferred to the people of the Fraser Valley. If the system closed before June 30, 1939, the property would revert to the Carnegie Corporation.

In 1939, Langley municipality voted to withdraw from the library, based on concerns about the amount of taxes going to the library, the sense that people should not have to pay for things they do not use and — according to the Public Library Commission — the "large foreign-born population" in poor economic circumstances. "They are fertile ground for the anti-library agitator," the commission said in a report.

It was the first break in the system's ranks since the library's creation in 1934, and local committees of readers went to work to get the decision reversed. In the end, they were successful; Langley came back in 1944.

Stewart went to work in other regions, applying the lessons learned in the Fraser Valley to the Okanagan Valley, Vancouver Island and the West Kootenay. Any new regional systems would not have the $100,000 boost that the Carnegie Corporation had given to the Fraser Valley; they would need to be started from scratch, using whatever resources could be found. Carnegie offered just $15,000 to help start other regional systems.

The library commission set January 1936 as a target for plebiscites on additional union libraries. That meant, Stewart said, that people in 200 rural districts and municipalities would need to learn about the concept so they could file petitions to trigger the plebiscites. Stewart began travelling from town to town, showing residents a selection of books that could be available in a union library. She carried the books in a little trailer that she towed behind her car.

In the end, union libraries were approved in the Okanagan Valley and on Vancouver Island, but failed, despite Stewart's best efforts, to go ahead in the Kootenay.

Okanagan Valley

A union library would be a major step forward for small communities. Okanagan Centre, a hamlet on Okanagan Lake just north of Kelowna, was typical. Its library was opened in 1921 through the work of the local Women's Institute, which collected $1 from every patron. The library's books — numbering from 300 to 500, depending on the year — were kept on a shelf in the Presbyterian Church. They

Downtown Kelowna was already booming when the regional library was established in the 1930s.
Okanagan Regional Library

were exchanged with neighbouring communities such as Oyama. The library bought some of its books and obtained more through the Public Library Commission's travelling libraries.

A union library would be different. Patrons would pay through taxes rather than user fees, and the selection of books would be much greater. Stewart reported that the library proposal drew strong support throughout the valley, and that 150 official endorsements were received from groups that ranged from "city councils to Japanese fruit packers."

The Okanagan endorsed a plebiscite in the fall of 1935. Larger communities acted first, then smaller ones. Representatives from all thirty-nine school districts said a union library would have strong support, and fifteen meetings throughout the valley approved a publicity campaign in advance of the vote. Leaflets printed to convince valley residents to approve the proposal stressed the value of pooling resources to create an up-to-date selection of 25,000 books on all subjects.

Plans called for a library serving from Sicamous in the north to Osoyoos in the south. Municipalities and rural school districts would join forces to build and operate a book collection of at least 20,000 volumes. The *Vernon News* noted that a union library would make 25,000 books available to the city at a lower cost per capita than was being paid at the time. The *News* called for an overwhelming vote in favour so that the library's benefits would be immediately available.

"The wide range of choice afforded by the large public library should form a most valuable supplement to our educational system, which, good though it be, is not in itself adequate to develop the intellect to the fullest extent unless backed by private study and the reading of the best literature," said the *Kelowna Courier*. The newspaper also said commercial libraries would have nothing to fear from a union library, which would not be able to match their fiction selections.

Votes were held in the cities of Armstrong, Enderby, Kelowna, Revelstoke, Salmon Arm, and Vernon on January 16, the districts of Glenmore, Peachland, Salmon Arm, Spallumcheen, Summerland, Penticton and Coldstream on January 23, as well as in forty-nine rural school districts. Most communities approved the library, which meant it could be started right away. The most critical gap was Penticton, where 630 of the 889 votes cast were against the library.

The first librarian, Muriel Page — soon to become Muriel Page Ffoulkes — arrived from the Toronto Public Library on

April 1, 1936, and discovered that she had a lot of work to do. The size of her assignment was evident in notes she wrote soon after her arrival. The library had a thousand catalogued books that had been left by Stewart, plus 6,000 more, uncatalogued and unsorted, on the shelves of the existing small libraries. The Public Library Commission also turned over all travelling libraries in the valley at the time.

It was not enough. "Library service had been promised for April," Ffoulkes wrote later. "Every town and school district in the valley expected a branch to open automatically in their midst that month. No van had been bought, no staff appointed." She said a person who had helped Stewart in her campaign knew the roads so was invaluable to the new library.

"Everywhere people quoted promises of 25,000 books ready with catalogue for use in April. Everywhere they expected large Carnegie funds to buy books. The outstanding difficulty of being in fifty-seven places at once while one really was expected to be at headquarters ordering books is quite obvious." Page said it had been estimated that the library would start with 20,000 books, but it had only half that number.

The chairman of the library board's finance committee resigned at the first meeting, saying there was not enough money to make the system work. The first branch was opened on April 24, 1936, in Vernon, using the building Stewart had rented as a base for her library campaign. As Kelowna was more centralized, Ffoulkes established the library's headquarters there in a building that doubled as the Kelowna branch. It was opened on May 24, 1936. The branch had only 300 books on opening day, and was down to thirty-seven when the doors closed in the evening.

A book van hit the road that May and was driven more than 10,000 miles in the next eighteen months. Like Stewart in the Fraser Valley, Ffoulkes learned to drive so she could deliver books. Unlike the Fraser Valley's van stops — where people could obtain books directly from the vehicle — the Okanagan van was used only to carry books to and from branches. Given the mud and the snow and the summer heat, getting it from place to place was sometimes a challenge. Okanagan Lake was between Kelowna and the road to the southern part of the valley, which meant the van had to use the lake ferry whenever it travelled to and from the south. That posed extra problems.

Patrons who had previously obtained books through Open Shelf, the Victoria-based mail service, were asked to check the union library for the future titles first. The library gave special attention to non-fiction books, although demand for new fiction remained strong. It also received

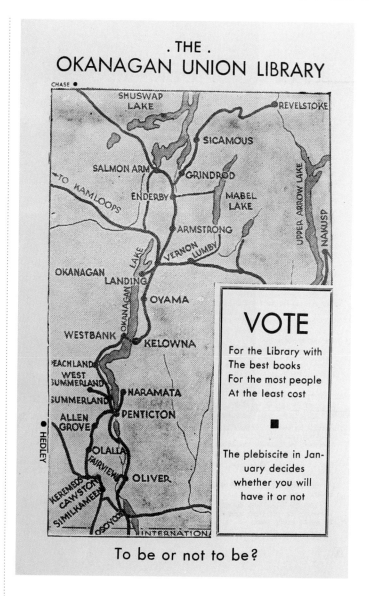

Map used to help convince voters to agree to library service in 1936. *Okanagan Regional Library*

$600 a year from the Department of Education for children's books.

Ffoulkes promoted library services any way she could. She told children's stories in a weekly radio broadcast. Her assistant, Adelaide Atkinson, wrote book reviews for local newspapers. Every fall, students from Kelowna's elementary school were taken to the library, class by class, so the children could become familiar with what it offered.

By 1938 the library had forty-two branches, some in proper buildings, some in schools, a few in houses and one on a wharf on the edge of Okanagan Lake. "There were branches in stores, in hotels, and in gas stations. Several were housed in community halls, and one graced a chicken house," Ffoulkes recalled later. That one was in Glenemma, between Vernon and Kamloops.

The glue that held the system together was on four wheels. "If you know the highways of the Okanagan you know the library van," the *Province* newspaper said in 1938. "In summer it swings over the blistering roads in a haze of fine dust; in winter it bucks snowdrifts and slithers around

Right: Okanagan book van at the branch at Naramata in the late 1930s. *Okanagan Regional Library*

Below: Okanagan Union Library's first book van crossed Okanagan Lake on a ferry. *Okanagan Regional Library*

ice-coated curves; it plunges onward in a muddy shower when spring breaks the hold of winter." The newspaper said the van was a symbol of the desire for culture and entertainment, and demonstrated that the people of the Okanagan were willing to help themselves through co-operation.

Tell that to the people in the van. "One morning the van drove aboard the ferry to make its southern trip," Ffoulkes recalled. "Slowly and painfully the boat plowed through drifts of ice until the further shore was reached. Then followed two hard days' trip through heavy snow until at last, and triumphantly, the van arrived to catch the ferry home again. But the ferry did not keep the tryst. She was frozen in the middle of the lake." So the two librarians — Ffoulkes and Atkinson — locked the van and walked across the ice to Kelowna.

On another trip, the library van went over the edge of the road, with one door jammed against a tree and the other opening into thin air. The two librarians honked the horn until they were noticed and rescued.

The union library agreement called for a three-year commitment to the arrangement. The Okanagan system suffered a serious setback in 1939, when that commitment expired, because Vernon, Coldstream, Armstrong, Salmon Arm, Spallumcheen, Hillcrest, Sicamous, Eagle Valley and Mara withdrew. The reason was simple: They had not seen any benefit from joining the union library. Their costs had gone up, but their book selections were no better than before. In time, however, they all returned.

Vancouver Island

Helen Gordon Stewart was relentless in her campaign for a union library on Vancouver Island. Three days after Christmas 1935, she was in Duncan to speak with community leaders and the committee that ran the Cowichan Public Library, urging them to join a regional library. In early January she was in Nanaimo to ask members of the Board of Trade to support a project. By pooling resources, she said, a much better selection of books would be available for all.

Stewart stopped in Ladysmith, Qualicum Beach and other Island communities, using everything from service club meetings to hobby shows as her venues. Everywhere she went, she carried her small selection of books to get people excited. "We are buying about 2,000 books, with the idea of illustrating through specific instances some of the things a large unit can do which a small one cannot."

Local committees backed the library proposal, and by the summer of 1935 Stewart reported good progress. "With two exceptions, every centre in Vancouver Island, from the Malahat to Courtenay and the Albernis, sponsored the scheme for a plebiscite, and resolutions poured in from every

conceivable kind of organization," she said in a report to the Public Library Commission.

Island residents were already thinking on a regional basis. As early as 1930, Nanaimo librarian Jean Elisabeth Whitman had noted that her library was "a small library in a very big community," as Nanaimo served residents from Qualicum Beach to Ladysmith, a distance of about seventy kilometres. "Our resources on books and money are very limited," she said, "and if all subscribers took out one book there would be nothing left but empty shelves."

The *Daily Colonist* in Victoria endorsed the union library. "The Fraser Valley people have evidently come to think of books and magazines as one of the necessities of life for which they are prepared to pay. With this stimulating example before them, the people of some sections of Vancouver Island might well consider the adoption of a similar union library plan."

Muriel Page Ffoulkes was born on May 19, 1895, in Deal, Kent, England. After working at the Toronto Public Library she came to British Columbia in 1936 to start the Okanagan Union Library. She was also involved in the groups dealing with music and the arts, including the Kelowna Arts Council. She retired in 1964 after twenty-eight years of service and died in Victoria on April 4, 1986.

Small libraries in Port Alberni, Courtenay, Cumberland, Nanaimo, Duncan and Shawnigan were in operation. Pooling the stocks and introducing a levy for maintenance would ensure books for every school district. The *Colonist* said a union library might start with 12,000 volumes, and would need about sixty deposit collections of books and magazines, housed in community halls, private houses, gas stations, stores or any convenient meeting place, run by volunteer helpers.

In the plebiscite, 1,983 voters were in favour and 983 were opposed. The vote was deemed a failure because the communities in favour did not have a combined population of 25,000 people. Despite this, the provincial cabinet passed an order in April 1936 to create a Vancouver Island regional library.

The new library would serve thirty-two rural school districts and three municipal centres. They included the cities of Alberni, Port Alberni and Courtenay, and the rural school districts of Beaver Creek, Bench, Bowser, Campbell River, Cedar (east, north and south), Cobble Hill, Comox

Vancouver Island's bookmobile, shown here in
1946, featured easy access to the collection.
Image I-30369 courtesy of Royal BC Museum,
BC Archives

Consolidated, Cowichan, Cowichan Lake, Departure Bay, Diamond Crossing, Errington, Fanny Bay, French Creek, Hilliers, Mill Bay, Minto, Montrose, Mountain, Nanaimo Bay, Oyster, Parksville, Qualicum Beach, Little Qualicum, Red Gap, Royston, Tsolum, Union Bay, Waterloo and Wellington.

Within a few days Nanaimo and Ladysmith joined the union, and Jean Stewart, the head of the Nanaimo library, was placed in charge of the union library. The headquarters were in Nanaimo — in an old dairy building on Wallace Street — with branches in towns and large centres.

Small basic collections were kept at deposit stations, changed about once a month and supplemented by the main stock. Borrowers could have a book for two weeks. These stations served closely settled areas and enabled a quick exchange of reading material. There were also van stops, served from a truck at the side of the road. The vehicle was a converted pickup with large panels that opened to reveal shelves facing outward. In 1938, the *Colonist* described what it was like on the Island's book van.

Children "crowded around the truck like so many tumbling puppies in their eagerness to see what the 'Liberry lady' had brought for them. They exchanged comments with each other as to their favorites, recommending and chattering in the way of childhood the world over. When the little group that had been waiting eagerly for Library Day had been satisfied, up went the sides of the van and away to the next port of call." The van was operated by librarian Peter Grossman and assistant Marjorie Kilgour. Grossman was a firm believer in the union library concept, having spent six years with the one in the Fraser Valley.

The *Colonist* described a deposit station in the Sunday school room of the local church. People came from all around to get books. "The scene resembles rather closely the old-time get-together around the cracker barrel of the village store — with the difference that in this case the conversation is rather more apt to be about what is going on in the world, which books have proved of most interest, and so on, rather than the latest local scandal."

The library even had a book on raising turkeys. It was invaluable to local farmers. They reported that as a result of what they learned from the book, they raised more than a thousand young turkeys for Thanksgiving and Christmas dinners.

There were seven routes, as far north as Campbell River and as far south as Mill Bay. All were day trips except one that required an overnight stop in Courtenay. If the union library did not have a book a patron wanted, it could borrow it from the public libraries in Vancouver and Victoria, the Provincial Library in Victoria, and the union libraries in the Okanagan and Fraser Valleys.

As the *Colonist* indicated, the benefits of a library could be intangible. "For instance, a man out of work, weary and discouraged, wanders into the library. He perhaps idly picks up a book, becomes interested in it, sees cuts of some little home-made gadget, decides to try his hand at making it, and is given a fresh start — at least, he is given food for thought. This is not at all an uncommon occurrence."

The three taxpayer-supported union libraries came to life during the Depression, when money was tight. The tough times did not discourage voters, but helped convince them that sharing resources could help them fill their needs. That meant giving up local control of their libraries.

"All those municipalities made a decision, in desperate times, in 1936. They were desperate to have library services," says Lesley Dieno, the executive director of the Okanagan Regional Library. "They knew they didn't have very good library services, with those little volunteer libraries that were around.

"Those women wanted a great education for their kids, that's what it was about. It was the Women's Institutes, it was the people who ran schools, it was the farmers who didn't want their kids to be farmers in a dust bowl. They wanted to open their kids' eyes to the wide world. They were desperate. Those city councils and those rural school districts had to be desperate to give up control."

Dieno says that losing control means saving money — but the equation is a tough sell when times are good, which is why the Depression was a perfect time to start the three regional libraries.

Libraries will get you through times of no money better than
money will get you through times of no libraries.
Anne Herbert, writer

9

THE GREAT DEPRESSION

The stock market crash in 1929 threw the global economy into chaos and brought on the worst depression in history. Then a drought on the Prairies forced thousands of farmers off their land, prompting many of them to come to British Columbia in a desperate search for work. The turmoil of the Great Depression meant public libraries were busier and more important than ever.

When the economy sinks, people turn to libraries for help finding employment or entertainment, or sometimes just because they wanted to be in a warm, welcoming building. "When times are difficult and unsettled as at present, people turn to the library for many reasons: To read and forget their anxiety and struggles; to pass the

....

Opposite: A hobo rides the train in the central Interior during the Depression years. *Vancouver Sun*

Above: Rev. Andrew Roddan at a cookhouse set up in the city dump at False Creek Flats. *City of Vancouver Archives Re N7 / Vancouver Sun*

time of idleness or insufficient occupation; as a recreation when other pleasures are too expensive," Alice Cruickshank of the Prince Rupert Public Library said in 1932.

"Libraries play a tremendously important part during times of unemployment when enforced leisure induces and gives opportunities to many people to read," Victoria's *Daily Colonist* reported. And there was plenty of unemployment; Vancouver's Collingwood East public library association estimated more than half of the people in the community were on relief.

> The richest person in the world – in fact all the riches in the world – couldn't provide you with anything like the endless, incredible loot available at your local library.
> Malcolm Forbes, publisher

But downturns also mean funding cuts, and in the 1930s the provincial government's cuts were brutal. Virtually every library faced shortages. The slashing was most severe at the Vancouver Public Library, which had to close its central branch for a summer and its Kitsilano branch for an entire year — despite the high demand for the service.

"The place is jammed from morning till night," Vancouver head librarian Edgar Stewart Robinson reported in November 1930. Robinson said the reference library was largely occupied by people seeking rest and shelter, to the disadvantage of those who wanted a spot to read and study. As a result, a notice was posted, asking people who had no legitimate use for the reference room to use the library's reading room in the old city hall building next door.

Despite the tough times, Robinson kept fighting on behalf of the library and its patrons. He lobbied to expand service in a time of cuts, and he kept reminding politicians that the outdated, outgrown Carnegie library at Hastings and Main streets had to be replaced.

Margaret Brunette, who worked at the Carnegie library during the Depression, remembered the smell in the reading room more than anything. "The men would come in first thing in the morning, and take off their socks and boots and put them on the radiators to dry," she recalled. "It wasn't the easiest place to work in." About 300 families attended Brunette's church in Vancouver's Kitsilano district

Men read at the tables in Vancouver's Carnegie library in 1937. *Vancouver Public Library, Special Collections, VPL 83999*

of Vancouver, but when the Depression was at its worst, only two of the men had jobs. Many men would visit the library every day to read newspapers and keep warm.

The book *God in the Jungles*, written by a clergyman named Andrew Roddan, is about the author's experience working with the homeless in Vancouver during the Depression. Many years later, his son Sam Roddan reminisced in the *Vancouver Sun* about the public library. "The reading room in those days was crowded with the unemployed," he wrote. "It was always warm and a washroom was handy for a quick shave." Roddan said the smell of damp, sour clothes and shoes and the sound of hacking coughs often filled the room. "It was here that the hoboes and drifters read their hometown newspapers, wrote letters home and stared through the dust-stained windows at the pigeons sitting on the ledges or fluttering to the street for a bread crumb.

"Many of the jobless were great readers and pored over books," Roddan wrote. "*Das Kapital, The Coming Struggle for Power, The Novel and The People*. Some of them made notes in cheap exercise books on *The Theory of the Leisure Class* and *The Regina Manifesto*. Scattered over the tables were copies of *Cry Havoc, For Sinners Only* and *Technocracy*.

"A magazine, *Canadian Forum*, was required reading for intellectuals. In its pages were articles on social reconstruction, work camps, the plight of the unemployed, hunger marches, plans for a better world. There were poems by Dorothy Livesay on man's inhumanity to man. In *Canadian Forum* one read Frank Underhill, F.R. Scott, Eugene Forsey, J.S. Woodsworth. And on occasion there was a poem or an essay about the Spanish Civil War by a young doctor named Norman Bethune."

Julia Carson Stockett of the reference department recalled a hectic time in the library. "Most of the city and interurban lines pass in four directions on two sides of the building, heavy trucks thunder by, street signals sound, crowds gather at the nearby market, the fire department dashes through, and organizations parade with bands. It is often a real achievement to answer a telephone question, especially when a building is being erected across the street or a general election is in progress."

Stockett noted the ethnic diversity in the neighbourhood. "The Japanese section lies on one side of the library, the Chinese on the other, and picturesque groups of Indians and East Indians mingle with crews from ports far and near, for the wharves are not many blocks distant. In these days of world-wide unemployment, Vancouver also has its crowds of men out of work and the library's location makes it a casual refuge, increasing the constant surge in and out," she said.

Despite the Depression, Edgar Stewart Robinson of the Vancouver Public Library believed that the city should have works of lasting value. To that end, he bought a 1431 prayer book from a Kamloops store, raising the $250 asking price through subscriptions. He also bought a single perfect page from the Gutenberg Bible, the first book ever printed. These items are still in the library's special collections. Robinson also obtained books that were retrieved from miners who had been burning them to keep warm.

Rev. Andrew Roddan visits one of the hobo areas near downtown Vancouver during the Depression. *Library and Archives Canada C027902*

The Vancouver Public Library started calling itself the Mental Relief Department. It could barely keep up with the demand. "One day last November nearly 8,000 books went over the desks of the system, and when a boy wheeled a book wagon of returned books into the stackroom there was a scuffle for some of the treasures it carried," the *Daily Province* reported in 1933.

The value of reading during tough times was reflected in the headline in the *Province*: "Books to the rescue." The newspaper described how reading had become more important during the Depression. "A young hobo in a camp

Right: Men work on road construction, one of the federal government's relief projects, in the Wasa area of the East Kootenay in 1934. *Library and Archives Canada A036089*

Below: Strikers board the train at Kamloops during the March on Ottawa in 1935. *Library and Archives Canada C029399*

near Kamloops saunters away from the shack and pulls out a book of verse," it said. "Soon he is thousands of years away, helping the tender-heeled Achilles in the siege of mighty Troy. A British Columbia logger, in the hills near Princeton, follows Genghis Khan and his hard-riding Mongol hordes into the centre of China. Next week he leaves for Puget Sound, where he expects to keep tryst with the Taj Mahal."

The *Province* quoted a Vancouver librarian who said the greatest demand for books on currency reform came from men with nothing in the bank. And that was just one example. "Few readers of *Crime Club* stories have ever carried guns. They do not need to. The lending library can send them to seven shootings a week, and it frequently does." The Depression changed reading habits. "Three brief years in a world which seems tumbling about our ears have made remarkable changes in our reading," the *Province* said.

"Folk who two years ago followed the fashions in Depression-cure crazes have given up on the task and have fallen back on three or four volumes which are becoming standard in modern radical economics. Cole's *Intelligent*

Man's Guide Through the World Chaos is probably the most popular of these. Technocracy is already losing its selling power and is rapidly joining the class of bridge books for which there was an insatiable demand not many months ago."

Libraries were busy but publishers were not, because people could not afford to buy books. And as individuals suffered, so did local governments. Six municipalities — Burnaby, North Vancouver city, North Vancouver district, Merritt, Fernie and Prince Rupert — could no longer pay their bills and went into receivership.

They did not have libraries to worry about. But Vancouver did, and while the big city did not face receivership, it still had to cope with a sharp drop in tax revenue. It cut costs wherever it could. The library system — the Carnegie library and the new Kitsilano branch — saw its budget slashed, then slashed again.

The library board, which wanted to cut its $110,000

Kitsilano branch, the first opened by the Vancouver Public Library, in the 1930s.
Philip Timms, Vancouver Public Library, VPL 3469

budget by $10,000, threatened to close the Kitsilano branch, which cost $7,000 a year to run, on May 31, 1931. It also told Robinson that he could only spent $14,000 on books, not the $18,000 he wanted.

"A Kitsilano mother" wrote in the *Province* that closing the branch would hurt the well-behaved youth in the community. "If our boys and girls cannot continue to secure good literature for their leisure moments, they will be prone to spend this spare time on the streets," she said. "Mother" argued that the library offered an ounce of prevention, far better than the pound of cure found in the detention home or the police court.

At the start of 1933, the city allocated $113,000 to the library, but five months into the fiscal year cut the budget to $65,000. That called for drastic measures. The Kitsilano branch, with 12,000 borrowers, was closed for a year. Seven staff members lost their jobs.

At the Carnegie building, opening hours were cut to thirty-eight hours a week from seventy-two. The board dismissed twenty-eight employees, including three janitors, five binders and twenty library assistants, with most forced to go on relief. It closed the main reading room, the boys and girls department, the bindery, the ordering and cataloguing departments — and portions of the reference and circulation sections. Employees had already seen their salaries drop by five to ten per cent; now, those who kept their jobs had to take another eight-per-cent cut. Some of the laid-off employees continued to work without pay because the library offered shelter and something to do.

Robinson fought the board, saying the cost-cutting plan "wrecks the whole system, providing no funds for books merely keeps the doors open." Then things got worse. The central library was closed for the entire summer, cutting off 60,000 readers. A few staff members remained on the job to handle returned books, but did not make further loans until September, when the library reopened.

The Kitsilano branch stayed closed until the summer of 1934, when it reopened for four hours a day, three days a week. It was also closed for the summer of 1935. The closures and cutbacks reduced traffic at the central branch, and the number of borrowers dropped to 40,000 from 60,000. The shelves were thinning; for the first time, book replacement was not keeping up with the discard rate.

In May 1935, about 250 striking men from relief camps entered Vancouver's main library, asked the staff to leave and settled into the museum on the top floor to protest the lack of jobs. They hung a sign saying "We demand relief" out of a window. Some had blankets; apparently they planned to stay for a long time. Mayor Gerald Grattan McGeer promised them five meals and said they could stay for two nights. McGeer then met with a committee representing the strikers and they agreed to leave. The occupation was followed by the

On-to-Ottawa trek, which ended with a riot in Regina that resulted in the deaths of a policeman and a protester.

Cost-cutting was also felt at the University of British Columbia Library. Over three years the university's budget was cut by two-thirds, to a low of $250,000 in 1932. Head librarian John Ridington said the cuts were so deep that the library's standards and reputation would be damaged.

Ridington protested that for seventeen years he had devoted his life to building a strong university library. "And now the prospect is — starvation, retrogression, I am weary at heart and sick of soul — and underlying every other emotion are feelings of impotence and rage." He reminded anyone who would listen that a good library was essential to a good university, and that the UBC library was the fourth best in Canada. The cuts would hurt so much that restoration would require "no end of funds."

One of the library's main features was its collection of scholastic periodicals that encouraged and supported scientific research. Ridington said that missing a year or two of these periodicals would seriously handicap the work of students and faculty. It would cost much more to fill in the gaps later. The university had been spending more than $5,000 a year on periodicals — yet the grant for the library was being cut by $10,000, to just $2,000. There was hope for a supplementary grant that would cover the cost of periodicals, but the purchase of new books would need to be abandoned.

It could have been worse. A commission led by George Kidd, a former president of B.C. Electric, submitted a report on government finances in 1932 that urged the province to cut $6 million from its $29 million budget. This could be done, the Kidd report said, through a wide variety of cuts — including reducing the number of MLAs, reducing the number of whiskey brands sold, sterilizing the patients in mental hospitals, ending free education at the age of fourteen, and giving scholarships to post-secondary students so they could attend university elsewhere, which would enable the government to close UBC. The provincial government considered the Kidd report but decided not to act on it.

Fortunately, the UBC Library received help from the Carnegie Corporation — a $15,000 grant, on the condition that "only books and current periodicals for general undergraduate reading in liberal arts colleges" would be purchased.

Fears were expressed that staff would be cut, forcing the library to open its stacks to students. That would increase the risk of losses. The idea was abandoned when one staff member offered to work half-time, allowing the library to hire two page boys. Then students volunteered to work for free, reducing the need for paid staff. These measures eased the crunch although the library still had to be closed on Saturday afternoons.

Victoria's public library reported that patrons were choosing "heavier" reading instead of fiction. "Many people are still refusing to resort to the pleasant sedatives of light and airy books," the *Daily Times* reported. There had been a noteworthy increase in the demand for books on mining; apparently people were looking for new ways to strike it rich.

Victoria Alderman J.D. Hunter, a doctor, said the reference department was being used by students from the college as well as from high schools and elementary schools. It stimulated an interest in good reading among children, helped teachers and provided adult education along professional and technical lines. "One young man supported

A few reasons given by people who have made use of the book collection of the Victoria Public Library during the past year are interesting to note. Some maintain that they escape from personal and economic worries; they are enabled to preserve a healthy mental attitude; to find out what caused the crash and a way out of the present economic condition; they are able to read the books they have often longed to read, but for which they have not had time until now; to prepare themselves for a different kind of job which will provide greater satisfaction of increased income.

Victoria Daily Colonist, 1931

Victoria Public Library's reading room for adults in 1939. *Times Colonist*

himself, his mother and three younger members of his family for three years by the exercise of his initiative and the study of books on mechanics," Hunter said.

New Westminster's library saw voluntary salary cuts and the loss of paid holidays. The library had about 5,500 members and the circulation had risen to 150,000, but the budget through the Depression was never more than $5,000 a year. In Nanaimo, the library imposed membership fees in 1933 in an attempt to balance the books.

> The library has given me so much of my education that I am especially and sentimentally attached to it. I almost lived in it, back in the dark thirties when time was about all one possessed. If you had provided beds in the rotunda, I am sure you would have had me for a star boarder.
> *Edward F. Meade, Victoria author*

The Depression affected the demonstration library in the Fraser Valley, which had been launched just months after the crash in October 1929. "Usually a country population is thought of as relatively stable, but the shifting about of men in search of work has been one of our problems during the year," director Helen Gordon Stewart said in her 1931 annual report.

"We have not as yet extended our service to the relief camps in our district, although we expect to send 100 or more books to Allco [near Haney] next week to help with their educational programme," she said. "As a result of this difficulty and of the closing of several mills, some of our branches have found it difficult to keep their circulation at the old level. The indications to the present give us ground for high hopes, if the Depression does not inundate us completely."

The relief camps in the Fraser Valley were among many established by the government to keep men out of trouble. The library commission expressed concern in 1932 about the lack of a comprehensive plan for reading and study by men in camps. "This enforced idleness on the part of hundreds of men has given an opportunity for a system of education which cannot be carried on at any other time," the commission said. "Isolated requests from these men for books which will help them to improve their present education, and to increase their knowledge in their various lines of work, show that an opportunity has been missed."

The commission was also concerned about its own survival, and the fate of the travelling libraries, which offered 45,000 books, and Open Shelf, which had 12,000 more. In 1933, commission chairman Hugh Norman Lidster announced that the Open Shelf system would be abolished, but promised that the commission would "try our hardest to keep the flag of the travelling library flying." Open Shelf ended when the manager's position was lost in budget cuts. It was revived a few months later, with the work shared among the remaining employees.

Some Open Shelf users cancelled the service because they could not afford the return postage. Others said they would rather pay postage both ways than lose access. "Pay cuts we could handle, but when our books were discontinued we realized there was a Depression," one patron said in a letter.

In 1934, commission superintendent Arthur Herbert Killam wrote that it was "only by the greatest of good luck" that his department was still open. There were no funds to buy books, he said, and not enough money to ship all of the travelling libraries that were in demand. The budget that year was just $9,500 — half as much as five years earlier. The commission had suspended grants to small libraries, which were already struggling to cope with the loss of funding from their own communities.

The commission's staff dropped to four — Killam, an assistant and a stenographer in Victoria, and Jeannette Sargent in the Prince George branch office, which had opened in the summer of 1931. Sargent, a trained librarian from Victoria, performed a remarkable job against all odds as she struggled to establish service in the north.

She started work in a small office in a former movie theatre on Prince George's main street. Her assignment was to deliver boxes of books along the Canadian National Railway line between Evelyn and McBride, as far south as Quesnel and Wells and as far north as Fort St. James. Sargent did not have a car, but relied on the twice-a-week passenger train to get from one library to the next.

"Daily demands are made by correspondence and by personal application for reading matter for isolated families, aids for newer farm methods, both agricultural and livestock, up-to-date books on machinery, geology, electricity, radio, carpentry, social problems and outlooks, world leaders and movements, anything and everything that will help form a connecting link with the outside world and give the necessary, though vicarious, social contact," Sargent said in her report for 1931.

In 1934 the commission lost almost all of its funding, and Sargent claimed just $36.70 in expenses. "The only personal contact work done was in those centres through which the librarian passed during her vacation. This is a cause of deep regret, as very little constructive work is possible unless the librarian can meet with at least the librarians in charge of the travelling libraries and the teachers."

Jeannette Sargent in the 1940s. *Hazel Lynn*

Jeannette Sargent was born in Pendennis, Manitoba, in 1899, and came to British Columbia with her family in 1908. Her father, William John Sargent, was a Victoria alderman who served as council's library board representative for several years. Jeannette took part in the librarian training program that was started by Helen Gordon Stewart, obtained a degree in arts from Queen's University and a degree in library science from the University of Washington.

In 1931 she opened the Public Library Commission's Prince George branch, serving the north-central region. She remained in the job for almost thirty years, and left a strong legacy of library service throughout the area. She married William Munro, a widower, in 1959, and left the commission the following June. She died at the age of 101 in October 2000 in Victoria.

She also said there had not been a teachers' convention in Prince George, so the only interviews she had had were with teachers who had come to her office on weekends. And she worried about the problems she faced convincing readers to broaden their interests. "If the physical food consumed is as lifeless and insipid as the mental food requested, we may expect the race to degenerate rapidly. It is not the fault of the youth that they were born in a part of the country where there are few external stimuli, but since this part of the country has been opened we must realize the responsibility of enlarging the vision of our future citizens."

Travelling libraries and elementary schools helped to a "very infinitesimal degree," she said. "Where parents have retained their vision in spite of forces working against them, we are cheered by the realization that their children are being given every possible opportunity. But those cases seem few."

Sargent worked alone for much of the Depression. She ran training sessions for the community librarians, handled fifty-six travelling libraries and sixty-six school libraries and provided books to individuals who came to her office. She could have done more, she said, if only she had help.

The commission sent books to one-room schools, matching the collections with the needs of the students. The age groups in the schools varied from year to year. That prompted Sargent to set up a book pool in 1939. She would take in books from every school in an area and redistribute them according to need.

Sargent enlisted thirteen schools to test the pooling theory. She had them send their books to her for checking and repair, then she assembled collections to suit the mix of students in each school. The thinking was simple: If a school had more students in the senior grades, for example, there would be no sense filling shelves with books for the junior grades. The idea worked, and before long all of the one-room schools in the north-central district were taking part.

After several tough years, the government restored some of the funds for library service. In 1939 the library commission expanded the Open Shelf mail-order service, thanks to a generous postal book rate granted by the federal government that spring. The commission passed on the savings, enclosing return-address labels with the books so patrons could return them at no cost.

Throughout the Depression, when money was in short supply, commercial libraries were still busy. Vancouver had between thirty and forty of these libraries, carrying 1,200 to 5,000 books each, and there were hundreds more around the province. Books were often available on small shelves in drug stores and in lending libraries operated by department stores. These libraries-for-profit did not try to build vast collections, offer reference services or bother with non-fiction. They dealt with popular fiction, and dumped books as soon as they fell from favour. The public libraries could not put the same emphasis on fiction because they had to spend their money on economic, social, technical and travel books.

The Library Rate, commonly called the Library Book Rate, was introduced in 1939 to help libraries serve rural and remote areas. Libraries receive a discount when they mail print materials to their users or to other libraries in Canada. The rate has survived for decades, and in 2010 it was estimated that three million shipments are made using the rate every year. About 2,000 libraries make use of the special rate.

Patricia Blake ran one of these commercial libraries in Chilliwack. In 1931, when she was in her early twenties, Blake invested a small insurance policy in 300 books and opened a library that charged borrowers 50 cents a month. Books were available for free from the Fraser Valley demonstration library, yet Blake's library was a success. Within four years she had 1,500 books, although she admitted the business was not always easy.

"There was too much competition — the district was thick with lending libraries — and we had too many friends," she said. "The place became a sort of studio headquarters for unemployed students. They descended upon us at all hours for meals, which we cooked on our tiny electric grill. However, we made a profit of $40 a month, and it tided us over the bad years." Blake added thirty new books every month, getting rid of old ones with sales twice a year. She sent lists of new books to out-of-town subscribers and let them borrow two books a week by mail.

In January 1935, a heavy snowfall followed by torrential rains caused a flood that knocked out electricity to Chilliwack and cut off the community. Blake's library, in the Empress Hotel by that time, was swarmed with customers — including 100 who signed up in one day. She had a candle at the window to show she was open, another at her desk, and a third for patrons to carry so they could find what they wanted.

Blake promoted her library through weekly book reviews

on CHWK radio, and had them dramatized by several voices, complete with sound effects. Her most popular book was T.E. Lawrence's *Seven Pillars of Wisdom*. She reported some people were reading it in a day. The book was also popular in Victoria, where the library had a two-year waiting list for a copy.

Library development was slow in the Depression. In some communities, library associations that had been formed with enthusiasm in the early 1920s died of financial starvation, while other areas reported good progress. In Kamloops, where taxpayers voted down a municipal library in a plebiscite, a handful of people organized an association a few years later to provide a book-lending service.

The Kamloops library grew steadily thanks to a major private donation and dozens of small ones. About 150 citizens put up one dollar each — enough for three books — for an annual subscription. Organizers sent out a circular asking for donations of books — and even specifying the names of the books. After the local newspaper provided publicity, Boy Scouts picked up between 2,500 and 3,000 volumes.

The association rented a room in the Federal Building, which housed the post office and was the busiest spot in town. A small donation came from the provincial government, and city council provided $500 for the first year. With proceeds from annual subscriptions, overdue fines and user fees, the library could buy 1,000 books a year. Before long, it expanded into a second room.

Christine McNamee, a trained librarian who had worked at the Provincial Library, moved to Kamloops with her husband and volunteered to organize the library. It proved so successful that when the Okanagan Valley's union library was started in 1936, the organizers of the Kamloops library decided not to take part. In May 1939, the library moved to a home donated by Una McIntosh Burris at Second Avenue and Seymour Street. The library took the bottom floor, and the city's museum took over the top floor.

In Victoria, children's librarian Hazel King took books to public schools, reminding young readers that they would find even more in the library. Since 1915 the boys and girls department had sent an average of 1,200 books a year to schools.

The Vancouver Public Library ended its support for school libraries in 1933 because of budget cuts, and the school board set up a central office to look after books for elementary schools. By 1939, six years later, all forty-nine elementary schools had libraries, making Vancouver the only city in Canada with that level of service. Public and school librarians worked together to pick the books. The

The library in Vancouver Tech Secondary School in about 1937. *Leonard Frank, Vancouver Province*

public library agreed to provide the quarters and facilities for ordering and processing books for the school board, which paid for the books, supplies and services.

Even as the Depression raged, some librarians were looking to the future.

Victoria librarian Margaret Clay said the public library "belongs to all, and should be free to all, regardless of creed, race, colour or financial status." It was the largest single adult education centre in the community and should serve all adult education groups, she said.

Clay stressed the value of school libraries and said they should include gramophone records and good periodicals. School libraries should be in attractive, well-lit and properly equipped rooms, and should be administered by trained librarians with special knowledge of books for children, the ability to direct pupils' reading with consideration of the needs of the individual child, and knowledge of the curriculum. There should be at least five books per child.

Edgar Stewart Robinson of the Vancouver Public Library said leisure time would surely increase as the economy improved, and that would have a huge impact on library service. "Libraries are in competition with other social agencies for a share of this time and whether or not they get it is one of the problems facing them," he said. "Nothing short of a definite programme of reading, supported by an unlimited supply of the best in literature, will win any great number of folk in competition with the motor car, the radio and the moving picture." Knowledge, he said, "increases geometrically, and grows upon itself."

10

THE WAR
AND ITS AFTERMATH

Canadians had little time to enjoy the end — or at least the relaxing grip — of the Depression. The world changed again in September 1939 when Canada went to war. British Columbia's librarians reacted quickly, providing books for soldiers and their families, changing the selection of books and even signing up for service.

"We cannot shut ourselves up in our ivory tower and isolate ourselves from something which, sooner or later, is bound to affect everyone and every activity in some way," the British Columbia Library Association said in its publication, the *Bulletin*. "It has already made itself felt by those libraries making book purchases

Opposite: Okanagan Union Library's branch at Naramata in the late 1930s. *Okanagan Regional Library*

Above: Cataloguing department in Victoria Public library in 1939. *Times Colonist*

abroad, especially in what is now an enemy country. It is now impossible to import any books or periodicals from Germany." British technical periodicals were being censored for fear of information getting into the hands of the enemy, and free documents from Britain were stopped due to war economies.

The Public Library Commission set up a book service for enlisted men. The war service library system started with one trained librarian, and branches were organized wherever there were soldiers, sailors or airmen. Brigadier William Wasbrough Foster, director of auxiliary forces, made the libraries an integral part of his work, and they soon provided a fine example of the power of collaboration.

The Public Library Commission stressed the value of libraries in wartime. "If a democracy depends for its existence on an enlightened electorate, there is no medium so effective, so universal, so unprejudiced and so disinterested as the book and the library whereby large masses of people may be influenced," the commission said in its 1940 report. "In the social revolution going on every day about us, it must be accepted that libraries are not luxuries but necessary and important agencies in a rapidly changing scene."

Willard Ireland. *Times Colonist*

Staff of the Provincial Library and the Public Library Commission volunteered to operate the war services libraries for Vancouver Island. A committee was formed in Victoria in September 1939 to distribute books — many supplied by the Imperial Order of Daughters of the Empire — from a base in the Metropolitan Building at Government and Courtney streets. An IODE book drive collected about 2,000 volumes and the public library gave its discards to the war effort.

The Public Library Commission said the books needed to be recreational, technical, educational and specialized, "such as those distributed by the medical service in connection with venereal disease." An estimated $10,000, to come from the government, was needed to buy technical and educational books. Recreational books — fiction, in other words — would come from the public. Potential donors were reminded to use common sense; *Care and Feeding of Infants* would not be of much use to a soldier.

A Vancouver group was formed in February 1940. The public library supplied books, and library staff sorted the donations of magazines and light novels collected by the IODE. Each staff member devoted ninety minutes a week to the task. About 2,500 books were sent out in the first year of the library. Librarian Edgar Stewart Robinson praised the work of the Canadian Legion War Services, especially the educational program that offered about sixty courses to members of the army. "These courses are so arranged that they follow the men wherever they go, and book service goes with them," he said.

In each military base, the libraries were run by the agency administering the canteen, such as the Salvation Army or the YMCA. When men were finished with the books, the collection was brought in, reconditioned and weeded, then sent to another depot, with the first unit getting a new set. The war services libraries also provided magazines — more than a million in the first year of the war. The magazines were sorted and sent in bundles of fifty, along with games and playing cards.

Victoria, Vancouver and New Westminster public libraries provided books to any men in uniform who asked for them. Libraries in smaller places did their best to get books to the men stationed nearby.

The Provincial Library, according to its annual report,

Willard Ernest Ireland served as provincial archivist for thirty-four years. For twenty-eight of those years he was also provincial librarian. When he became archivist in 1940, he joined three other staff members on the third floor of the provincial library. When he left, the archives had a staff of thirty and a new building beside the provincial museum. Ireland served as president of the British Columbia Library Association, the Canadian Library Association, the Pacific Northwest Library Association and the British Columbia Historical Association. He was on the University of British Columbia Senate and University of Victoria's board of governors. He kept busy as a public speaker, giving presentations about the library and the archives to national organizations, local clubs and everything in between. Ireland retired in 1974 and died five years later.

served "virtually as headquarters for this service, which in 1942 sent out over 10,000 donated books to naval, military and air force stations in every part of Vancouver Island." Professional librarians worked after hours sorting books, typing up author and title cards, pasting corners and labels and putting together libraries to be sent to service canteens, outposts and military hospitals.

A collection of 100 books was also placed on each ship built in Victoria. In October 1943, the Royal Canadian Navy started establishing libraries. Members of the Women's Royal Canadian Naval Service, recruited for the purpose, looked after books that came from the IODE. The Royal Canadian Air Force also appointed librarians, but the army made no provisions for buildings or books; its service depended on volunteers.

The war services libraries in Victoria distributed about 40,000 books. Spencer's department store in Victoria was a major supplier, donating new books every two weeks. As new books arrived, the quality of the collections increased and by war's end in 1945 the stock of the war services libraries was considered to be similar to that of public libraries. On January 15, 1946, the war libraries office in Victoria was closed and its books were sent to the IODE in Vancouver for use in military hospitals and any remaining camps.

Many library employees signed up for service. Most of them were from Vancouver and Victoria, which had the largest libraries and therefore the most employees. Two of the first to sign up were John Moloney and William Muncy of the Victoria Public Library, who joined the Royal Air Force in 1939.

The Women's Royal Canadian Naval Service, which was formed in July 1942, attracted Joan Bramley and Georgina Wilson of the provincial library, Doreen Woodford of the University of British Columbia and Arabel Peirson, Peggy Marshall, Isabel Stirling, Margaret Creelman and Monica Hodges from the Vancouver Public Library.

Unlike most of the other librarians who signed up for war service, Creelman and Hodges were asked to work in their chosen profession. They were among the first Canadians to be assigned to supply Canadian reading material to the Royal Canadian Navy in the United Kingdom. They started with a reading room in Londonderry, Northern Ireland, where Creelman was the base librarian to the Canadian Naval Administrative Authority, then went to the Canadian Naval Mission Overseas in London.

Library staff members who joined the women's division of the Royal Canadian Air Force included Kathleen Armstrong, Isabel McTavish, Joan Ellingham and Jessie

Maitland, from the Vancouver Public Library; Eileen Heaton of the University of British Columbia and Nancy Stiell from the Okanagan Union Library.

Other Vancouver employees who joined the services were Beverley Robinson, Sam Sullivan, Arthur Bolster and Alex Forbes. Peter Grossman of the Vancouver Island Union Library, Roman Mostar of the Fraser Valley Union Library and John Lort of the provincial library went to fight.

Sydney Weston and Willard Ireland of the provincial library and Hope Hodges, Donald Bell and William McCaghey of the Public Library Commission volunteered as well. The provincial library, the archives and the library commission contributed more personnel than any other division of the Department of Education.

Two Victoria staff members were interned by the Japanese — Beth Harris in Manila and Frances Dodds in Hong Kong.

The departure of so many staff members brought a radical change, reflected in a November 1941 headline in the *Daily Province* newspaper: "Public library may hire married women." For the duration of the war, the Vancouver library board had decided, married women who were trained librarians could work part-time in the library if suitable single women were not available. Head librarian Robinson said the need for trained help was "quite desperate." Married women had never been officially barred from working at

Margaret Jean Clay, Victoria's head librarian from 1924 to 1952. *Times Colonist*

the library, he said — it's just that the library had only hired single women and had required single women to resign if they married.

The shortage of males caused a problem in the Fraser Valley as well. Roman Mostar, the assistant librarian, had been driving the book van, and when he joined the Royal Canadian Air Force the library could not find a trained male librarian to replace him. The board felt it was not practical to hire a female librarian for the job — even though Helen Gordon Stewart had proven years earlier that women could do it. The board opted for a First World War veteran from Sardis who was not a librarian, but at least he was a man.

Vancouver Public Library staff members pitched in to help the war effort in many ways. They provided clothing for evacuee children in 1940. They gave money to the Red Cross and made 260 garments for prisoners of war and relief in China, Russia and Greece. They raised $36 for records and a player for a merchant navy ship. They also attended meetings of the district Air Raid Precautions organization, supplemented by courses in first aid and anti-gas measures.

The Japanese bombing of Pearl Harbor in December 1941 resulted in the removal of Japanese Canadians from the coast. That brought a dramatic change to the clientele at Vancouver Public Library's central branch. The number of young readers was cut in half. Library board chairman G. Stanley Miller said the exodus of Japanese Canadian children was the main factor. "They were always great readers and they were handy to Main and Hastings, where the library is located. Most other children find the library is too far away."

The war years at the University of British Columbia library were quiet — and dark. Part of the collection was hidden in vaults in case the building was bombed. Windows were covered with tarpaper and, to comply with blackout regulations, most reading room lights were turned off each evening.

Nobody knew whether British Columbia would come under attack. That uncertainty helped the university build its collection, because the Provincial Library in Victoria sent over duplicate copies of British Parliamentary debates. The understanding was that if the set in Victoria was destroyed, the volumes at the university would replace them. If the Victoria volumes emerged unscathed, then the university could keep the books.

UBC head librarian John Ridington was succeeded in 1940 by William Kaye Lamb, who at thirty-six had already been the provincial librarian and archivist and the superintendent of the Public Library Commission. One of Lamb's first assignments was a pleasant one: Dealing with a collection of 3,500 books left to the university by Judge

Frederick William Howay, a noted historian and a supporter of libraries for many years. Howay requested the books be kept together, with restrictions on their use.

"There is no finer collection," Lamb said. "I was amazed at what the judge had done. I have known him for many years and knew about his library, but I found there were sections of which I knew nothing. The gift is a wonderful contribution to the university." When the Howay books were combined with another major gift — the collection of Robie Lewis Reid — the UBC library could claim to have Canada's greatest collection of Pacific Northwest Americana and British Columbiana.

Lamb spent eight years at the university library. In his time there he gave a lasting gift to every Canadian library that used the Library of Congress cataloguing system. Recognizing that it was not always appropriate for Canadian books, he devised a way to classify Canadian material within it.

The war gave British Columbia a new college with a new library. On October 21, 1942, the Canadian government opened a naval college in the former Dunsmuir home, Hatley Castle, west of Victoria. The castle, along with buildings for family members and gardeners, staff and servants, sat on 229 hectares. The government had spent $75,000 to acquire the property in 1940, and had named it Royal Roads after an offshore anchorage in Juan de Fuca Strait. The library was set up in the castle's master bedroom. In 1946, air force personnel were admitted, followed by army recruits the following year. The name was changed to Canadian Services College Royal Roads. As the number of students increased, so did the book collection; soon the library took over the entire second floor.

The war also brought library changes to Prince Rupert, far up the coast. Dim-outs ordered because of the war prompted many people to stay at home in the evenings and, according to the library commission, they did "a greater amount of intelligent reading." Prince Rupert became a key transit point for the military, and the U.S. Army set up a library to serve its troops there. When they left, the books remained and many local residents were able to boost their home libraries with American discards.

The Carnegie Corporation provided $5,000 for general reference and technical books in civilian libraries in the north, including Prince Rupert and Whitehorse. The library commission said in its 1940 report that books were a key part of the war effort. "It is thus one of the tasks of the commission to join in the struggle against totalitarianism by helping to forge the most potent weapon of defence, the advancement of knowledge and the increased understanding of democratic principles and practice. Through the Open

Shelf of more than 30,000 volumes it makes this defensive armour available to thousands of eager readers throughout the length and breadth of the province."

Once again, war changed reading tastes. Early in the conflict, the Victoria library reported long waiting lists for Adolf Hitler's *Mein Kampf* and Nora Wain's *Reaching for the Stars*, about four years she spent in Germany with her husband in the 1930s, as well as recent books about European politics. *All Quiet on the Western Front* was popular, in line with renewed interest in memoirs of the Great War.

Patrons wanted books about engineering. The reference department had more requests on subjects such as signalling, airships and naval vessels. Atlases and gazetteers were in continuous use. Men from throughout the British Empire who came to the Patricia Bay airfield under the Commonwealth Air Training Plan made use of the Victoria Public Library for technical books.

Public libraries continued to put a major emphasis on non-fiction so readers turned to commercial libraries for fiction. There were plenty to choose from; in Victoria, for example, the Saturday books page in the *Daily Times* featured advertisements from stores such as Diggon's, the Blue Window Library, the Marionette Library, and the Hudson's Bay Company, which had a library on its mezzanine level, and Spencer's department store, with one in the basement.

In 1944, *Quill and Quire* magazine said Victoria was the best book city in Canada. Victoria had as many book shops as Toronto, which had ten times the population. The report prompted the *Daily Colonist* to note, using figures provided by the Public Library Commission, that twice as many books per capita were borrowed in Victoria as in Vancouver.

"If libraries are to survive they must be provided for in much the same manner as schools," the *Colonist* said. "New buildings would do much to raise the level of work done as well as to extend the type of service given. Music and art, as well as practical subjects such as economics, sociology, politics and the various technologies, depend to a large extent on libraries, especially for the literature on those subjects.

"Adult education is inextricably tied in with libraries, regardless of the subject or method of study employed. Yet how can any of these developments be encouraged or tried out in buildings and with equipment long since inadequate to meet even the most ordinary public needs?"

Funding was a major concern. In 1944, Vancouver spent just 39 cents a person on library service, down from 50 cents in 1932. Still, the money helped pay for the central library, the branch in Kitsilano, the Kerrisdale branch that opened in 1943, four deposit stations and service to hospitals and institutions.

Gasoline and tires were in short supply during the war so the union libraries had trouble keeping their book vans on the road. Before the war, the van in the Okanagan travelled more than 1,000 kilometres a month. Its schedule was cut in half, so many books were delivered by local freight services. Library boards eliminated all but one meeting a year. The B.C. Library Association asked the Wartime Prices and Trade Control Board for special priority for tires, arguing that libraries were important to wartime morale and were therefore part of the war effort. They had little success, and had to make do with used or retreaded tires.

Public library service continued to expand. Stewart J. Graham, the principal of Creston Valley Junior-Senior High School, built his school library from scratch and opened it to the public in 1943. The library commission provided it with 200 books. A similar joint library was opened in Williams Lake in 1945.

The war's end in 1945 brought remarkable prosperity to British Columbia. The return of the province's soldiers and the resulting baby boom, coupled with high levels of migration to the province, created a sense that anything was possible. The stage was set for unprecedented development, with new schools, libraries and entire communities appearing where before there had been just trees and rocks. New dams providing electricity caused entire valleys to disappear under water.

Just as reading interests changed when the war started, they changed again after the fighting stopped. Victoria's Margaret Clay reported less interest in personal narratives of the war and increased interest in the problems of the post-war world. Books on businesses, trades, house planning and building were in special demand. In fiction, *Forever Amber* and *Gone With the Wind* were seldom left on the shelves.

Private libraries thrived in the 1940s. Gertrude McGill had a special one, the Children's Garden Library, in her back yard on Tattersall Drive in Saanich. It was designed to give children from four to eight years some play group activities during the summer months, and guided reading to children aged nine through twelve the entire year. The library was in a building that measured eight feet by ten feet, with window boxes, tiny curtained windows and a rounded doorstep. The little library filled with books attracted seventy children a day in the summer.

Detective books were also popular, although there were not as many to choose from as before the war.

"Getting away from it all is the fashion today, both in writing and reading," said Nina Napier of Victoria's cataloguing department. "The simple country life, individual independence, are what people seem to seek. There is a craving for settlement in life and a nostalgia as readers look back on happier times. It is most apparent in the books that depict prewar and pre-First War Britain. Judging from the demand for a series we have of *Britain in Pictures*, there must be a lot of homesickness for the Britain of other days."

The New Westminster Public Library started lending phonograph records to 100 borrowers who had signed up for the service. The library gave occasional concerts of recorded music in the reference room, and a loudspeaker broadcast summertime concerts to those eating lunch on the library's lawns.

The Vancouver Public Library started lending records in 1947 with the help of a $1,500 donation from the Kiwanis Club. The library's 1,000 records were mostly orchestral, but included vocal and instrumental selections. "We have attempted to start a collection of the best from the world of music, but it may be expanded later to include some popular music," head librarian Edgar Stewart Robinson said. The records were available on one-week loans.

In September and October 1944, Nicholas and Ivy Morant of the National Film Board shot a two-reel film on regional libraries in the Fraser Valley. Particular emphasis

Fraser Valley book van visits the Glen Valley store, east of Fort Langley, to deliver books to the residents in the 1940s.
Fraser Valley Regional Library

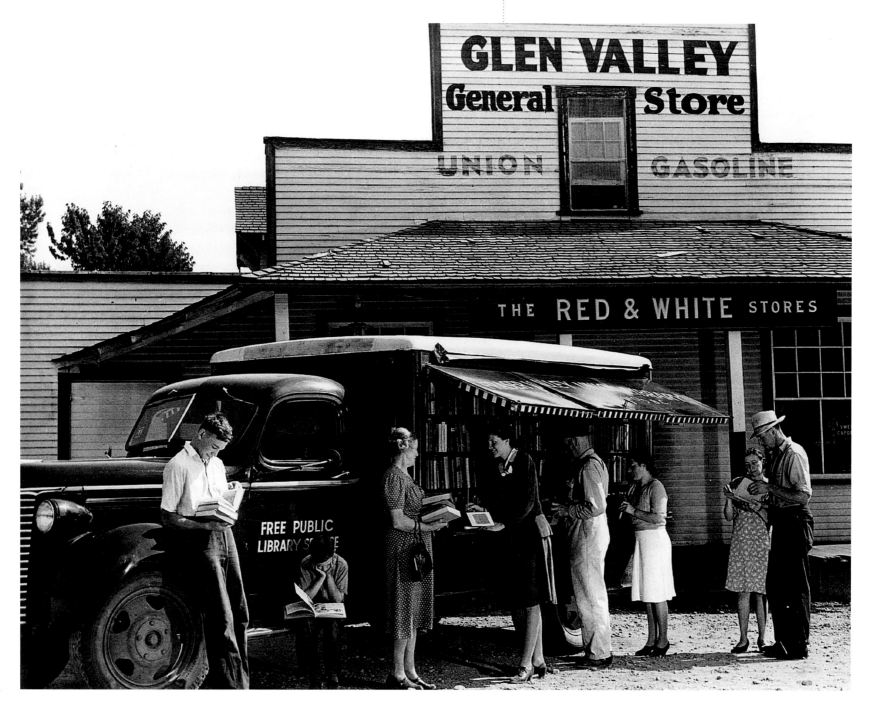

was paid to the mobile work from Hope to Crescent Beach. The Morants — also known for their work on the Canadian Pacific Railway — shot many scenes at book van stops. They also took still photographs in the library and on the road, showing the van serving borrowers in front of a country store, welcoming children and leaving stacks of books at schools. Three hundred people attended the premiere of the movie *Library on Wheels* in Abbotsford on September 22, 1945.

By 1946, public libraries in Vancouver, New Westminster and Victoria as well as the Okanagan union library were getting films from the National Film Board for their new film departments. Librarians led discussions after screening films such as *As the Twig is Bent*, about juvenile delinquents, and *Every Drop of Water a Safe One*, about water purification.

Surveys in 1940 and 1945 paved the way for a new strategic plan to encourage library development. The war meant little was done with the 1940 survey, but the 1945 survey set the course for several years. Entitled Programme for Library Development in British Columbia and developed by a committee organized by the B.C. Library Association and the Public Library Commission, it recommended again that the government provide grants to libraries. It also suggested nine library units — metropolitan libraries in Greater Vancouver, Greater New Westminster, Greater Victoria; union library districts on Vancouver Island, the Fraser Valley, the Okanagan and the West Kootenay; and commission branches in Prince George and in the Peace River — that could provide library service to 80 per cent of the population.

The committee recommended a director of school

libraries be named. It also said the University of British Columbia should start a librarianship school so there would be "an assured flow of trained people" to run libraries.

The Public Library Commission opened a branch in Dawson Creek to serve the Peace River area, a region that had, according to commission head Charles Keith Morison, a dearth of libraries. He said travelling libraries sent to the Peace had been "simply swallowed up and never heard from again." One-room schools had ancient travel books and "choice items," he noted sarcastically, such as *God Wills It*, a 1902 book by William B. Stearn. Morison said well-meaning

Volunteers work on the second library building in the Cloverdale district of Surrey in 1941. *Surrey Public Library*

Adrian Raeside

people from across Canada had been sending discards to the Peace for years.

"I had the privilege of acting as a scourge to cleanse the Peace of dog-eared paper that could only serve the purpose of turning people, old and young, away from books," he wrote later. School collections were so bad, he said, that the only choice was to extract the few books that mattered and toss the rest away. This he did, with the help of commission staff member Beth Quinsey, in a spectacular fashion. They took the discards to the middle of the suspension bridge that crossed the Peace River at Taylor and dumped them over the side.

"The best procedure is to burn this kind of stuff, for it is marvellous how a discard will otherwise come back like a lost cat, but it was impossible to find sufficient fire for tons of books in mid-summer, so they were committed to water instead," Morison wrote later. "It was an odd sight to watch from the top of the arch a long line of white pages stringing along downstream, looking for all the world like a lot of confetti from the height of our vantage point, and floating off into the distance on their way, perhaps, via Mackenzie to the Arctic Circle."

Morison purged books from libraries throughout the province. He had particular disdain for the Hardy Boys and the Bobbsey Twins.

Okanagan bookmark.
Okanagan Regional Library

In 1946, Maxwell A. Cameron brought major changes to libraries with his report on education — even though it did not mention them. Cameron spent several months talking to educators before recommending a massive consolidation of school districts. British Columbia ended up with seventy-seven, about 10 per cent of the former number. Cameron argued that consolidation would reduce inequalities. Students should have equal access to good schools no matter where they were, he said.

Changing the school districts also changed the union libraries, because they were made up of municipalities and school districts. Before Cameron submitted his report, the provincial government had specified that if more than half of the school districts making up a new, larger district were in a union library, the district being formed would become part of the union library. If less than half were involved, the new district would be out of the library.

That created a problem in Penticton, which had voted against being part of the Okanagan Union Library. The old Penticton school district had not been part of the union library, but it was merged with four others, including three — Summerland, Kaleden and Naramata — that had belonged to the library. Therefore, the municipality had to join.

Penticton council protested to the government. "Are the taxpayers not intelligent enough to vote on this question?" asked Reeve Robert Lyon in a letter to the attorney general and the provincial secretary. "Is this a new system of democracy, or just plain fascism, where the higher-ups take matters into their own hands?"

Councillor J.W. Johnson said Penticton would have to spend $7,000 a year on library service under the union concept, much higher than the $2,000 the existing library cost. And, he said, joining the union library would mean the city had only a share of 23,000 books, rather than owning 8,000 books outright. "Years ago, Penticton ratepayers voted on the union scheme and rejected it," the *Penticton Herald* reported. "Objections taken locally to Penticton's forced inclusion in the union library are based upon cost and the alleged fact that the union cannot provide as good a library as is at present available."

Muriel Page Ffoulkes, the head of the union library, tried to calm Penticton's concerns by pointing out the skills of her staff members. "These librarians are trained to maintain a well-balanced mental diet on your shelves just as your hospital is trained to give its patients a well-balanced physical diet," she wrote. "They will consider it a privilege to serve the Penticton people in the future."

Clement Dix, the chairman of the Penticton library association, was upset. "As a lifelong socialist such a move as proposed by the union library has my sympathy, but what is left in my mind is a somewhat hazy conception of how all our responsibilities can be justly dealt with," he said in a letter to Ffoulkes. Again, she tried to calm the fears. "There will be no dark shadows in our relations with Penticton," she told Dix. "The occasional squall, perhaps to bring our fortitude into play, but I for one enjoy the wind."

The Public Library Commission tried to convince Penticton of the benefits it would gain, noting that 2,800 people in Kelowna belonged to the union library, while in Penticton, which had a similar population, only 240 people were members of the local library. A more extensive collection, the theory went, would entice more people to join.

In January 1947, after twenty years of having its own library, Penticton reluctantly joined the Okanagan system. Penticton council had provided the local library association space in the municipal building for free; now, it billed the union library $100 a month for its use. Resentment over the way the union library had been imposed lasted for years.

The Cameron report required other communities to join union libraries, while others lost library service. The Salmon Arm area, Hedley and rural areas of Kelowna had to join the Okanagan library, which saw its population served jump to 44,544 from 23,384. Maple Ridge joined the Fraser Valley library. Qualicum Beach, Duncan, North Cowichan and other areas had to join the Vancouver Island library.

The rush to expand service caused logistical problems for the union libraries. In the Okanagan, for instance, many new patrons were in small hamlets off the beaten path.

"To the north we have taken in a large number of small communities, up in the hills and across lakes, and off the highway in every direction," librarian Ffoulkes reported. "We have not yet been able to find them all, this not being the time of year to leave the highway unless one is sure of one's way."

The Open Shelf service was struggling to keep up with demand for its books. The pre-war cut in the postage rate for books resulted in a lasting increase in activity. Adult fiction in Open Shelf was restricted to the classics and "a discriminating selection of modern novels that might rightly be regarded as literature." The juvenile collection included a full range of fiction and non-fiction — "a portent that good reading tastes may yet prevail against the pulps and the comics," as the commission's 1946 annual report said.

Travelling libraries were still popular. "It may be a collection of sixty volumes loaned to a little brown school-house at Lone Butte or Cape Mudge, or a library of fifty to 200 books exchanged two or three times a year for readers at Bella Coola, Skookumchuk, or Queen Charlotte City, or a collection for a lonely lighthouse at Cape Beale or Langara Light," the commission's 1946 report said. "The travelling library provides a renewable collection of the best classical

North-central branch office of the Public Library Commission opened in 1947. *Public Library Services Branch*

and modern books, fiction and non-fiction, adult and juvenile, to people living in outlying parts of the province

"We are all fishermen, isolated from Prince Rupert by a bi-monthly mail service, also twenty miles of water (bad). Our ages are from fifty years to seventy, most of us have been sailors. We like books of and about the sea, which includes, piracy, salvage, fighting on sea battles, exploring, etc. ... In the winter we overhaul our boats and do various chores made necessary by our isolation. In the long evenings a good book out of your box of pleasure is something to look forward to. One fellow here, an Irishman, never read a book in his life until he came here. The first one he got took thirteen months to read. Now he eats them up, though he won't read fiction."

A letter to the Public Library Commission, 1942

— in mines, logging camps, fishing villages, ranching communities, etc. — who would otherwise be starved of good reading, recreational or educational."

Rules for access varied by community. The book depot at the Sooke Supply Store, for example, was open for two hours on the days when the store was open.

In 1948, provincial legislation was changed to allow public libraries to pool their resources. The following year, libraries in Prince George and Burns Lake tried sharing what they had, with the help of Jeannette Sargent and the Public Library Commission. The other eight libraries in the north-central region soon joined; they were too small to provide adequate service on their own, but too far apart to have a regional library such as the one in the Fraser Valley.

The university in Vancouver and the college in Victoria were under pressure from returning soldiers who wanted an education. By 1948, enrolments were three or four times higher than during the war. Craigdarroch Castle quickly became too small for Victoria College, and students marched in protest of the lack of space. In response, the college was

Library in Victoria College after it moved to the Normal School in 1946. *Image I-01897 courtesy of Royal BC Museum, BC Archives*

Left:In the 1940s, more than 2,000 books were kept in a fireproof vault in the UBC library.
Vancouver Sun

Below: UBC library worker Pearl Cameron checks an original map of British Columbia in 1948.
Vancouver Sun

W. Kaye Lamb, right, in 1951 with Neal Harlow, one of his successors as librarian at UBC.
University of British Columbia Archives 3.1/361

William Kaye Lamb was born in New Westminster. He graduated from the University of British Columbia with a degree in history, did three years of graduate work in France, returned to UBC for his master's degree, then completed his doctorate at the London School of Economics. He was provincial librarian and archivist from 1934 to 1940, and was superintendent of the Public Library Commission from 1936 to 1940. He founded the *British Columbia Historical Quarterly* in 1936.

In 1940 he became the head librarian at the University of British Columbia. In 1948, at the age of forty-four, he moved to Ottawa to become the dominion archivist. He created the National Library because, as he said at the time, Canada needed one. "There is no co-ordination of books and literature in the various dominion government departments at present, and there are many valuable books that should be collected and filed centrally." Lamb served as the first national librarian. He retired to Vancouver, and died there in 1999 at the age of ninety-five.

moved to the Provincial Normal School, where teachers were trained. In 1946 the college hired its first trained librarian, Marjorie Griffin, who served for one year.

The Victoria College library was tiny compared to the one at UBC, which had 300,000 volumes in 1948. UBC's campus was designed to serve 1,500 students, but had 9,300 by that time. That October, the library opened its north wing, larger than the original building, which gave it room for 600,000 books and seating for 800 students.

The university added courses in law, pharmacy, architecture, agricultural engineering and social work, and the library needed materials on those subjects. It was difficult to get extra copies of standard books, and textbooks were scarce. Still, the library sent books to borrowers around the province, in keeping with librarian William Kaye Lamb's philosophy of sharing resources.

"Nowadays the UBC library looks upon itself as a partner of the Provincial Library, and the public libraries in Vancouver, Victoria and other cities," Lamb said. "It is part and parcel of the whole library system of the province, and insofar as the campus demands permit, aims to make its specialized collections available wherever they might be needed.

"If the smallest library in the province happens to serve a reader who has serious need of books it does not itself possess, it should be able to tap the resources of the whole library system of the province to secure the books required."

Lamb also believed that major research libraries should specialize because "a well-rounded library is always a mediocre one." He argued that a library is supposed to serve other libraries, and be served by them. Continent-wide planning was needed, he said, to ensure that one copy of every book published would be in at least one library in the United States or Canada.

"Time was, not so long ago, when libraries tended to hoard their treasures," he said. "All this is changed, and as far as possible, libraries borrow freely from one another, and so make good their individual deficiencies. Indeed libraries — and in particular research and university libraries — are tending more and more to think on regional terms. Experience has shown that many books that are important and valuable are, nevertheless, actually used relatively seldom. Under these circumstances one copy in a region is sufficient; for as long as it can be borrowed when it is needed, there is no necessity for every library in the area to have its own copy."

UBC students were two decades away from being allowed to browse the shelves for themselves without restrictions. Samuel Rothstein, who later founded the university's School of Librarianship, first saw the stacks for himself in his third year. Other students quickly asked him what it was like in this "place of mystery." Rothstein says open stacks made

a huge difference because students could see what was available, although they take up more space and require more security.

The 2,500-volume library at Essondale mental hospital in Coquitlam was expanded in 1947. A trained librarian was appointed, along with an advisory committee made up of the psychologist and three doctors. "The emphasis at first was placed on book selection, by itself a negative approach. Some patients may become absorbed in what they are reading and forget for a short time their own abnormal patterns of thinking. Others, however, may only fortify their delusions," librarian Jean Irving reported.

"Every patient requires individual attention for recommended reading, but books pertaining to some subjects are avoided in general. Those dealing with material derogatory to the medical profession, mentally ill persons, suicide, morbid situations and horror tales are not acceptable. Books concerning psychology, psychiatry, religion, mysticism, numerology and similar fields may be disturbing and are also kept from circulation."

Medical and technical volumes were kept in the nurses' training office. The New Westminster Public Library helped by recommending and lending reference books not in the Essondale collection. Bibliotherapy, Irving noted, was positive and active.

The Elizabeth Fry Society provided library service to jails for several years. In 1949, the provincial attorney general's department appointed a full-time prison librarian. John C. Lort, who had been on the staff of the provincial library as well as librarian at Ketchikan, Alaska, was assigned to organize services for the Oakalla Prison Farm, the New Haven institution in Burnaby and the provincial jails in Prince George, Kamloops and Nelson.

In 1948, a survey of hospitals revealed most only had donated books in their patient libraries. One hospital had assigned a nurse to look after the library for a few hours a week. "Progressive hospital authorities and progressive librarians agree that a good book service in hospitals serves a definite therapeutic purpose," the Public Library Commission said, and recommended that public libraries establish hospital services. It argued that Vancouver should have a hospital librarian and an assistant, the union librarians should appoint hospital librarians and in the smaller communities, nurses or volunteers should look after hospital libraries.

After the war, libraries faced severe staff shortages and rapidly rising costs, and struggled to find qualified people and the money to pay them. Since the start of the war, few students had entered library schools and many librarians left to enter the armed services or seek more lucrative fields. "Amongst the women a larger proportion than usual entered the field of matrimony," the Public Library Commission noted, which threw a big load on those who remained.

While women had made progress on the road to equality during the war, when the men returned from service things went back to normal. "Library work is done by women, but it is run by men," Samuel Rothstein of the University of British

In 1945, the Fraser Valley Union Library needed a new regional librarian. The board asked the secretary to advertise in the *Library Journal*, the *Toronto Star* and the *Winnipeg Free Press*, stating the starting salary would be $185 a month, but to "leave mention of truck driving out of the ad."

Columbia library said in the B.C. Library Association's *Bulletin* in 1949.

"Though there may well be some doubts as to the justice of the situation, it is an undeniable fact that there

Children gather in the Vancouver Public Library for 1949's Young Canada Book Week. *Artray photo, Vancouver Public Library, VPL 81075*

exists in the library world a strong prejudice in favour of men, especially when the question of appointment to administrative and supervisory positions arises, so much so, that a well-known director of a library school has been left to declare that any male librarian may expect to rise to the position of department head within five years, if he is only reasonably competent." The bias toward males in management was not confined to libraries; it was typical in most fields. Nor was it confined to the 1940s.

In 1947, the Vancouver library expanded into the Pender Street wing of the old city hall. By then it had 150,000 books and a budget of $23,500, of which only $2,000 would go to fiction. Librarian Robinson said the library had to concentrate on books for business and trades people.

By the end of the 1940s the three Carnegie buildings were pushing the half-century mark, and had been out of space for years. The Victoria library moved ten tons of books, periodicals and pamphlets to a storage room in the public market building adjacent to city hall, leaving only sixty per cent of the collection open to patrons. A major expansion was announced in 1949.

Vancouver voters approved — with a majority of eighty-three per cent — spending $150,000 for three more branches. Another $1 million was set aside for a new central library. The plebiscite was a first in British Columbia; never before had voters agreed to spend money on a library building.

Service was still hard to find in many areas; even urban areas such as Burnaby, West Vancouver, Richmond, and North Vancouver were without modern libraries. Another problem was that books were in short supply. Hardly any new ones had come from Europe, and American books were scarce, too expensive and had poor quality paper, binding, and print.

The shortage was alleviated by a new form of book — the paperback. "Comprised largely of the more popular and ephemeral class of literature and supplied in a cheap format, these books are now purchased in great quantity by people who formerly borrowed this type of literature from the public library," the Public Library Commission noted in its 1945 annual report.

Microforms have been in British Columbia since the 1940s. In 1947, the reference department at the Vancouver Public Library acquired a microfilm reader, allowing patrons to read archived newspapers such as the *Daily Province* and the *Vancouver Sun*. The new Canadian Library Association also announced plans to make historical materials, particularly early newspapers, available on microfilm. Microforms — microfilms, which are reels of film, and microfiche, which are flat sheets — have allowed libraries to have, in one small room, as much material as would fill an entire floor in conventional printed format. Typical collections include newspapers, government reports and technical reports. Microforms enable libraries to obtain materials that could not be obtained in print form or which are rare or too expensive. Both formats need to be magnified and projected onto a screen to be readable, but images can then be printed.

"This does not mean that libraries will discontinue catering to the recreational reader, but it does mean that they will be able to pay proportionately greater attention to books and services of an informative and educational nature.

"The paperback has thus released resources which can advantageously be applied to other library services which will be appreciated by the businessman, the student and the serious reader. This is but another of the revolutionary changes brought about by war and the shortage of materials, one which promises to be accepted as permanent practice."

11

THE FABULOUS FIFTIES

At the start of the 1950s, library service in British Columbia was under pressure. The three Carnegie libraries were bursting with books, but in smaller towns volunteer associations were doing the best they could after two tough decades. Libraries were still struggling to develop a presence, and scrambling even to find space.

John Adams Lowe, a public library expert from Rochester, New York, did not mince words when he visited British Columbia in 1949. The Vancouver Public Library, he said, was "deplorable," and while he praised the book collection, the building was "inconceivable" and had to go. "It is in Chinatown, a decadent part of

Opposite: Margaret Turnbull, the librarian in Vancouver's new bookmobile, takes books to eager readers Cora Edgett and Penny Brabant in 1956. *Don McLeod, Vancouver Province*

Above: Volunteers at the Creston library sort the latest selection of books from the Public Library Commission. *Public Library Services Branch*

the city. A central library should cater to the entire city, with the building in the centre of the business section."

He was just as unimpressed with the Victoria Public Library's newspaper reading room, which he said had no place in a public library because it "attracts the lowest down part of the community." Lowe said people should buy their own newspapers. "We do not furnish an old man's home. There should be social service institutions to take care of that problem. They take up space that should be used by people seeking information from reference books."

Lowe said expanding the building would be pointless, even though plans for an addition had been prepared. "This building should have been shelved twenty-five years ago," he said. "It is a monumental building. Today we plan a building as a functional working library."

If Lowe was horrified by what he saw in Vancouver and Victoria, it's a good thing he did not visit some of the smaller communities. North Burnaby had its own building, as did Greenwood, in the Boundary area, and Telkwa, in the Bulkley Valley. Westview, near Powell River, had a building but efforts were being made to move the library into the old school. The libraries in Collingwood East and Tate Creek were in community halls. Revelstoke, Merritt and Smithers were in municipal halls.

The Cranbrook library was split, with the adult section in a downtown room and the children's section in the school. McBride and Fernie were in schools, although Fernie was negotiating for a room in the post office, like the one used in Grand Forks. The Burns Lake library was in the old drafting office for the engineering firm which installed the municipal water system. Castlegar was in the basement of a board member's home. Dawson Creek and Prince George were in reconditioned army buildings; Prince George shared the accommodation with the Boy Scouts and Girl Guides.

Field was in the YMCA building at the Canadian Pacific Railway depot; Hazelton in the rear of an old church building; and Kamloops in an old residence that had been bequeathed as a combined library and museum. Ocean Falls was in the recreational hall owned by Pacific Mills. Port Mellon was also in the recreational hall, but was in limbo because the major employer, the Sorg pulp mill, had shut down and the population had dropped. Kimberley had a small upper office in the company store.

Rossland was in the courthouse. The Vernon and Quesnel libraries had closed after losing their space. North Vancouver City was in the former administration building of the Central Mortgage and Housing Corporation until it moved to an old one-car garage at Lonsdale and Sixteenth.

In 1951, after the Burns Lake library moved to a new home, the library sign still hung above the door of its old building. *Image I-00702 courtesy of Royal BC Museum, BC Archives*

Dramatic changes would mark the 1950s. Two of the three Carnegie libraries moved to new quarters, and the third had a massive expansion — even though Lowe would not have approved. And the 1958 centennial of the founding of the colony of British Columbia would bring new library buildings to several communities.

Victoria

The wave started in Victoria, whose building was described by the Public Library Commission as outmoded and "one of the poorest in British Columbia." The library board had been calling for a new building since 1921, and finally, in October 1949, it announced that a proposal for a four-storey addition to the original Carnegie library would go to the voters for approval. The building had been designed to house 15,000 books, but by 1949 there were 93,000 on the shelves. In 1906, Victoria had had 24,000 people and 1,000 library patrons, but by 1949 it had 103,000 people and 27,000 borrowers.

"Since 1906 one department store has expanded and another has been opened. One large and at least three medium sized hotels have been built. Several large office buildings have been added and many smaller ones. Eleven schools have been built in Victoria city alone, but the library has been carrying on its work in the same building," a library board report said.

Ten tons of books were in storage in the public market building next to city hall. Then, as now, about twenty-five per cent of the book stock was on loan at any given time, helping to ease the burden. A new location was not considered. Margaret Jean Clay, the head librarian, believed that a library had to be in the heart of the city. She said the Victoria library had one of the most desirable locations in Victoria, and one of the best library locations in North America.

The expansion would use land purchased in January 1939 using, legend has it, the proceeds of book fines. Plans included a massive remodelling of the Carnegie building, with an entrance removed and two elevators added. The architects went for a modern look for the addition rather than trying to match the style of the Carnegie structure.

The expansion would allow the library to offer story hours, puppet shows, hobby exhibits and other features. It would be an effective answer to the easy accessibility of movies and crime comic books. "It is the best way we know of meeting a very grave menace in the current newsstand literature for children," said Hazel King, the children's librarian.

Voters approved the $250,000 project on December 8, 1949, and work started almost immediately. In January 1950, borrowers were allowed to take as many books as they wanted, making it easier for the library to move to temporary quarters in the Pantorium Building at Fort and Quadra streets. Much of the reference collection was boxed up and placed in storage.

When part of the old building was demolished a large lead box was found in the cornerstone. Included were 1903 reports from city council and the board of trade, a 1902 city bylaw signed by Mayor Charles Hayward accepting the gift of $50,000 from Andrew Carnegie, and copies of the *Daily Colonist* and *Victoria Daily Times*. The materials were sealed in a new cornerstone along with new items.

Margaret Jean Clay, who was born in Moose Jaw in 1891 and marched in women's suffrage parades in Victoria in 1916, succeeded Helen Gordon Stewart as the head librarian in Victoria in 1924. She served in the position for twenty-eight years, and after retirement she catalogued books for the Vancouver Island Regional Library in Nanaimo for six years. She was president of the B.C. Library Association and the Pacific Northwest Library Association, which made her a life member in 1952. She chaired the 1946 meeting that led to the creation of the Canadian Library Association. She was on the Public Library Commission from 1948 to 1966. Clay received an honorary degree from the University of Victoria in 1973, and died in 1982.

While at the temporary location, the Victoria library became the first in Canada to adopt the latest technology — an Eastman Recordak photocharging machine, which helped automate book borrowing. When people signed books out, the book cards and the patron's library card were placed in the machine, there was a click and a whir, and the numbers were recorded on microfilm. The machine was basically a slow-motion movie camera that could take 4,000 photos per roll of film — three days' worth of activity. The film was sent to Vancouver for developing and returned within twenty-four hours. It could be checked at any time to determine the status of loans.

Under the old system, staff members had to write four sets of numbers for every book marked. They sometimes handled 2,000 books in a day. It was calculated that the new system would save twenty-six seconds on each book checked out. Recordak photocharging machines were used in libraries into the 1990s.

Victoria's library expansion opened on October 17, 1951, with Mayor Percy George cutting the ribbon. The vast

Expansion of Victoria's Carnegie library building in 1950. *Image I-02302 courtesy of Royal BC Museum, BC Archives*

increase in space would satisfy the library's needs for the next three decades.

Soon after, an anonymous donor provided a record-playing machine for the library's music room. "We hope we will be able to build a collection of records and have concerts of recorded music from time to time," Clay said. "It is part of the policy of expanding music facilities. Circulation of records is becoming more and more a part of library services, just as is the use and circulation of films." The library did not begin to lend records until after Clay retired. Starting in 1956, a patron could borrow one opera, one symphony, one musical comedy or three mixed long-play records. The library also started a series of bi-monthly talks on fine arts.

John C. Lort, Victoria's head librarian in 1956, said television had helped stimulate reading. After the novelty wore off, TV viewers settled down to a few favourite programs each week. Those programs meant that viewers skipped the movies in the local theatres, but before and after the shows they had time to read. That explained, Lort said, why library circulation had been rising along with the sale of television sets.

Vancouver

In Vancouver, it took longer to make a decision on a larger central library. The board hired Lowe and John Stewart Richards, Seattle's public librarian, to review facilities. The two men reported in 1950 that Vancouver had too few books, too few librarians, too few library buildings — and too little money.

The central library at Hastings and Main, they said, had "wretched ventilation" and "inadequate restrooms" and was "hazardous in case of fire." The odours from the adjacent market and alley were so obnoxious that windows had to be kept closed. They hinted that the building might be condemned. The library had only 0.44 books per capita, compared to the accepted minimum standard of 1.5.

Vancouver voters had approved $1 million for a new central library in December 1945, but nothing was done for several years. The city chose a location on the northeast corner of Robson and Burrard in 1951 and bought it the following year.

In 1953, the Carnegie library was described in the *Vancouver Sun* as being at the centre of the narcotic trade in Vancouver. "Addicts Alley" and "Peddlers Promenade" ran beside the library in the most sordid section of the city. The Public Library Commission said the library was "over-conveniently close to some of Vancouver's best-known blind pigs" — establishments that illegally sold alcohol. It was the only civic department still in its first permanent quarters. The library board said it had outgrown the building in 1917, after just fourteen years of use. By 1953 it had thirty-five times as many books as when it opened.

A busy, drafty corner beside the door to the annex — Vancouver's old city hall — was home to the library's collection of patent records in 1950. *Vancouver Province*

The library ended its record loan service in 1953 because of the high cost of replacing discs. At the time, the library had 250,000 books and 40,000 records, and still lent projectors and educational films. Popular movies were increasing interest in certain books. Thanks to Danny Kaye and Walt Disney, *Andersen's Fairy Tales* and *Peter Pan* were in high demand. Other popular books among children in the early 1950s were Helen Bannerman's *Little Black Sambo*, first published in 1899, Beatrix Potter's *Peter Rabbit*, *The 500 Hats of Bartholomew Cubbins* by Dr. Seuss, and *Curious George* by Hans Augusto Rey and Margret Rey. Another popular series was *Freddy the Pig*, by Walter R. Brooks, about a pig who was an improbable success as a detective, pilot and many other professions.

Older children were interested in the classics — *Treasure Island*, *Robinson Crusoe*, *20,000 Leagues Under the Sea*. At the time, only about ten children's books were published in Canada each year, compared to 1,500 in the United States. Well-liked Canadian offerings included Katherine Clark's *The Sun House*, about B.C., and *Ook Pik, the Eskimo Boy*, by William George Crisp. The library started a teen section in the 1950s because many children were regular users until they became teenagers and stopped visiting.

The Vancouver Public Library started a bookmobile service to the city's outlying areas on March 20, 1956. A total of 1,600 books would fit in the vehicle, drawn from a stock of 14,000. There were two desks, front and back, and service was provided to eleven stops four days a week. The van was said to be the only bookmobile in North America with a translucent roof.

As planning for a new central branch continued, Lowe returned to Vancouver to help influence its design. One of his ideas, revolutionary at the time, was to ask members of the library staff for opinions on what the building should look like and how it should be organized.

The planned location did not win unanimous approval and several other sites were suggested, although council confirmed the Robson location in September 1954, and architects Harold Semmens and Doug Simpson went to work on plans. The Vancouver Tourist Association offered its help, saying that if the library had "sombre lines" it would cost the city hundreds of thousands of dollars in reduced property value in the adjacent area.

Harry Boyce, Peter Grossman and Colin Robertson in Vancouver's bookmobile in 1957. *Vancouver Public Library, Special Collections, VPL 3403*

Sod was turned on April 18, 1956, and the building went up quickly. The Carnegie library was locked on Saturday, October 19, 1957, and staff started moving books to the new building, which was to be opened on November 1. It was bad news for the old men who had been keeping warm and dry in the reading rooms of the Carnegie building. Library officials expressed hope the men would not come to the new building. Peter Grossman, the assistant librarian, said several groups were working on plans to provide places where the men could sit in warmth with something to read.

"Some of the old chaps will be heartbroken. They come in day after day, mostly to read newspapers from home and places they have lived. It's their life," one library employee said. For Albert Crawley, sixty-six, the Carnegie library had been an escape from his heatless room on Main Street. "I couldn't have had a better place, these last few years. Most times, when the weather was bad, I was there all day. My room is cold and very nasty-smelling." Crawley said he was looking for a new room close to the new library.

On October 19, the day the old library closed, head librarian Edgar Stewart Robinson had a heart attack in Victoria, where he was attending a meeting of the Public Library Commission. He died in Victoria's Royal Jubilee Hospital five days later — just eight days before the new library building opened. He was sixty years old.

Robinson's influence had extended beyond Vancouver. For almost twenty years he had served on the Public Library Commission, including a stint in the chair. He helped shape policies that contributed to a great expansion of libraries throughout the province. Throughout his thirty-three

Above: In 1957, a "closed" sign was finally placed on Vancouver's Carnegie library. *Vancouver Sun*

Left: Excavation work at the corner of Burrard and Robson in Vancouver, the new home of the Vancouver central branch in 1956. *Vancouver Public Library, Special Collections, VPL 3401*

Edgar Robinson looks at a page from the library's Gutenberg Bible in 1950. *Vancouver Public Library, Special Collections, VPL 86728*

Opening day in November 1957 brought crowds to the new Vancouver Public Library central branch. *Vancouver Public Library, Special Collections, VPL 3407*

Marion Watts Thompson became the first head of the children's department at the Vancouver Public Library in 1924, and set up an inviting room where children and books could come together. Unfortunately, when she lost her hearing due to illness, she had to move to the cataloguing department — but she retained her interest in children's books.

In 1960, the library honoured Thompson by giving her name to a special collection of children's books.

The collection, with books dating from the 1870s to the 1940s, had been started in the 1940s when staff started putting aside the older books. The collection is now part of the library's special collections department.

"Books, like people, find their just reward. The good live on but the bad are soon forgotten," Thompson said. In other words, a good book fifty years ago was still a good book. She gave as examples *Little Women*, *Wind in the Willows*, *Alice in Wonderland* and *Black Beauty*. She said the books that were preachy, with morals or messages, simply disappeared. "All children of all times have loved fairy tales, stories about horses and stories that make them laugh."

Thompson died in 1969.

Vancouver's central branch at Burrard and Robson served the city from 1957 to 1995.
Vancouver Sun

Above: Ruth Cameron, New Westminster's head librarian from 1936 to 1954. *New Westminster Public Library photo 3347*

Below: Amy Hutcheson, New Westminster's head librarian from 1954 to 1973. *New Westminster Public Library photo 3197*

years as Vancouver's head librarian he had fought for a new building, but did not live long enough to see crowds cramming in to celebrate its opening.

Vancouver had about 400,000 people when the new library opened at 750 Burrard Street. In 1903, when the Carnegie building opened, the city's population had been 34,000. The new library was overdue. It was notable for another reason: It won a Massey Medal, Canada's highest architectural honour.

The bottom two floors of the old Carnegie building were taken over by the Vancouver Museum, a tenant on the third floor since the building opened. The museum stayed for a decade, until it moved to Vanier Park. From 1968 to 1980, the Carnegie building was vacant and at risk of being torn down, but was saved by a concerted community effort. It came back to life as a community centre in 1980, and included a branch of the Vancouver Public Library.

More and more homes were getting television sets, but that did not hurt the library. As Margaret Brunette, the head of the extension department, said in 1958, family members were often nearly married to the television when it was new, but they returned to books in time. "The library must have a constant source of supply to compete with TV or newspapers," Brunette said.

New Westminster

The New Westminster library board started seriously talking about a new building in 1946. A few years later the board considered remodelling the Carnegie building and adding a bookmobile service, but finally decided that there was only one viable choice.

"The building has outlived its usefulness," said Owen Armitage, the library board chairman. "The population growth to the west and east has left it in a position where it no longer serves the mass of people." The Carnegie library was in the middle of the property, making expansion impractical, and on the crown of the property, so access was difficult.

Amy Hutcheson started her library career working for Helen Gordon Stewart in the Fraser Valley system. After graduating from library school and working as a children's librarian in Hamilton, Hutcheson returned to British Columbia. In 1942 she started working at the New Westminster Public Library, and became head librarian when Ruth Cameron died in 1954. Hutcheson guided the library through its move to a new building. She retired in 1973.

On February 18, 1954, the library board and the city's finance committee confirmed plans to move the library to a new home. Two days later, head librarian Ruth Cameron, who had been at the library since 1936, died. She had been ill for several months.

In 1956, the board chose a location at the corner of Sixth Avenue and Ash Street, close to a new Woodward's shopping centre. Voters approved the site on October 25, 1956, and three months later voted in favour of the plans for a $350,000 building that would have all public departments on the main floor and a mezzanine for technical processes and administration.

Governor General Vincent Massey opened the library on November 19, 1958, 100 years to the day after the creation of the colony of British Columbia. New Westminster's population at the time was about 33,000, five times the number of residents when the old Carnegie building went up. There had been a need for a new library; circulation rose by sixty-eight per cent from the previous year, and the number of registered borrowers climbed to forty per cent of the population. The reference department saw a tripling of queries.

In July 1960, the old Carnegie library was torn down. The 1958 building, much expanded over the years, is still in use today.

West Vancouver

In December 1947, West Vancouver did not have library service, and its residents decided that a library would be a suitable memorial to the community's war dead. In 1949, volunteers started canvassing for funds for what would become the West Vancouver Memorial Library. A site was picked in the 1900 block of Marine Drive, and plans were drawn that called for $28,000 for the building and $7,000 for equipment.

The library had a wall dedicated to the memory of Lieut. Horace Gordon Stone, who was killed in action in 1918. The wall included a stained glass window that had been commissioned in 1931 by Henry Stone, a founder of the Vancouver Art Gallery, and his wife Beatrice Stone, as a memorial to their son. It was created by John Henry Dearle, chief designer for the London firm of Morris and Co., and was a reproduction of Sir Frank Dicksee's painting *Harmony*. The window had been displayed in the Vancouver Art Gallery until the Second World War, when it was removed for safekeeping. When the West Vancouver Memorial Library was under construction in 1950, Elsie Gentles, Lieut. Stone's sister, presented the window to the library.

The library was opened on November 11, 1950 and reflected a spirit of co-operation that was unusual for the time; it was operated in conjunction with the Vancouver Public Library. It quickly became an essential part of life in

Left: Circulation desk at New Westminster's Carnegie library was overcrowded long before 1956, when this photograph was taken. *New Westminster Public Library photo 2983*

Below: Governor-General Vincent Massey opened the New Westminster Public Library's new building on Nov. 19, 1958. *New Westminster Public Library photo 2982*

Memorial window is a focal point in West Vancouver's library. *West Vancouver Memorial Library*

number of students, faculties or buildings. Samuel Rothstein, the assistant librarian, noted that industry was making increasing demands for research. The library, the storehouse of records of research, should be the starting point.

Harlow believed it was important to know what was happening at other university libraries, and in 1958 he spent three weeks touring libraries in Canada and the United States. He also attended a seminar at McGill University in Montreal and determined that new technologies, such as the IBM computer, were not yet suitable for library use. Manual methods for indexing and cataloguing were still the most effective ways to store and find information, he said.

In 1956, the Friends of the Library of the University of British Columbia was founded, and offered to help provide new materials. One of its first major acquisitions was a 20,000-volume collection of Canadiana, purchased in Montreal in 1958. The next year, the Friends acquired a 45,000-volume library considered one of the most important collections of Chinese books and manuscripts in the world. It contributed to UBC's reputation as one of the leading centres in North America for the study of Chinese history, philosophy, literature and geography.

In Victoria, the college library had 10,000 volumes by 1952 and 35,000 by 1956. It also had an extensive phonograph record collection, and every Tuesday at noon students gathered in the basement to listen to selections.

The Public Library Commission continued to push for library development through the 1950s, offering carrots and using sticks in its attempts to motivate local areas to support libraries.

By 1950, the commission had twenty-nine people in its Victoria headquarters and its branches in Prince George and Dawson Creek. Its budget was $113,000, with $19,950 in grants going to libraries in Burns Lake, Castlegar, Cranbrook, Dawson Creek, Fernie, Field, Grand Forks, Greenwood, Hazelton, Kamloops, Kimberley, Merritt, McBride, North Burnaby, North Vancouver, Ocean Falls, Prince George, Revelstoke, Rossland and Westview in Powell River as well as the union libraries serving the Fraser Valley, the Okanagan Valley and Vancouver Island. Grants were also given to the B.C. Library Association and the Canadian Library Association.

The commission had been giving small grants to small libraries since 1944. In 1951, the grants became much bigger, and were given to large libraries as well. The commission gave $50,000 to the seven taxpayer-supported municipal libraries, which were grateful for the windfall; they had needed help for some time. The money helped provide books, films, microfilms, microfilm readers

West Vancouver, despite the competition from television, movies and other forms of entertainment. Children liked the travel and adventure books, while adults liked the do-it-yourself and gardening books.

University of British Columbia and Victoria College

After the post-war rush of students, the University of British Columbia became somewhat quieter in the 1950s. The campus had 2,500 students a year before the war and 9,500 immediately after, but enrolment dropped to 6,500 by the middle of the 1950s.

In 1952, the university's first branch library was opened. The Bio-Medical Branch Library at Vancouver General Hospital served the clinical departments of the Faculty of Medicine and the B.C. Medical Centre.

It was an established fact that a good library was at the heart of any university. In 1956, head librarian Neal Harlow took the argument a step further, saying a university's character was determined by its library — not by the

Students use the University of British Columbia library in 1956. *Bob Olsen, Vancouver Province*

and photocharging systems, and made possible special collections and bookmobile services.

Voters in Vernon turned down membership in the Okanagan library system and voters in Central Saanich rejected a deal that would have given them access to the Victoria library. In both cases, Open Shelf was cited as a factor in the failure of the plebiscites. As a result, the Public Library Commission announced it would no longer offer Open Shelf to Vernon residents. There was a different conclusion in Central Saanich; the municipality agreed to pay for library service after the Victoria library enticed it with the promise of a bookmobile.

In 1953, the commission announced an end to Open Shelf service in Richmond and Burnaby, an effort to convince local residents to support local libraries. It worked; Richmond voters agreed to join the Fraser Valley system and Burnaby started its own municipal library.

The Public Library Commission kept an eye on the province's major developments. Open Shelf and travelling libraries were available to the construction camps at Nechako Dam, Kemano, Tahtsa Lake and at Kitimat, where the commission provided advice to the Aluminum Company of Canada regarding permanent library services for the city to be created.

It wasn't easy to open a library in Wells. When Dorothy Wall moved there in 1951, she drummed up support based on her experience at the Vancouver Public Library. Wells residents collected money for a library in the old community hall and obtained sheet metal from mines for a partition to hide a billiard table. When the local liquor store got new lights, it donated its old ones to the library. Curtains and books were put in place, and the opening was set for February 15, 1952 — but had to be postponed when it was declared a day of mourning for King George VI.

The library opened a few days later, with books available one afternoon and one evening every week. Wall obtained books, including westerns and mysteries, from the Public Library Commission in Victoria. She also ordered books in Italian because Wells had a large Italian population. The day before the books arrived, the commission's annual report noted, the Italians had left Wells.

Charles Keith Morison was born in Ormstown, in Quebec's Eastern Townships, in 1891. After serving in the First World War, he worked in a variety of jobs in Canada, the United States and Mexico before enrolling in the librarianship program at McGill University in Montreal. He was hired as a van driver in the Fraser Valley and became the first librarian there when the union library was established in 1934. In 1940 he became provincial librarian and superintendent of the Public Library Commission.

He retired in 1956, aged sixty-five, and then became the children's librarian at the Vancouver Island Regional Library. He followed that with a job at Victoria College. When he left the college he built filing drawers and shelving for libraries throughout Vancouver Island, and wrote a book about his experiences as the head of the library commission. He died in 1977.

The Dawson Creek office, opened when Charles Keith Morison was commission superintendent, covered 110,000 square miles, still sparsely settled despite a population surge during the war. The branch had 25,000 titles for borrowers such as trappers along the Alaska Highway from Dawson Creek into the Yukon. Dog teams were sometimes needed to get books into communities inaccessible to the book van.

The commission opened a branch in Cranbrook on October 1, 1956, and its staff encouraged rural libraries throughout the East Kootenay. Within three years ten libraries served small communities in the area. The Kingsgate library, south of Fernie, was in the home of Dolly Bell, the book custodian. In Wynndel, books were at the Co-Operative Fruit Growers building, sponsored by the Women's Institute, and S.H. Moseley was the librarian. Mrs. J.A. Phair was in charge of the Sparwood-Michel-Natal library, sponsored by the local community club. W.B. Johnston was the librarian at Jaffray, with the parent-teacher association as the sponsor and the school providing space.

The library in Marysville, near Kimberley, was under the Lions Club and the Parent-Teacher Association, and

Bill Orr and Marlene Sutton check the film selection at the Public Library Commission's Cranbrook office, which opened in 1956. *Public Library Services Branch*

housed in a former church. In Invermere, the library was divided; adult books were at the fire hall under Major T.C. Bell and children's books were at the school under Mrs. T.N. Weir (and later Lil Obee). North of Radium, Mrs. Lloyd Watkins had books for Brisco at her home, and Mabel Hall looked after the books at the Parson school. Mrs. C.D. Bearns had books for Donald and the Upper Blaeberry at Donald School. A library was also established in Mrs. J.O. Bergenham's home in Moberly.

The three regional libraries — the word "union" was replaced in 1951 — continued to serve through branches

The Okanagan Regional Library would go to any heights to deliver books to readers. In the 1950s it had a branch at the Nickel Plate mine, high above Hedley in the Similkameen district. Books were changed every six weeks, sent up and down the mountain on the shaft truck that took groceries, oil and other necessities to the miners.

Top left: Muriel Page Ffoulkes served as the head librarian in the Okanagan Regional Library system from 1936 to 1964. *Okanagan Regional Library*

Top right: Comox Municipal Library provided service when Comox withdrew from the Vancouver Island Regional Library between 1953 and 1972. *Times Colonist*

Left: Fraser Valley Regional Library's branch in Chilliwack in the 1950s. *Bette Cannings*

Above: In 1951, the Vancouver Island Union Library's headquarters also served as the Nanaimo branch.
Vancouver Sun

Top right: A library was one of the important services offered in the "instant town" of Kitimat, with a dedicated building opening in 1958.
Kitimat Public Library

and bookmobiles, although all three systems needed larger administration buildings. The Fraser Valley library was the first to get one, moving to a single-storey building in Abbotsford in May 1953. It continued to seek better accommodations for its branches, which had to be provided rent-free by the member municipalities.

The Okanagan Regional Library's headquarters shared a building with the Kelowna branch until December 31, 1954, when it was closed. Premier W.A.C. Bennett, the MLA for the South Okanagan, opened the new building at Queensway and Ellis Street on April 15, 1955.

In the same year the Vancouver Island Regional Library moved out of the basement of the old library building in Nanaimo into its new home on Strickland Street at the corner of Needham. The library's two bookmobiles — nicknamed Gert and Reo — provided service to 274 stops, including towns, villages, hamlets and private homes, travelling 150,000 miles a year.

The Island's home librarians — people such as Berthe Colvin of Cowichan Station, who kept a shelf of books in her residence — slowly disappeared as branch service improved. The Island had sixty home librarians in the early days, when part-time branches were also opened in grocery stores and dry-cleaning outlets. By the 1950s the board wanted its branch libraries in premises used exclusively for that purpose.

A growing interest in libraries was evident in communities such as Kamloops, Kitimat and Williams Lake. In 1950 voters in Kamloops approved a municipal library, which hired a professional librarian and took over the books collected by the community library association. In 1956, the

old house that had been used as a library for eighteen years was torn down and replaced with a new building.

The instant town of Kitimat, built to serve an aluminum smelter, got its first library in 1954. It shared the fire hall with a truck and a jeep, and on busy days, weather permitting, the vehicles were moved outside to make more room for library patrons. The Kitimat Chamber of Commerce collected books with a drive in March 1955. Two months later the library was incorporated with volunteers, including members of the fire department, in charge.

Broadcaster Dorwin Baird spread the word about libraries for years through his radio programs, *Silent Friends* and *Book Mark*. They were broadcast on radio stations throughout the province in the 1950s and 1960s. Baird died in 1972.

In 1956 a new fire hall was opened and the books went to the municipal hall until the dedicated library building was finished in February 1958. More than 100 volunteers kept the library going, with 1,300 adults and 1,500 children holding library cards. Kitimat's population was estimated at 11,300, and the library had about the same number of books, with an average cost of $2.75. As the library expanded, more staff members were hired, reducing the need for volunteers to sort and shelve the books.

The Williams Lake library opened in 1945 in an old school annex, then moved to the back of a radio repair shop and then into a basement room at St. Peter's church hall. In 1956, volunteers led by the Kiwanis Club built a new library. Shelves and drapes were donated, elementary school students raised money for chairs and tables, and Boy Scouts bought floor tiles through hot dog sales. Door-to-door book drives built the collection. In 1958, proceeds from a library-sponsored wrestling match raised enough money to pay off the construction debt.

In Ganges, a library was opened in November 1959 at the back of the Mouat Brothers store when plans to build a centennial museum fell through. The library had 1,200 books donated by Salt Spring Island residents as well as some from the Public Library Commission.

School libraries saw dramatic improvements during the 1950s. In 1956, when the Faculty of Education was established at the University of British Columbia, training for school librarians was offered, and students could major in school librarianship. The UBC faculty replaced Normal Schools in Vancouver and Victoria that had been used for teacher training for decades.

By 1959 every secondary school had a library, with book collections and reference material. The Public Library Commission provided single-room country schools with small libraries through its headquarters in Victoria and its branches in Prince George and Dawson Creek. A report by the Department of Education reinforced the importance of school libraries and led to a commitment for more of them, although many disappeared from schools in the 1960s when the postwar baby boom caused a space crunch.

Special libraries were developed and expanded as well. There was a 7,500-volume library, for example, in St. Joseph's

Marjorie Colquhoun Holmes worked in libraries for more than fifty years, so was well suited to write the 1959 book, *Library Service in British Columbia: A History of its Development*. Holmes joined the Victoria Public Library as a student apprentice in 1915, and stayed on staff until 1936, when she went to the provincial library. She was assistant librarian when she retired in 1954. But she wasn't finished; she ran the libraries at Victoria Press — the publisher of the *Daily Colonist* and the *Victoria Daily Times* — and the Art Gallery of Greater Victoria. She died in 1990.

Hospital in Victoria in 1958. Only books with happy endings were allowed, and the shelves did not hold any books that were sexy, morbid, profane or anti-Catholic. "As the sign on the wall says, we accentuate the positive," said the librarian, J. Madeline Clay — no relation to Margaret Clay, the long-time head librarian in Victoria.

The St. Joseph's library included humour, light romance, rugged adventure and mysteries. Any patients who were able to visit the library were welcome, and for the ones unable to get there, a book barrow was wheeled through the rooms each day. Reading "passes the time and keeps patients thinking," Clay said. "It helps to take their minds off themselves." She said that some patients liked reading so much, they would stay in hospital a few extra days to finish the book they were reading. "Our only stipulation is that patients don't take books home."

Top: *Adrian Raeside*

12

THE FIRING OF
JOHN MARSHALL

All John Maitland Marshall wanted to do was help people get books from Victoria's new bookmobile. But in 1954, he found himself at the centre of a major controversy and a victim of the Red scare that reached into Canada — and its libraries.

Marshall was fired two months after he was hired, before the mobile service even hit the road. He lost his job because before he came to British Columbia, he had been connected with groups that leaned to the political left. Before things cooled down, there were calls for book-burning parties, Marshall had left the province and

Opposite: John Marshall in the early 1950s.
Marshall family

Above: *Adrian Raeside*

qualified librarians were boycotting the Victoria Public Library.

It was the McCarthy era. Fears of the Communist threat swept through North America, sparked by United States senator Joseph McCarthy's hunt for Communists in positions of authority. Freedom of speech and association were under attack. The Red scare had already begun when Irene McAfee of the Vancouver Public Library attended the American Library Association's annual convention in Chicago in 1950.

"The Americans knew they were in the midst of a national emergency and were shaping their policies accordingly," she reported to the British Columbia Library Association when she returned home. "They were conscious of the dangers to free thinking, reading and speaking, and were presenting a more united front against them than ever before. The word 'McCarthyism' has evidently been taken into the language as the term indicating what the free spirit of man is fighting against in the United States."

Marshall, the son of a banker, was born in Saskatchewan in 1919. He and his wife, Christine Smith, had two small children, John and Kathleen. He had been the children's librarian for the Fraser Valley Regional Library for eighteen months before he was hired in Victoria in December 1953. Marshall did not seek the Victoria job; he was asked twice to apply before he agreed. There had been no complaints about his work — and he was certainly well prepared for it, with a Master's in English from the University of Saskatchewan and a Bachelor of Library Science degree, with honours, from the University of Toronto.

Victoria Daily Times, January 25, 1954

But his qualifications or the mouths he had to feed did not matter to the Victoria library board. What mattered was that "a group of public-spirited citizens," as the board put it, had uncovered some dirt in his past. Marshall had been educational director of the People's Educational Co-op in Winnipeg in 1947 and spent six months as assistant editor of the *Westerner*, a leftist paper. He had attended the Canadian Peace Congress in Toronto in 1949, 1950 and 1951 — and the congress, many believed, was a Communist front.

Fears about Communism were not far below the surface in the early 1950s, and the Marshall case was not the first time that British Columbia's libraries had to deal with the implications of "Reds" holding public positions.

In June 1950, the B.C. Library Association objected to a clause added to the constitution of the Trades and Labour Congress of Canada that would prevent known Communists from holding congress offices. Other local affiliates of the congress had adopted similar clauses, but the library association argued that the body should not concern itself with politics. The Labour Progressive Party, considered to be Canada's Communist Party, was a legal organization, the librarians said, so the congress had no right to discriminate against its members.

The next year, Vancouver Mayor Charles Thompson declared that all city employees would be screened and any Communists fired. The plan was abandoned when Fred Hume replaced Thompson as mayor.

In September 1952, controversy erupted when Kay Gardner, a clerk in the Vancouver Public Library's East Hastings branch, went to a peace conference in China with her husband Ray, a B.C. Peace Council official. "This is something that shouldn't happen," said Hume, the mayor. "Our boys are dying in Korea every day in the fight against Communists."

The next month, the library board fired Gardner, giving as its reason the fact that she had obtained her leave "under misrepresentation." She had told the board her husband worked for a large newspaper syndicate and they were going to Europe. In fact, he was connected with the Communist newspaper *Pacific Tribune* and they had gone to Asia. Gardner appealed, saying she had been fired for political reasons, but the library board ruled that she had been absent without leave. Her firing stood.

City Librarian Fired As Red Taint Hinted

(Continued on Page 11)

The Victoria Public Library Board has decided to dismiss John M. Marshall, 34, from the library staff and informed sources say the reason for the board's action is Marshall's alleged past association with Communist-front organizations.

Board chairman J. F. K. English today confirmed that Mr. Marshall was to be advised his services would not be required after Feb. 1, and that he would be paid a month's salary in lieu of notice.

Mr. English refused to state any reason for the dismissal. He said that since Mr. Marshall's probationary period had not expired, the board was not obliged to give any reason.

Informed sources said the board voted to dismiss Mr. Marshall after being advised he had been assistant editor of the *Westerner*, a leftist paper in Winnipeg, and attended the Communist-inspired Canadian Peace Congress in Toronto in 1949, 1950 and 1951.

Mr. Marshall was engaged by the library board to take charge of its recently-acquired bookmobile. The bookmobile will be put into operation soon, distributing books in the outlying municipalities.

Mr. Marshall today said he had not been notified of the board's action and therefore could not make any specific comments about it.

months with the Westerner before it folded up operations. Mr. Marshall said he was entitled to his own views on political and economic affairs, but, in fact, has devoted himself entirely to library work for the last three years and ceased any public connection with political matters. He is not now and has never been a card-carrying member of the Labor-Progressive Party.

Mr. Marshall added that any steps he may take as a result of the board's action will be considered when he receives formal notification.

Strike Hits London

LONDON (Reuters)—Electrical construction work stopped on scores of important building sites in the London area today as almost 8,000 members of the Communist-led Electrical Trades Union launched a week's strike for higher wages.

Rail Dispute Board

OTTAWA (BUP)—Supreme Court Justice R. L. Kellock has been named chairman of a conciliation board set up to try to settle the country's railway dispute, Labor Minister Milton F. Gregg announced today.

Tories Active Again

EDMONTON (CP) — The Progressive Conservative

In Victoria, Marshall was shocked by his firing in January 1954. He learned of the dismissal when a story about it was reported in the *Victoria Daily Times*. He was unprepared for the loss of the job as well as the challenge to his reputation. He told the newspaper he was entitled to his own views on political and economic affairs, but swore he was not, and never had been, a card-carrying member of the Labour Progressive Party. Marshall said that he had ceased any public connection with political matters when he decided to become a professional librarian. "There has been no question of my competence or ability to perform the duties for which I was hired," he said.

Marshall appealed the firing and took aim at the "public-spirited citizens" who had accused him. "Groups or individuals which carry on secret investigations into a man's beliefs and past associations, and put pressure on his employers to fire a fully qualified employee without giving him the opportunity to defend himself, are undermining our democratic freedoms," he said.

One library board member told the *Daily Colonist* newspaper it was good the Marshall matter had been made public. "If they are labelled, they are useless to the party," the unidentified member said. "We should always be on the watch for them." The board ordered a review to find and remove "subversive pro-Communist" books from the library. One member said those books did not belong in a library supported by public funds in a democratic country.

Victoria Mayor Claude Harrison favoured burning any subversive literature in the library. "There's going to be no pussy-footing at all," he said. "It's very easy to see which is Communist literature. I know one thing, I'll soon find them. No difficulty at all. And I know what I would do with them — throw them in my furnace." The mayor said he did not know of any specific Communist books, but vowed it would be possible to get rid of them quickly. Books that tried to undermine Canada's democratic system should never have been written or bought by the library.

Alderman Brent Murdoch said any seditious or subversive books should be removed — "and any member of the library staff who belongs to a Communist organization will go out behind the books." It was time, he said, to clean up libraries. Harrison and Murdoch both stressed they were

Daily Colonist, January 27, 1954

not opposed to books of a historic nature, such as those about Stalin, the Russian revolution or the writings of Marx and Engels.

Their comments sparked a huge outcry, with supporters lining up on both sides. Even Premier W.A.C. Bennett got involved, saying that book-burning would be "a bunch of foolishness." He said he was opposed to any investigation of the Provincial Library, and threw his support behind Marshall. "I am 100 per cent opposed to what people call McCarthyism and witch-hunting." Willard Ireland, the provincial librarian, also said he was opposed to book burning.

Marshall had several other defenders. Roderick Haig-Brown of Campbell River, a magistrate and one of Canada's best-known authors, said Harrison was "dim-witted" and "not very thoughtful, nor intelligent." Saanich Reeve Joseph Casey said Marshall should get a hearing, adding that if subversive books were to be taken from the library shelves, *Mutiny on the Bounty* would have to go. W. Harry Hickman, the principal of Victoria College, when asked if the college would remove books considered subversive, replied "I should hope not!" Dr. Norman MacKenzie, president of the University of British Columbia, said Harrison's stand was a "dangerous proposal."

But the anti-Communist fervour was widespread. Victoria MLA Lydia Arsens, for example, said the books should go. "If we remove all books about Communism and by Communists we are not denying any citizens freedom."

Doris Lougheed, a Victoria library board member, said it was time to start fighting Communism in Canada. She accused the Victoria newspapers of taking a "very Communistic attitude" in handling the controversy. The press, she said, had been trying to smear honest citizens who were trying to fight Communism.

One citizen, Peter Hartnell, said that he had been keeping an eye on Communist books in the Victoria library since 1937. Head librarian Margaret Clay had, he said, directed a policy of procuring Communist-authored books.

Don't join the book burners. Don't think you're going to conceal faults by concealing evidence that they ever existed. Don't be afraid to go in your library and read every book.
Dwight D. Eisenhower, U.S. president 1953-1961

The *Daily Colonist* weighed in. "Unless McCarthyism is to raise its ugly head in Canada, something better than hearsay will be required to support assertions of subversive literature on the shelves of the Victoria Public Library," it said. "There have been no bonfires of books in this land, no edicts such as Hitler's or Stalin's that one book or another must be consigned to the flames. Good taste on the part of the public in selecting its reading, and maturity of thought in perusing it have proved far more effective than any form of censorship."

The *Victoria Daily Times* called for common sense and quiet analysis. "No honest Canadian wants the library to become a propaganda agency for Communism," it said. "On the other hand, no thinking people want excitement over such a possibility to restrict desirable library service or to eliminate from circulation books, magazines or journals which throw informative light on the activities of those interests that swear allegiance to Moscow." It noted the library board's position was that its role was to provide as much material as it could on as many subjects as possible — within the law — and to trust readers to form intelligent conclusions. "We believe that is the right attitude."

The *Vancouver Sun* said it hoped the "stupidity of those responsible" for the talk of burning books would give way to enlightenment.

Victoria's Junior Chamber of Commerce — which the newspapers had identified as the source of the allegations against Marshall — went on record as deploring the idea that books should be burned. Still, with rumours that eight other Communists were in public offices or responsible positions in Victoria, the junior chamber said it was committed to highlighting the perils of Communism.

The library's staff association defended Marshall, saying the board should explain why he had been fired. "Never before in this library has an individual, whether temporary or permanent employee, been dismissed without reason," the association said. It argued that Marshall was competent and enthusiastic.

"We have always understood that as city employees and public servants we have no politics. This we interpret to mean that we do not use the library, nor our official positions for political purposes of any kind. Mr. Marshall has not been accused of breaking this rule," the association said. Private individuals had the right to freedom of thought, "one of the principles upon which a library is founded," the association said.

In Vancouver, library board chairman Harry Boyce said it was possible a person with subversive beliefs could be hired — although references were demanded and checked closely.

Another board member, Alderman Anna Sprott, said that a book-burning campaign would be "too small town" for Vancouver.

Vancouver librarian Edgar Stewart Robinson said a library should not tell people how to think. "Its duty is to present both sides of the question and let them make up their own minds," he said. "We have all kinds of books on Communism and the people want to read what we have, both for and against Communism." One of those books was *Five Stars Over China* by Mary Endicott, the wife of Canadian Peace Congress leader Dr. James Endicott. The Vancouver library also had *Peace Review*, the monthly magazine published by the Congress.

The nearby Burnaby library had been offered the same publications, but turned them down because they were "not the kind of books" wanted in Burnaby. The North Vancouver city library found on its shelves a few books that were Red and a few that were only pinkish — but vowed that the books would not be burned.

The person who knew the most about Marshall's work ethic was Ronald Ley, his former boss in the Fraser Valley and that year's president of the B.C. Library Association. Ley sent a telegram defending Marshall to the Victoria board. The Public Library Commission spoke out against the burning of books, saying a library should help citizens reach intelligent decisions on all issues — and that can only be done when all sides of questions are available.

Marshall was fired with only a few days left in the library board's annual term. He was given a chance to argue his case before the new board the following week. One of the new members was Robert Wallace, a Victoria College mathematics professor, who said he was amazed by the idea of removing books. "Libraries are the greatest single contributing factor to education in its broadest sense."

Marshall pulled no punches. "I challenge the board to produce any proof that I have since becoming a librarian abused my position in any way, or allowed my opinions — whatever they might be — on matters outside the profession to influence me in any direction in the performance of my professional duties," he said.

"It might be held that because of what I am or what I believe, I may in some way abuse my position in the future. This assumption comes dangerously close to justifying, on the part of employers, an attempt to enquire into the political, social or economic beliefs and in the religious principles of an employee.

"No employer has any such right in a democratic country."

Marshall's plea failed; with only Wallace speaking in his defense, his firing was confirmed in a three-one vote. Chief

Victoria Daily Times,
January 27, 1954

A History of Service to British Columbia | **155**

librarian Thressa Pollock resigned in protest. Pollock, who had been at the library for twenty-seven years, said she would only stay if the three board members who opposed Marshall resigned.

On February 21, the British Columbia Library Association held a special meeting in Vancouver to discuss the Marshall case. More than 100 members attended. "I firmly believe in the democratic way. I am also a loyal Canadian," Marshall told them.

The members passed two resolutions. "It is our conviction that sound personnel procedures must necessarily imply that the employment or dismissal of any person shall be based only upon his competence to perform the professional and technical duties involved, and that any personal beliefs become pertinent only when they interfere

Daily Colonist, February 23, 1954

Personal Integrity Endorsed
Marshall Backed By Association

All library groups in Canada and the U.S. will be informed of the "personal integrity" of a dismissed bookmobile director, John Marshall.

A meeting of the B.C. Library Association, called to discuss the firing of Mr. Marshall, was held in Vancouver, Sunday.

It was decided to give Mr. Marshall a letter of recommendation and at the same time Victoria Library Board came in for some strong criticism.

NOT PARTY MEMBER

Mr. Marshall told the 100-odd members who attended the meeting that he was not a member of any political party. "I firmly believe in the democratic way. I am also a loyal Canadian," he said. He charged that he had been wrongly dismissed.

After hearing Mr. Marshall, the association passed two resolutions which will also be forwarded to library groups throughout North America. They read:

"Sound personnel procedures must imply the assumption that the employment or dismissal of any person shall be based only upon the competence to perform the professional and technical duties involved and that any personal beliefs become pertinent only when they interfere with the quality of the service rendered:

"That we as an organization go on record as firmly believing in the Canadian ethical and legal concept that a man must be considered innocent until he is proven otherwise and we

highly deprecate and condemn the present attempt to damage a person's reputation without proving that he has failed to maintain ethics of his profession or meet his obligations as a citizen."

CAREER JEOPARDIZED

The association felt that the action of the board had seriously jeopardized Marshall's professional career.

Meanwhile, the Vancouver and Lower Mainland branch of the Canadian Authors' Association also passed a resolution condemning the board's action. "We view with grave concern both the suggestions that certain books should be removed from the shelves of Victoria Public Library and the dismissal of John Marshall from the library staff," read a statement from branch president Edmund Pugsley.

CENSORSHIP DANGER

The statement said the public should have access to all books and such censorship "is very dangerous in principle."

T. K. Willis, president of the Victoria and Islands branch of the same association, disassociated his branch from the Vancouver statement.

"We are strictly a cultural group," he said last night.

A public hearing will be held by Saanich municipality. March 1 at 7.45 p.m. on the application to have property at the south-west corner of Shelbourne Street and Feltham Road re-zoned for commercial use.

with the quality of the service rendered," said the first.

"We, the members of the British Columbia Library Association, in special session assembled, wish to go on record as firmly believing in the Canadian ethical and legal concept that a man must be considered innocent until he is proven otherwise; and we highly condemn and deprecate the present attempt to damage a person's reputation without proving that he has failed to maintain the ethics of his profession or to meet his obligations as a citizen," said the second.

These resolutions were forwarded to the Canadian Library Association, the Pacific Northwest Library Association, British Columbia library boards and British Columbia library staff associations. The B.C. Library Association wrote a letter of recommendation for Marshall and urged its members to refuse positions in Victoria until a new library board was in place.

"Can — or should — a member of the BCLA apply for any position in the Victoria Public Library as long as the policy of the board remains what it is?" the association's *Bulletin* noted in April 1954. "It is in the answer to this question that the association's real attitude toward witch-hunting may be made known. Let us hope we have the conscience and courage to say 'no.'"

By May, six of the eleven full-time professional librarians at the library had resigned and the library had not been able to replace any of them. Georgina Wilson, the acting head of the circulation department who resigned so she could marry, used her letter of resignation to plea "that the present board support the principles of tolerance, intellectual freedom and high standards of service that were characteristic of early and excellent boards."

Nora Dryburgh, who had been appointed to replace Marshall, was among those who resigned. Her departure meant the mobile service had three librarians before it delivered a single book to Victoria's suburbs.

In June, the BCLA resolution was adopted at the annual conference of the Canadian association, which prompted a sharp rebuke from the *Vancouver Sun*. The newspaper's editorial, with the headline "No place for Reds in our public libraries," appeared just below the *Sun's* commitment to "progress and democracy, tolerance and freedom of thought."

"It would be a very dangerous thing to have a Communist, or for that matter a fascist, in a position of public trust where he or she could influence the minds of a very large section of the public," the editorial said. "There's no doubt that librarians are ideally placed for this."

The newspaper noted it was not illegal to be a Communist or have Communist sympathies. "It could be argued — very successfully perhaps — that any person having an intellectual bias towards Communism isn't very bright. But that's not the argument that appeals to the public — and to library boards — so much as the feeling that persons who actually have direct or indirect associations with Communists are not loyal Canadians but have given their true allegiance to a foreign power and a foreign ideology."

Professional competence is less important than a person's character, the *Sun* said. "The majority of Canadians today believe that Communists and those who sympathize with them are working to undermine our country and its way of life. In the context of world and national events there's nothing naive about looking on such people as 'bad' characters."

The editorial drew a strong response from a reader in Burnaby, Alan Crocker, who said public library patrons "are the very last people in need of protection against subversive influences." The wealth of literature that is the heritage of western democracy "is more than a match for Communist propaganda so long as we continue to practise the values of freedom and tolerance we prize so highly," Crocker said. "When we resort to suppression or persecution we make a mockery and provide the Communists with their strongest argument."

After his firing, Marshall took his family — wife Christine, one-year-old Kathleen and five-year-old John — to Yorkton, Saskatchewan, where he got a job with the rural school library service. After four years there, he spent two years as the first professional librarian in Kitimat, and then moved to Toronto to become the head librarian at a new branch in North York.

He capped his career by spending seventeen years teaching in the faculty of library science at the University of Toronto. He loved books, and loved reading books about books. He also edited *Citizen Participation in Library Decision-Making: The Toronto Experience*, which was published in 1984.

The Victoria library paid a heavy price for the Marshall affair. It had trouble attracting qualified librarians until the board members involved in the firing were gone. John C. Lort, hired to replace Pollock as the head librarian, spent several years restoring the library's stature in Victoria and in the library community.

In 1998, the board of the Greater Victoria Public Library apologized to Marshall, flying him and his wife to Victoria so he could receive the apology in person. "What goes around, comes around," Marshall said at the ceremony. "So be it."

John Marshall in the 1990s.
Marshall family

Neil Williams, the library board chairman, told Marshall that the events that had happened would have been unjust at any time. "The fact that they took place within a library, in my mind, pushes them over the border into obscenity." Robert Wallace, the former board member who had argued on Marshall's behalf, expressed regret that he had not been able to convince the others. And with that, as Marshall's son, Dr. John Marshall, said later, "the dark cloud over his career was finally lifted."

The B.C. Library Association gave a plaque to Marshall. It also renamed the association's intellectual freedom award in his honour.

Marshall died in Toronto on October 26, 2005. His obituary, written by his family, described him as "a passionate bibliophile and ardent supporter of social justice."

1927	Library associations formed in Alberni, Kimberley and North Burnaby
1927	Vancouver opens Kitsilano branch
1927-28	First province-wide library survey is conducted
1928	Conservatives form government; Simon Fraser Tolmie becomes premier
1928	Library associations formed in Armstrong, Kamloops, Quesnel, Revelstoke and Vernon
1928	New Westminster names a library board
1928	Ocean Falls Company library started
1929	Creston library association formed
1929	Terrace library opens
1929	Vancouver Public Library expands into old city hall
1929	Wall street crash sparks Great Depression
1930	Fraser Valley demonstration library starts service with branches in Chilliwack, Mission, Abbotsford, Langley, Haney, Ladner and Cloverdale
1930	John Ridington of UBC conducts national library survey
1930	Shawnigan Lake library destroyed by fire
1931	Public Library Commission establishes a branch in Prince George
1931	Vancouver Art Gallery opens, and includes an art library
1933	Alberni and District library started
1933	Liberals elected; Thomas Dufferin Pattullo becomes premier
1933	Library act amended to allow union library districts
1934	Fraser Valley demonstration converted to a union library
1934	Ladysmith library opens in city hall
1934	William Kaye Lamb becomes provincial librarian, provincial archivist and superintendent of the Public Library Commission
1936	King Edward VIII abdicates
1936	Library started in Lake Cowichan
1936	Supervised library study periods started in high schools
1936	Okanagan Union Library and Vancouver Island Union Library formed

1936	Prince George public library association formed
1937	Nanaimo Harbourfront branch opens
1937	Smithers and Vanderhoof start library associations
1938	Library courses for teachers started at UBC
1938	Fraser Valley Union Library broadcasts on CHWK
1938	Library started in Qualicum Beach
1939	Books distributed to members of the armed forces, who also get free access to libraries
1939	Vancouver library starts working with schools to develop libraries in them
1939	First association of school librarians is formed
1939	Federal government cuts mail rate for libraries
1939	Library association formed in Field
1939	Five municipalities, including Vernon and Armstrong, leave the Okanagan system
1939	Kamloops library moves into donated house
1939	North Burnaby library moves to its own building
1939	Rossland library association formed
1939-1945	Second World War
1940	Charles Keith Morison becomes the provincial librarian
1940	Fraser Valley's Port Coquitlam branch moves to city hall
1940	John Ridington retires as UBC librarian; succeeded by W. Kaye Lamb
1940	Langley withdraws from Fraser Valley system
1940	Provincial library survey is conducted
1940	Public Library Commission publishes a guide for school librarians
1940	Public Library Commission opens a branch at Dawson Creek
1940	Radio broadcasts on CJOR deal with library matters
1940	Revelstoke library association revived
1940	Royal Roads military college opens
1940	Saanich gets service from Victoria after eight-year break
1940	Willard Ireland becomes the provincial archivist
1941	Chemainus suspends library service for the duration of the war

1941	Coalition government is formed; John Hart becomes premier
1941	Libraries created in prisons
1941	Masset library started
1941	Pearl Harbor; Canada arrests Japanese nationals
1942	Alaska Highway project announced
1942	Public libraries come under the Minister of Education
1943	Creston opens joint school-community library
1943	Port Moody public library association starts
1943	Vancouver opens Kerrisdale branch in former Point Grey municipal hall
1944	Allies launch the D-Day assault
1944	Burns Lake library starts in the hardware store
1944	Commission restores grants in aid after a 10-year break
1944	Esquimalt contracts with Victoria for library service
1944	Greenwood public library association formed
1944	Vancouver school board appoints a full-time librarian
1944	Langley returns to Fraser Valley system
1944	National Film Board makes *Library On Wheels*, about the Fraser Valley Union Library
1944	New Westminster library starts broadcasts on CKNW
1944	Pacific Northwest Bibliographic Center opens in Seattle
1945	Celebrated artist Emily Carr dies
1945	CKPG brings radio service to Prince George, and the library gets a weekly show
1945	Fernie library revived in the high school
1945	Greenwood library association formed
1945	Programme for Library Development published
1945	Shawnigan Lake votes 100 per cent in favour of joining the Vancouver Island system
1945	Vancouver opens the Gordon House branch in the West End
1945	Tate Creek library association formed
1945	Williams Lake sets up a joint school-community library
1946	Burns Lake library association formed
1946	Clearwater Women's Institute opens a library
1946	Grand Forks library opens in the old post office
1946	Kinnaird library started
1946	Library commission office opens in Dawson Creek in an old army hut
1946	Maxwell Cameron's report on education reshapes regional library systems
1946	Port Mellon library association formed
1946	Prince George library offers free service
1946	Revelstoke library reopens
1946	Special collection established for boys at Oakalla
1946	Vancouver Public Library open 12 hours a day for the first time since 1933
1946	Canadian Library Association is formed
1946	Victoria College moves to Provincial Normal School
1946	Willard Ireland named provincial librarian and archivist
1947	Cumberland library opens in city hall
1947	Delta joins the Fraser Valley Union Library
1947	Kimberley library association revived
1947	Library associations formed in Castlegar and Dawson Creek
1947	Library commission moves to new quarters in Prince George
1947	Armstrong, Spallumcheen and Mara return to the Okanagan system
1948	Alberni library moves to city hall
1948	Okanagan system starts a mail-order service
1948	Okanagan opens two new branches in Summerland
1948	Library associations formed in Hazelton and Westview
1948	Travelling libraries offer free shipping both ways
1948	UBC library's north wing is opened
1948	William Kaye Lamb leaves UBC library to become dominion archivist
1949	Burns Lake library opens
1949	Chemainus library moves to Masonic hall
1949	Chilliwack branch of Fraser Valley moves to new quarters
1949	Library commission starts a reference service on CBC Radio

1949	Library commission gets new quarters in Dawson Creek
1949	McBride library association formed
1949	North-Central Co-operative Library started in Prince George
1949	Port Mellon library closes when pulp mill closes
1949	Trail votes to start a library
1949	Vancouver circulates one million books
1949	Vancouver opens Hastings and South Hill branches
1949	Vernon votes to rejoin the Okanagan library
1950	Campbell River joins the Vancouver Island system
1950	Fire destroys libraries in Tate Creek and Westview
1950	Fort St. John library association started
1950	Libraries offered to Indian residential schools
1950	Nakusp library reopens after 15-year closure
1950	Notre Dame College opens in Nelson
1950	Port Moody library association formed
1950	Programme for Library Development revised
1950	Provincial grants offered to libraries
1950	Quesnel library moves to Loghouse building
1950	Rossland library moves into courthouse basement; first library with free rent in a provincial government building
1950	Vancouver opens Dunbar branch
1950	Vernon rejects the Okanagan system
1950	West Vancouver Memorial Library opened
195	Author and suffragette Nellie McClung dies
1951	Creston library association formed
1951	Fraser Valley opens Haney branch
1951	Kamloops community library gets municipal status
1951	Kimberley moves to location above the bus depot
1951	Ladysmith, Campbell River move to new quarters
1951	Nakusp library association revived by Women's Institute
1951	North Burnaby opens its East Hastings branch
1951	Port Moody establishes a public library association
1951	Pouce Coupe library association formed
1951	Union libraries renamed regional libraries
1951	Vancouver opens Collingwood branch
1951	Victoria Public Library more than doubles in size
1951	Wells and Williams Lake library associations formed
1951	White Rock branch moves to bigger quarters
1952	Courtenay and Parksville get new quarters
1952	Fernie library moves into post office
1952	Langley Prairie branch moves to bigger quarters
1952	Library associations formed in Capilano, Cranberry Lake, Gibsons and Terrace
1952	Peace River District co-operative library started
1952	Social Credit takes over government; W.A.C. Bennett becomes premier
1952	Vancouver Island Regional Library starts its fifth bookmobile route
1952	Vanderhoof library association re-established
1952	White Rock branch of Fraser Valley opens
1953	Abbotsford branch moves into municipal building
1953	Coldstream votes in favour of a library branch
1953	Comox quits regional library, starts municipal one
1953	Courtenay library moves to city hall; had been in a private residence
1953	Fraser Valley opens Whalley branch
1953	Fraser Valley moves into its new headquarters in Abbotsford
1953	CBUT, British Columbia's first television station, goes on the air
1953	Golden library association formed
1953	Kaslo library reactivated
1953	National library established in Ottawa
1953	Port Mellon library association revived
1954	South part of Burnaby gets its first public library
1954	Fraser Valley opens Cloverdale branch
1954	John Marshall firing shakes Victoria Public Library
1954	British Empire and Commonwealth Games held in Vancouver
1954	Library associations formed in Tofino and Ucluelet

1954 Okanagan opens branches at Coldstream, Lavington and Kaleden

1954 Okanagan opens new headquarters and Kelowna branch

1954 Vancouver Island opens Union Bay branch

1954 Vancouver's Kerrisdale branch gets new home

1954 Victoria Public Library starts bookmobile service

1955 Kimberley library moves to the old police station

1955 Langley City branch opened by Fraser Valley Regional Library

1955 Library associations formed in Kemano, Kitimat and Squamish

1955 Okanagan Regional Library gets new headquarters

1955 Prince George municipal library opens

1955 Queen Charlotte City library opened by volunteers

1955 Richmond joins the Fraser Valley Regional Library with two branches, Steveston and Brighouse

1955 Vancouver Island Regional Library gets new headquarters in Nanaimo

1955 Williams Lake opens "log library"

1956 Britannia Beach library association formed

1956 Burnaby public library opens, and assumes assets of North Burnaby association

1956 Dogwood becomes B.C.'s official flower

1956 New libraries in Courtenay and Penticton

1956 Programme for Library Development revised

1956 Public Library Commission drops service to most schools larger than one room

1956 Public Library Commission opens branch in Cranbrook

1956 Vancouver starts bookmobile service

1956 Vernon votes to join the Okanagan system

1957 Dorwin Baird starts weekly radio broadcasts about books, called Silent Friends

1957 Fort St. John library opens in provincial government building

1957 Kamloops library moves into new building

1957 Library associations formed in Mount Sheer and Powell River

1957 Elvis Presley performs in Vancouver

1957 Revelstoke joins the Okanagan system

1957 Richmond opens Bridgeport branch

1957 Trail sets up a library board; library opens in 1958

1957 Vancouver opens new central building; closes Gordon House branch

1957 Vernon, Lumby branches open in Okanagan system

1957 White Rock joins the Fraser Valley Regional Library

1958 Alert Bay library association formed

1958 New libraries open in Armstrong, Enderby, Hazelton, Nakusp, Naramata, Ocean Falls, North Vancouver city, Squamish, Summerland and Woodfibre

1958 Fort Nelson library opens

1958 Kitimat library gets its own building

1958 Bookmark newsletter started for teacher-librarians

1958 Ripple Rock, a navigation hazard in Seymour Narrows, is blown up

1958 Lake Cowichan library moves to municipal hall

1958 New Westminster moves to new library

1958 Capilano library opens in North Vancouver

1958 Revelstoke joins the Okanagan Regional Library

1958 Smithers library moves to town hall

1958 Whalley branch opens in Surrey

1959 Chetwynd public library started by volunteers

1959 Kimberley moves to the Fisher Block for a week – then the weight is declared unsafe and it has to move again

1959 New libraries in Salmo and Salt Spring Island

1959 Quesnel municipal library formed

1959 Tate Creek library renamed Tomslake

1959 Vancouver opens Oakridge branch, first library in a shopping centre in Western Canada

1959 Wildwood Heights library incorporated at Powell River

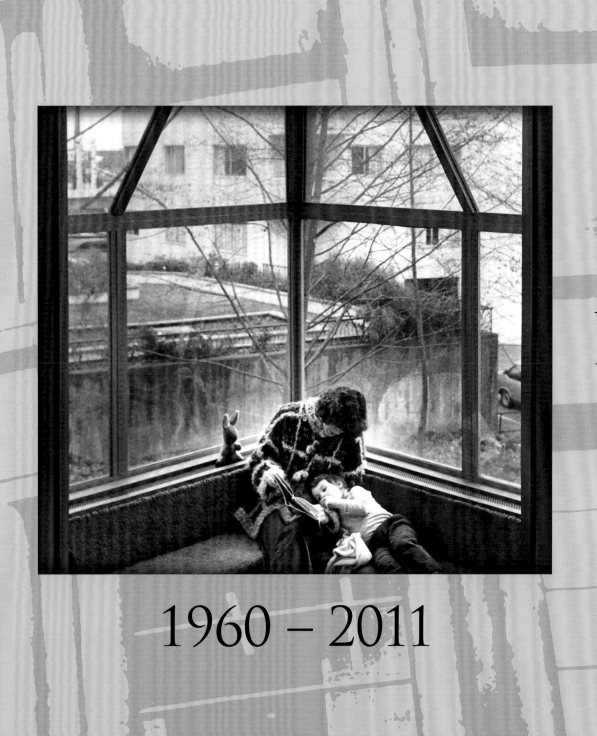

PART 3

1960 – 2011

13

A RENEWED PUSH
FOR SHARING

The 1960s and 1970s saw a renewed emphasis on one of the basic ideas behind libraries — that by sharing resources, an entire community can benefit. This time, however, libraries rather than individuals were talking about sharing, and the entire province stood to gain from it.

Rose Vainstein, a professor at the University of British Columbia's School of Librarianship, was responsible for much of the momentum as the province's libraries worked toward regional co-operation. The provincial government backed the idea until 1978, when it suddenly pulled its support. But that did not detract from Vainstein's greatest accomplishment: She helped British Columbians see that

Victoria Public Library had
plenty of room in 1960.
Times Colonist

than ever, but there were still problems. Small communities made do; in Rutland, just east of Kelowna, the library was in the back of a radio repair shop, while the Westbank library was in a private home. On Vancouver Island, more books circulated through the regional library's two bookmobiles than through its two busiest branches, in Nanaimo and Duncan.

Some people paid directly for service, others paid through taxes, and still others got service for free. People in Vancouver could get a recent book from the library, but readers anywhere else would probably be out of luck. "You might as well just go out and buy the thing," remembers Ray Culos, one of the leaders in the push to develop library services.

Something had to be done. In 1962 Vainstein was asked to compile two reports, the first on Greater Victoria and the second on the entire province. In both, she encouraged development, growth and collaboration between libraries and library systems.

The first study took a matter of months. The Victoria Public Library was serving four municipalities from its downtown location, and Vainstein proposed branches in Esquimalt, Oak Bay and Saanich as well as a second bookmobile. She urged all libraries to work together, saying small libraries could not afford strong reference departments, vast circulating collections or skilled staff.

Soon after Vainstein delivered her report on Victoria, the Public Library Commission and the School of Librarianship asked her to start the larger study that would cover all of British Columbia. Vainstein visited the Open Shelf mail-order and travelling library departments at the commission's headquarters in Victoria as well as the branches in Prince George, Dawson Creek and Cranbrook. She went to all twelve municipal libraries, the three regional ones, and forty-four of the forty-nine local associations. Soon after, however, Vainstein had health problems. She did not complete her report until 1966, almost four years after she started work.

they could have better service if libraries worked together.

Vainstein compiled one of two significant 1960s reports that helped shape library service for decades to come. The other, by UBC president John B. Macdonald, encouraged the development of post-secondary options, leading to the creation of more colleges and universities.

When Vainstein arrived in 1961, libraries were better

Rose Vainstein was born in Edmonton on January 7, 1920, the youngest of four children born to a rabbi and his wife. The Vainsteins moved to Pennsylvania in 1924. Vainstein graduated from library school at the end of the Second World War, and then served as an army librarian in occupied Japan, a county librarian in California and a library consultant with the United States Office of Education in Washington. She also wrote books on librarianship.

When her work in British Columbia was done, she returned to the United States. She set up public library service in a wealthy suburb of Detroit, then went to the University of Michigan to teach librarianship. She retired at the age of sixty and spent her final years in a retirement facility near Philadelphia. Vainstein died on August 24, 1999.

Vainstein praised groundbreaking efforts such as the Fraser Valley demonstration library of the 1930s, travelling libraries, Open Shelf and the commission's branch system. She also liked the commission's public relations program, including radio broadcasts promoting library use, a short-course training program for librarians, province-wide library surveys, and lists to help librarians select books.

Beyond that, Vainstein expressed disappointment. A quarter of a million people, she said, did not have access to a local public library, and service for many others was inadequate. There were huge differences in service. British Columbia had ten communities with 25,000 or more people,

The Gold River secondary school library on Vancouver Island in 1968. *Vancouver Province*

The Business section at Vancouver Public Library had an extensive card catalogue. *John Denniston, Vancouver Province*

all within Greater Vancouver or Victoria. One, Coquitlam, had no legally organized library, but its residents borrowed books from Open Shelf, the library commission's free service. Since they were getting service without paying for it, there was little incentive for residents of Coquitlam, or several other communities, to start their own library.

Hugh Norman Lidster died at the age of seventy-eight in New Westminster on January 2, 1967, one year after retiring from the Public Library Commission. He had served on the commission since 1929.

He became a lawyer in New Westminster in 1917, and was elected to council in 1925. He became chairman of the city library board and then, in 1927, a member of the provincial library survey committee. He worked for the city as a solicitor from 1934 until he retired in 1957, at which point he started devoting even more time to his library commission work. The New Westminster Public Library was closed for two hours for Lidster's funeral.

In Greater Victoria, Open Shelf even served as a local library. The Sooke School District did not have library service but its residents could go to the Open Shelf office to borrow books. There were other inconsistencies: Much of Greater Victoria was served by book vans from Victoria and from Nanaimo. Powell River, with a much lower population than Greater Victoria, had four libraries run by volunteers.

Vainstein said libraries kept books long after they were useful because they were trying to fill shelves or make a collection look more extensive. Ruthless weeding, she said, would result in more useful, dynamic and attractive collections.

Vainstein wanted services that would transcend local boundaries, similar to those for education, health, recreation, water resources and even sewage. Her vision was for a network of thirteen service areas, and she admitted that the idea was not new; a 1945 report on library service had recommended districts based on the Vancouver, Victoria and New Westminster metropolitan areas.

She believed British Columbians needed convenient and regular access to a large, diverse collection, but needed to be able to draw from other, larger collections for specialized materials. The most costly, specialized resources and services should be in only one library, but made available to all — and to that end, a rapid communications system was needed

to make it easier for libraries to exchange requests.

Vainstein said the provincial government should provide leadership and guidance, but she warned that local effort, local decisions and strong community support would be needed. To win that support, she said, libraries would need to encourage and cultivate the reading tastes of their communities. "Not until adults have had an adequate demonstration of the difference which quality public library resources and services can make will they be willing to support increased budgets," she said.

She recommended that the Public Library Commission's grants to local libraries be extended to cover the costs of establishment and operating libraries, and also the costs of regional reference and inter-library loan services. Grants should be based, she said, on population, service areas and the need for incentives. The government should pay one-quarter to one-half the cost of new buildings.

The provincial sales tax on books was removed in three stages. In 1962, the tax was removed from all books used in courses in schools, universities, trade schools and vocational schools. In 1966, the law was changed so libraries did not have to pay the tax. The tax on books bought by individuals was lifted in 1974.

Vainstein recommended the appointment of a full-time school library consultant for the province, and at least one school librarian in every district. She said British Columbia's schools had 350,000 students but not one school librarian with both teacher and librarian credentials. Schools without libraries had shelves of books in each classroom.

She discouraged joint public and school libraries, saying they had key differences. Public libraries needed to be near shopping and transportation, while schools needed to be near playgrounds and lawns. The public libraries had to be open longer hours and in the summer. Vainstein said that while some projects to link school and public libraries had worked, most had failed. Adults, she said, did not like to use the libraries during school hours. Libraries in schools served the school communities first; adults found the book supply too limited.

After Vainstein started work, but before she released her report, the provincial government approved central libraries in elementary schools and adopted a list of 4,000 recommended books for school libraries. As a result, there were complaints that her recommendations on schools were outdated. The public library community embraced her work, however, and for several years Vainstein's report was considered the essential guide to library development.

The Vancouver and Victoria libraries backed the Vainstein report by agreeing to serve as reference libraries. And Coquitlam finally got a library — a joint venture between the municipality and the school board, opened after voters twice rejected a municipal library.

The Public Library Commission cautioned that local officials fretted about costs and were too often skeptical of professional advice. "Without the acceptance of the idea of co-operation among libraries, a multiplicity of workshops, seminars and conferences would come to naught — and yet the idea is not immediately embraced in all quarters," said the commission, warning that most local libraries were operating near starvation level.

The move toward collaboration suffered a blow in 1968 when taxpayers in Penticton voted to pull out of the Okanagan Regional Library. There had been complaints about the regional service in Penticton since the city had been forced to join twenty years earlier. Penticton residents said the card catalogue was inadequate and complained of delays in getting books from regional headquarters in Kelowna. The final straw was a change in financing that increased the costs to larger communities, Penticton included.

Penticton Alderman Joe Coe started a petition urging that the city withdraw. Other council members supported him, saying the city could provide service for less money. Penticton paid $35,595 to the regional library in 1968, but the proposed budget for its own library was $32,700. Alderman Frank McDonald said Penticton's own library would be second to none, and would have 19,000 books, more than it had as a branch of the larger system.

William Rentoul Castell, the head of the Calgary Public Library, supported Penticton's bid to pull out. He said the Okanagan library did not have a complete cataloguing system, its collection in Penticton was too small, and the local staff could not fully use the resources at headquarters. Castell assured Penticton's readers that they would still be able to get books from the Okanagan system through inter-library loans.

In a plebiscite in December 1968, Penticton taxpayers voted 1,763 to 1,060 to withdraw from the regional system, and the divorce was made final, thanks to mediation by the provincial government, in April 1969. The regional library had to give Penticton the fixed assets in the branch

and 16,000 of the 16,225 books in the Penticton branch. Penticton's new library board told the librarian to select 225 books of little value and send them to Kelowna.

Despite that setback, the Public Library Commission remained committed to improving service and increasing co-operation under a new name: the Library Development Commission. New legislation specified that the minimum population for a new municipal library would be 5,000 people — a change designed to encourage small communities to join regional networks. Libraries would also get financial incentives to work together.

The commission did not want to give grants to "struggling, self-isolated" libraries doing only half the job of a regional system. A library that declined to improve, the commission said, should not expect a subsidy. In 1970, the commission went further, saying it would not give money to libraries whose municipality, electoral area or school district could join a larger unit of service but failed to do so.

That was bound to get attention. B.C.'s libraries of all sizes are perennially short of money. Just before Peter Grossman retired as Vancouver's head librarian in 1970, he noted that the provincial government had made $300,000 available to all of its libraries, while a single library might get that much in Ontario.

The *Vancouver Sun* chastised Grossman for being too gentle, arguing that the Vancouver library had been suffering for years, and as a result was mediocre. "The trouble with librarians is that their calling demands they spend their lives under signs saying 'silence.' But when wringing from politicians the money needed to bring a library up to acceptable standards, hushed tones, as the record shows all too clearly, get them nowhere," the *Sun* said.

"What's needed to give Vancouver the sort of library we should have is a little of that hard-nosed, money-grubbing, go-for-the-jugular instinct of our aquarium people. Once

Peter Grossman was born near Chilliwack in 1910, and in 1930 became the first bookmobile driver for the Fraser Valley Demonstration Library. He obtained a degree in librarianship from the University of California in Berkeley in 1938, but the Second World War broke out before he could pursue his career in libraries. He was severely wounded in Italy, but returned to head the Fraser Valley system before going to Nova Scotia for six years, serving as the provincial librarian. In 1954 he returned to British Columbia to become assistant director of the Vancouver Public Library, and became head librarian on the death of Edgar Stewart Robinson in 1957. He served as president of the British Columbia Library Association, and also of the Canadian Library Association. He retired in 1970 and died three years later.

Right: Alice Bacon in front of a decorative poster in the Burnaby Public Library in 1971. *Ralph Bower, Vancouver Sun*

our librarians show the same determination to acquire Melville's *Moby Dick* as the fishy crowd in acquiring live whales, maybe future directors will have more believable swan songs."

The editorial drew a sharp response from Bryan Bacon, the chief librarian in Burnaby, who said the problem of financial support was even greater in smaller libraries. "Sure, the provincial government grant is pitifully inadequate, but this is one of the lean years — not that the fat ones were any better," he said. "Meanwhile federal aid to public libraries has been limited to a handful of books, half of which were (happy chance) in French, distributed with liberal abandon bordering on recklessness during Canada's centennial year. It will probably be another hundred years before libraries get another such windfall from Ottawa."

Bacon argued that libraries were too often "small inefficient units, jealously guarded by external rivalry, internal complacency and misplaced civic pride." Libraries needed public support, he said, but to get that, they had to give the public what it wanted. Sharing resources would improve efficiency, which would be better for patrons. Before that could happen, Bacon said, the government had to change legislation so libraries could operate on a regional rather than municipal tax base. He said the priorities of local governments were persistently "in the vicinity of drains and sewers."

In 1971, about 250 people gathered in Victoria for the Centennial Citizens' Conference on Libraries, which had the theme of Libraries: Vital to Tomorrow's World. Only about

Alice Simpson — later Alice Bacon — was a graduate of the first class at the University of British Columbia's School of Librarianship. She worked in libraries in New Westminster, Vancouver, Burnaby and Bellingham, Washington, before becoming the regional director in the Lower Mainland office of the Library Development Commission in 1970. With Lois Bewley she organized the 1971 conference on libraries in Victoria. She ran the province's taped books program, and served on a national task force on library service to the visually and physically handicapped. She helped create the Greater Vancouver Library Federation, and served as an adjunct professor at the School of Library, Archival and Information Studies at UBC. She retired in 1988.

fifteen per cent of the attendees were librarians; the rest were citizens and government leaders.

"We still have to convince some of our own members that they should be offering a service, instead of acting as custodians for the books," said Alice Simpson, a field consultant for the Library Development Commission and one of the conference organizers. "Most people still think of a library as a place to go when they want something to read. They don't realize what a library can do for them."

Simpson blamed librarians for this lack of understanding. "We've sat and waited for people to come to us. Not one public library in this province has a full-time, or even part-time, public relations officer on staff. No business would operate this way." Simpson argued for co-operation between libraries, saying that the Lower Mainland had nine public libraries, but people from one municipality could not use libraries in other municipalities. Some areas had no service at all.

Enid Dearing of North Vancouver District and Harry Newsom of the School of Library Science at the University of Alberta touched on another kind of co-operation — between school and public libraries. They argued for the co-ordination of services on a regional basis, including agreement on collections, buying and processing materials and backup services. The future, they said, must bring co-operation between public, post-secondary and special libraries.

The conference resulted in several recommendations, including a province-wide library card so each individual could use every library — finally offered more than thirty years later as the BC OneCard — and more co-operative services and programs.

After the conference, Ray Culos of Burnaby, the head of the trustees' section of the B.C. Library Association, wrote in the *Victoria Daily Times* that a lack of money was the biggest obstacle to library development. "We have imaginative, far-sighted people throughout the library system who are anxious to turn libraries from a mere collection of books into true community resource centres. But their efforts are stymied because of the lack of financial resources."

Culos said a library must reflect "the vital link between information output centres, leisure time and entertainment, audio-visual needs, continuing education and the ever-increasing demand for instant communication. In short — a community resource centre."

Above: Ray Culos. *Courtesy Ray Culos*

In the 1970s, access to the book collection was the most important service offered by local public libraries. *Times Colonist*

Ray Culos, a member of the Burnaby Public Library board, was active in the Canadian and British Columbia library associations. He was named to the Library Development Commission in 1970 and elected its chairman in 1973; he served until the commission was eliminated in 1978. He was hardly a political appointee, given that he was put on the commission by a Social Credit government, a New Democratic Party government and then by the Socreds again. He was the Canadian Library Association's Trustee of the Year in 1974. In his day job, Culos was in charge of community relations at Pacific Press, the publisher of the *Vancouver Sun* and the *Province* in Vancouver.

Regional conferences were held in Kamloops, Nelson, Burnaby, Prince George and Prince Rupert, and an extensive report on organizing systems throughout the province was issued in December 1971. It built on Vainstein's report, although it recommended eleven library service areas, using the boundaries of the new regional districts, instead of Vainstein's thirteen areas.

In 1972, Provincial Secretary Wesley Black introduced the Public Libraries Act, which would allow regional districts to form federated and integrated library systems. The Kootenay seemed most ready, and 200 people attended a conference that May in Nelson to discuss a regional system. The city helped draft plans for a regional headquarters in Nelson. The idea was scrapped, however, when the New Democratic Party won the provincial election that summer, and priorities changed. The new West Kootenay Library Association opted instead for better communications and co-operation between libraries that would remain independent.

In September 1973, the Library Development Commission published a plan based on the report two years earlier. Ten of the eleven proposed public systems were to integrate their services and the eleventh, in the Greater Vancouver Regional District, would be a federation that combined services of municipal libraries without integrating them. The government offered to cover twenty per cent of the operating costs of recognized systems, with more money for new branches. To qualify, however, libraries would need to be regionalized.

The government was accused of trying to blackmail

libraries. In Prince George, for example, the library board unanimously rejected the regional proposal, and the Fraser-Fort George Regional District struck a committee to fight it. The resistance came even though the Prince George board had applied for and received a grant from the Library Development Commission to create a regional resource collection.

The first integrated system based on the commission's new program was launched in January 1974 in the Thompson-Nicola Regional District. It was a bold move: outside of Kamloops, the region had relatively few people spread over a wide area. Kamloops, Merritt and Ashcroft had municipal libraries; libraries in other communities relied on volunteers. The councils in Ashcroft, Cache Creek, Kamloops, Logan Lake and Merritt agreed to take part without a public referendum. The concept was put to voters in the other three municipalities and the ten electoral areas that fall, and eighty-eight per cent were in favour.

The system served from Merritt north to Clearwater, and from Clinton east to Chase. The Library Development Commission provided financial assistance, helped set operating standards and assigned librarian Mary Leask to Kamloops to help. In 1975, voters in the Cariboo Regional District agreed to join, and the expanded service became known as the Cariboo-Thompson-Nicola Library System.

Mary Leask spent fifteen years on the staff of the External Affairs department, and served in Ottawa, Japan, and four European countries. After that she attended the School of Librarianship at the University of British Columbia, then went to work for the Public Library Commission. She spent two years in Kamloops after being assigned to help set up the integrated library system in the Cariboo and Thompson-Nicola regional districts. She also started a training program for community librarians that helped to raise the level of service throughout the province.

Ray Culos, by then the chairman of the Library Development Commission, said the new system would assure access to information no matter where the patron lived. "You won't have to live in Vancouver to get services of a major library."

Changes came to Greater Vancouver after Albert Bowron, a Toronto library consultant, was asked by the Library Development Commission to study the service there. He said it was hurt by parochialism, and he called for an end to restrictions based on municipal or community boundaries. For a start, he said, there should be common library cards and registration procedures, standardized hours of operation, standardized loan periods and free use of all libraries by all residents. Later, libraries could adopt centralized technical services, speedy inter-library lending, and coordinated planning.

Bowron suggested that Surrey, White Rock, Richmond and Delta leave the Fraser Valley Regional Library to become part of a system based on the boundaries of the Greater Vancouver Regional District. He also said Port Moody, Port Coquitlam and Coquitlam should have one system, with two branches served by a central library in Coquitlam.

Spurred on by the new Public Libraries Act and by Bowron's report, seven Lower Mainland library boards — Vancouver, West Vancouver, North Vancouver city and district, Burnaby, New Westminster and Port Moody — formed a federation in 1973 to allow cardholders to borrow from any system. Patrons in outlying areas could draw on the resources of Vancouver's central library by using telephone or Telex, a system of printers connected to telephone lines that allowed for the transmission of text messages, and books would be delivered to the local branch by motorcycle and truck.

The Greater Vancouver Library Federation was finally launched in November 1975, and included twenty-five branch libraries — fourteen in Vancouver, four in Burnaby, three in North Vancouver district and one in each of the other areas. The amalgamation was the first of its kind in Canada. Each member of the federation continued to be municipally funded and retained control over its own expenditures, operations and policies. People in Coquitlam, Surrey, Richmond and the University Endowment Lands — outside the area covered by the federation — could get non-resident library cards for $25 a year.

Also in November 1975, voters in Richmond decided to withdraw from the Fraser Valley system. Richmond had been the largest contributor to the region's budget so the loss of its five branches caused major financial problems. Fraser Valley cut the hours of its twenty-five remaining branches by twenty-five per cent and bought only 40,000 books in 1976, down from 56,000 in 1975.

The divorce got ugly. In April 1976, the regional library filed a Supreme Court action against Richmond, claiming $109,012. It took six months to settle the dispute, which ended when Richmond paid the bill and agreed to return

Joy Scudamore, the co-ordinator of the Greater Vancouver Library Federation, which was started in the late 1970s. *Ralph Bower, Vancouver Sun*

25,000 books, which the regional system used to stock new branches in Cloverdale, Port Coquitlam and White Rock. The Fraser Valley and Richmond boards agreed to allow residents to borrow books from all branches in the two systems.

Richmond had no regrets about the split, reporting later that it had improved its book stock, set up a quality reference service and developed an efficient automated catalogue that was available on microfiche at all branches and in school and college libraries.

A few years later, Surrey also left the Fraser Valley system, but the split was easier thanks to the lessons learned with Richmond. The library board worked out terms in advance, and the separation agreement gave the regional library half the books in the Surrey branches, or the equivalent in money.

At the Library Development Commission, Culos and the other four commissioners — all working for free — continued pushing to make quality libraries accessible to everyone in the province. The commission was determined to use its budget to develop better, more equitable library service.

There was talk of major change on Vancouver Island, but as the provincial secretary noted in a report, "apparently irreconcilable views" blocked progress. The Greater Victoria board wanted to take over all service south of the Malahat, while the Vancouver Island Regional Library board wanted to take over Victoria. The lines between the two systems were blurry. The Vancouver Island system had opened a branch in 1963 in a Colwood shopping centre at the request of voters in the Sooke school district. New books were brought from the Island system's central headquarters in Nanaimo, even though Greater Victoria's central library was closer.

In the Okanagan Valley, the library board — made up of school district and municipal representatives — started working on plans to reorganize along regional district boundaries, as recommended by the Library Development Commission. In the Kootenay, the idea of an integrated library system was back, and a referendum was planned for 1976.

Then all plans were put on hold. The New Democratic Party government, which had supported integrated systems, was defeated in 1975, and the new Social Credit government wanted financial restraint. The commission no longer had seed money for library projects.

The drive to regionalize and integrate came to a crashing

Above: Provincial Secretary Ernie Hall sends books on their way at the Okanagan Regional Library's new headquarters in Kelowna in 1974. *Okanagan Regional Library*

Right: Okanagan's 1974 headquarters offered plenty of room for the cataloguing staff of the day. *Okanagan Regional Library*

halt in May 1978, when Recreation and Conservation Minister Sam Bawlf — responsible for public libraries — announced that grants would be concentrated "on the provision of the most essential resource in our public libraries — books."

The government cancelled the incentive grants and declared that any decision to participate in a regional library or integrate service would be local, without financial pressure from the government. Annual grants were to be based on the population served — $1 per capita for areas of 6,500 or more people, and up to $2 per capita for areas of 6,500 or less. Operating costs became the responsibility of local boards. The government also promised to increase its funding to $3.5 million in 1979-80 from $3.2 million in 1978-79.

The Library Development Commission met with Bawlf to protest the changes, saying the new grant structure would be particularly damaging to the pilot project in the Cariboo and Thompson-Nicola regional districts, which had been getting more money than other areas.

The next month, Bawlf disbanded the commission, saying it would be replaced with an advisory council. Final responsibility for public libraries would be with the ministry's new Library Services Branch. These changes ended a program of library development that could be

traced to Vainstein's report — and essentially to the creation of the Public Library Commission in 1919. The dream of eleven new library districts, bringing shared resources and equitable, comprehensive service to every community, was over.

The commission had made a lot of progress in a short time. As Culos says, before the late 1960s and 1970s, library patrons could not count on their library having the book they wanted — and a reader in Burnaby could not borrow a book from Vancouver. In many communities, librarians had been relying on donations to keep shelves full, and local residents did not understand the potential of libraries. In just a few years, all of that changed.

"All of a sudden people who were readers were able to fulfill their needs. All of a sudden people who didn't think of the library as the first source of information and entertainment and education had the opportunity," Culos says. The library federation in Greater Vancouver was perhaps the most notable change to follow the work of Vainstein, but the concept of sharing had been strengthened throughout the province.

The years between 1960 and 1978 brought many changes

Spacious library branch in downtown Kelowna in the 1970s. *Okanagan Regional Library*

Above: Public Library Commission used a station wagon to move books among libraries in the East Kootenay in the 1960s. *Public Library Services Branch*

Top right: Exchange of books in the Marysville library in 1964. *Public Library Services Branch*

to library service — new libraries, new technology and even a new type of library book. In 1962, the Fraser Valley Regional Library had become the first library in Canada to offer paperbacks. The average cost was 40 cents, which meant the library could obtain eleven paperbacks for the price of one hardcover. Paperbacks were not as durable but they provided twice the number of circulations per dollar. Almost half of the new books acquired by the library that year were paperbacks.

The idea caught on. Vancouver Island libraries added them in 1963. Two years later, the Vancouver Public Library offered paperbacks in its central library, and added them to its eight branch libraries in 1966. These books were not expected to last as long as hardcover books so they were not catalogued in the same way, which saved time and money. Paperbacks arrived at the Peace River branch of the Library Development Commission in 1972, and as the branch's annual report noted, they offered "simplified processing, portability, and the book in cool form."

Howard Overend, who ran the Peace River branch, travelled about 25,000 miles a year. His route included sixty schools, twenty-eight rural communities, isolated oil and construction crews, lonely farms and ranches. Once a year Overend's book van made the 1,000-mile run up the Alaska Highway, taking books as far as the Yukon border. His branch served about 35,000 people in an area of 110,000 square miles.

Overend delivered to schools four times a year. He recalls taking up to fifteen boxes of books into a schoolroom,

spreading them out on the floor and letting the children dive in. The children would pick the ones they wanted, to a maximum of 100 per classroom. Overend's visits provided teachers in one-room schools a rare contact with the outside world. Some teachers never adjusted to the loneliness, he says, and would appear more withdrawn with each visit. These teachers would leave at the end of the school year, never to return.

Overend's work made him a star on the silver screen. A director and cameraman from the National Film Board joined him on an Alaska Highway trip, and their colour documentary *Journey From Zero* showcased scenery as well as the work of the commission. It had its B.C. premiere in Dawson Creek in May 1962. The documentary brought national attention to the commission through the photographs and information the film board provided to the print media. Overend's story appeared in several daily newspapers, about fifty rural newspapers in Western Canada and other publications.

Overend kept busy. He started a quarter-hour weekly program, *The World of Books*, on CJDC-TV in Dawson Creek, and wrote a column for the local newspaper. He also obtained a bookmobile — the tenth walk-in model in the province and the first in the service of the library commission. On top of that, families from outside Dawson Creek could borrow books from his office.

The Public Library Commission stopped sending books to schools during the 1960s, saying that they had to develop their own libraries. But libraries continued to struggle to find

Left: Howard Overend worked for the Public Library Commission in Cranbrook and Dawson Creek in the 1950s and 1960s. *Public Library Services Branch*

Below: Public Library Commission van at Azouzetta Lake, on the John Hart Highway between Prince George and Dawson Creek, in the 1960s. *Public Library Services Branch*

Bottom: Students were welcome to skip class at Vancouver's Prince of Wales Secondary School in 1967 — as long as they spent their time in the school's library. *Deni Eagland, Vancouver Sun*

the best way to combine service for public school students and the public.

School libraries came a long way, as was noted by Samuel Rothstein, the founder of UBC's School of Librarianship. In the early days, school libraries were often makeshift collections of books in the principal's office and "whoever was no good at teaching would be in charge." In time, the libraries offered substantial collections and librarians had a high level of training.

The Vancouver Public Library started an experiment in the Killarney Secondary School in 1968, adding 10,000 books to the library and providing a librarian from 4 to 10 p.m. The library did not attract members of the public, however, which meant a trained librarian was supervising a study hall. When the trial ended in 1978, few patrons seemed to care. More successful Vancouver school branches were Strathcona, which opened in 1972 in an elementary school, and Britannia, which opened in 1975 in a massive school and community complex on 18 acres.

In 1974, Vancouver opened its Joe Fortes branch, with the King George Secondary School library in the mezzanine

Sheila Egoff and Judi Saltman at the University of British Columbia. *University of British Columbia Archives 41.1/644*

Sheila Egoff received a diploma in library science from the University of Toronto in 1938, and worked as a librarian in Ontario before joining the University of British Columbia faculty in 1961. As a professor of librarianship and the first tenured professor in children's literature, she was responsible for more than simply training children's librarians; she helped establish children's services as they exist today. She inspired a generation of children's librarians, who still quote one of her favorite sayings: Only the best is good enough for children.

Egoff, who retired in 1983 and died in 2005, led many initiatives to increase the quality of children's literature in Canada and abroad. In 1994, she was the first professor of children's literature to be named an Officer of the Order of Canada. Egoff was a recipient of the Ralph R. Shaw Award from the American Library Association in 1982, an Outstanding Public Library Service Award from the Canadian Association of Public Libraries in 1992 and the 2004 Anne Devereaux Jordan Award from the Children's Literature Association. Egoff received several honorary degrees. The children's literature prize from the B.C. Book Prizes is named in her honour.

level. The Fortes branch — the first in the West End since 1958 — developed a collection in line with the needs of the area, the highest-density neighbourhood in Canada. There were a lot of young single adults but not many gardens and not many cars. As a result, books on gardening and auto repair were kept to a minimum, but there was an emphasis on the occult, photography, arts and crafts, interior decorating and bestsellers.

Joint projects were tried elsewhere. In Greater Victoria, two high school libraries were opened four evenings a week, and students were able to check reference books or work on assignments. One of the schools, in Esquimalt, stopped the experiment after three months because of a lack of use. The Vancouver Island system tried combining public and school libraries in Port Alberni, but found that not all adults were willing to share a library with children. The Kitimat public library opened a branch in Kildala School, but circulation was low and the branch closed after a year. The poor results prompted the Library Development Commission to declare its opposition to the combination of public and school libraries.

In 1971, the Greater Victoria Public Library stopped offering bookmobile service at the five schools that had received the service. The bookmobile librarian, Terry Smith, said a bookmobile could not match a visit to a library. Besides, he said, the bookmobile might be doing more harm than good if schools were not being encouraged to develop their own libraries.

For public libraries, bookmobiles were still an important means of reaching borrowers. The West Vancouver Memorial Library obtained its first bookmobile in 1968, paying $2,000 to Burnaby for a van that was no longer needed because of the expansion of school libraries. The van was stationed a day each in the Horseshoe Bay, Glenmore and Chartwell areas.

Libraries were also seeing the leading edge of the computer revolution. In the 1960s, large university libraries turned to computers to keep track of books, and the library commission predicted that more changes were coming. "The size of the body of recorded information is beginning to stagger the imaginations even of those who have grown up with it, and the problem of storing, organizing it and using it has become paramount," the commission said in a report.

It was becoming common to hear, the commission said, expressions such as "information retrieval," "random access memory," "machine readable form," "information-processing services" and so on. And there were several notable predictions about technological change.

Jesse Shera of Cleveland's Western Reserve University

told a B.C. Library Association conference in 1967 that a computer or push-button library would someday pool all the written and computerized knowledge in all the libraries on the continent. "We will interrogate the computer by asking for a list of books that pertain to the particular subject sought," he said. "This information, gathered from libraries across the continent, will be obtained in seconds and appear on a television screen." He said universities could have completely computerized library systems within forty or even thirty years — by the start of the twenty-first century, more or less.

Lawrence Leaf of the University of British Columbia's curriculum laboratory told Greater Victoria school librarians that students would one day be able to obtain a taped lesson by telephone. These lessons could come on videotape, he said, or be dialed from home. He said the librarian would become a "media specialist" skilled in directing students to information stored in many forms, not just in books.

Phyllis Baxendale of the IBM Research Laboratory in San Jose, California, predicted that users would be able to talk in ordinary language to the computer via keyboard and the computer would reply by displaying information on an adjacent screen. G.R. Campbell, systems analyst at the University of Victoria library, boldly predicted that computers would eventually help libraries check out books, produce overdue notices and become more productive.

Campbell had high praise for the Vancouver Island Regional Library, which had developed a computerized listing of its holdings and made it available in every branch and bookmobile. The project had not been easy. It took three months to enter every book, by author, title and subject, into IBM key-punch machines, and then the results were transferred to tape. The computerized system replaced the card-index system at library headquarters in Nanaimo. In 1970, the Okanagan Regional Library also introduced a computer-based catalogue with copies in twelve branches.

Microfiche catalogues based on computer printouts meant every branch could have a listing of what was in the system. In a few years, microfiche would be left behind, but computers were not quite ready for prime time. In the late 1970s, the Fraser Valley system installed a computer terminal in its Whalley branch as a test. It was a good thing that patrons could still use microfiche because, in 1980, the system was out of order for forty-seven days, or eighteen per cent of the year.

Technology opened up other possibilities as well. In 1969, to fight a serious theft problem, the Vancouver Public Library put magnetic strips in books and gates at the exits. The strips would sound an alarm when they went through the gates without being de-sensitized during checkout. Most other libraries adopted similar measures, because the cost of

stolen books was much higher than the cost of adding the magnetic strips.

Several libraries and library branches started in the 1960s and 1970s and helped reflect the communities they served. In 1966, the Sliammon reserve near Powell River opened a library with about 600 books for the 300 residents. Library patrons could take out one book at a time and keep it for a week. Chief Leslie Adams made some of the band's books, including encyclopedias, available in the library. Today, residents can use the Powell River Public Library, which still services the library on the reserve.

In 1970, the first aboriginal library in the province was opened in Bella Coola. It had 400 books about the community's history, traditions, art forms and language. "This is an Indian library and it is making the Indian heritage a living force in the Bella Coola community," said Chief Jim Kelly. The collection included illustrated books on West Coast Indian arts and crafts for the Kwakiutl artist and student and technical how-to books on painting and carving. There were books on Indian legends for children, on West Coast history and geography, and on the history of Indians in Canada.

> In 1975, about 12,000 overdue books were returned to Victoria because of a special amnesty promotion. Fines would be forgiven, and free McDonald's milkshakes would go to people who returned the books. Some of the books returned had been out for six or seven years.

The library was housed in a replica of a West Coast longhouse, a cultural centre and meeting place of the community, with twentieth-century touches such as a coffee bar and recreational centre. It was also a spot where Kwakiutl language and dances could be taught again, and craftsmen could produce and display their work.

The Bella Coola service led the way for libraries in many other First Nations communities. Most have full libraries with research collections dealing with aboriginal rights and titles, as well as archival material including oral histories. In time the B.C. Library Association established a First Nations interest group to foster library development in First Nations communities and the training of library technicians and librarians from those communities.

The Burnaby Public Library recognized the right of every child, no matter how young, to have a library card — and also the right of every child to experience the world of imagination stimulated by stories in library books. With those beliefs in mind, the library hit the road in 1974 with a brightly coloured Ford Econoline van that it called the Storybus. The specialized bookmobile served day-care centres, housing units and churches. It carried a portable puppet stage along with 1,500 hardcover picture books.

Burnaby's Story Bus was in the road until 1984. *Deni Eagland, Vancouver Sun*

When Victoria's Craigdarroch Castle became home to the school board, one room was devoted to a library for teachers — seen here in 1967. *Times Colonist*

In 1973, the Burnaby Public Library opened a neighborhood library in the Crest Shopping Centre that was designed to break down the barriers of traditional libraries. It wasn't like a regular library; its collection had 9,500 paperbacks. "Because we haven't a catalogue the old-time librarians throw up their hands in dismay," said Bryan Bacon, the chief librarian. "They'll never find an obscure seventeenth-century edition of surgical book manufacturing in the Maritimes, but that's not what we're all about. Pretty soon we plan to get in a bunch of gramophone records so we can lend them as part of our service."

The Burnaby library also exempted children and senior citizens from fines on overdue books. Bacon said there was no sense in penny-pinching when the goal was to get people reading.

In 1974, the Library Development Commission took over a project called Vancouver Taped Books, which provided books and other special reading materials for the blind and physically handicapped. The service had been started under a Local Initiatives Program grant to create employment. The commission made it available to members of the Greater Vancouver Library Federation, and soon expanded it so libraries throughout the province could buy books on audiocassette.

Some new libraries served select groups. The Fraser Valley Regional Library started bookmobile service to Agassiz Mountain Prison in 1973, and forty-two inmates became avid readers, borrowing an average of ten books each that year. A lending library was created in 1972 by the Narcotic Addiction Foundation of B.C. with funding from the B.C. Council on Drugs, Alcohol and Tobacco. The collection of books devoted to drugs and drug problems was based at the foundation's headquarters in Vancouver.

In 1975, the B.C. Law Library Foundation was organized to manage the collections of legal information throughout the province. The foundation was the first of its type in North America, offering a library system governed by the

financial institutes that supported it and the various groups that used its services. During the 1970s, the number of law libraries in B.C. rose to twenty-seven from eighteen.

Libraries continued to find ways to work together, and sometimes the collaboration crossed the line between public and post-secondary libraries. In 1972, for example, the Fraser Valley Regional Library and the Douglas College library agreed to honour each other's cards. A similar deal was struck between Camosun College and the Greater Victoria Public Library. There were benefits for both sides; the public libraries had huge fiction sections, while the colleges had more non-fiction and technical books.

Books for East Kootenay libraries filled the shelves in the Public Library Commission's Cranbrook branch in 1964. *Public Library Services Branch*

14

THE BOOM
IN CAMPUS LIBRARIES

The post-war Baby Boom changed most aspects of North America, including libraries. The impact was perhaps most dramatic in colleges and universities. In 1958, there were two options for students who wanted a degree — the University of British Columbia or Victoria College. The two institutions served a population of 1.6 million as British Columbia celebrated the province's centennial.

Then the Baby Boom wave, which had already sparked a huge expansion in elementary and high schools, began reaching university age. Their numbers, along with the increasing importance of a post-secondary education in the new British Columbia, brought extraordinary growth.

Opposite: Part of the extensive card catalogue at the University of British Columbia in the 1970s. *University of British Columbia Archives 41.1/2712-4*

Above: Malaspina college's first library, in 1969, was in the old Nanaimo hospital. *Times Colonist*

Within ten years, British Columbia had a dozen more post-secondary choices. Each needed libraries to serve a growing student population, and professional librarians to build and manage those new collections. The UBC Library, which had 450,000 books in 1960, launched an aggressive expansion program. It took the library almost fifty years to obtain its first half a million materials, but in less than a decade, from 1960 to 1967, it added one million more.

Sam Rothstein in the UBC's new library stacks in the early 1960s. Peter Holborne photo, University of British Columbia Archives 1.1/12282

Samuel Rothstein was born in Russia and brought to Canada when he was two years old. He served in the Canadian army in the Second World War, then learned librarianship at the University of California Berkeley and the University of Illinois. He was the first Canadian with a doctorate in librarianship. In 1961 he was associate director and acting director of the University of British Columbia Library, and director and professor of UBC's new library school. Rothstein served as a president of the British Columbia Library Association and the Pacific Northwest Library Association. He was named an honorary life member of PNLA in 1987 and was given an honorary doctorate by UBC in 2004.

There were major changes in library training as well. In the post-war boom years there were plenty of library jobs, but not many trained librarians to fill them. Low salaries and a lack of suitable training limited the supply of potential employees.

British Columbians had to leave the province to complete their education in library service. Their options in Canada were McGill University in Montreal, where the country's first librarianship program was created in 1904, or the University of Toronto. More programs were available in the United States. Graduates had their choice of jobs when they completed their studies, because there was great demand for qualified librarians across the continent.

The need for a library school at UBC had been recognized many times, starting soon after the university opened. In the late 1950s, President Norman MacKenzie, librarian Neal Harlow and associate librarian Samuel Rothstein decided to make it happen. The first step was a summer course offered in 1960 with the help of the British Columbia Library Association, the Public Library Commission and the university. Eighteen branch custodians — as librarians in the regional libraries were known — took part in the brief, concentrated course in the administration of small public libraries, with the cost underwritten by the commission.

The summer school was offered again in 1961, but the big change came that fall when Rothstein opened the School of Librarianship, offering a one-year post-graduate Bachelor of Library Science degree. Rothstein was the school's first director. He had a busy year; he was also the interim librarian after Harlow left to take a job at Rutgers University. Rothstein promised that the school would attract people from the Prairies as well as B.C., and would train them to fill the many vacancies in Western Canada.

The library school had four faculty members and thirty students in its first year. All but two graduated. The school was certainly needed because, along with new colleges and universities, public libraries were expanding, and these libraries needed trained professional librarians. In 1971, the library school shifted to a two-year Master of Library Science program. A Master of Archival Studies program was added in 1979. The school evolved into the School of Library, Archival and Information Studies, and started a Master of Children's Literature program in 1999 and a PhD program in 2003.

By 1961, when the school was started, UBC was one of the three most important post-secondary institutions in Canada. Its library, with a capacity of 500,000 volumes, reflected its stature, and it continued to evolve and expand with the changing times.

The library's new $1.7-million south wing was named after Vancouver industrialist Walter Koerner, who had provided twenty-five per cent of the funds. The balance came in grants from the Canada Council and the provincial government. The expansion allowed a major reorganization, with divisional reference rooms opened for the humanities, social sciences and sciences, and the creation of the special collections and Asian studies divisions. One section, known as the College Library, was filled with material for first- and second-year students. This library was eventually renamed the Sedgewick Library after Garnett Gladwin Sedgewick, the head of the Department of English from 1920 to 1948. It became popular with all undergraduates and soon had more patrons than it could handle.

Victoria College had a library with 64,300 books and thirteen staff members in 1960, the year it was converted to a four-year college. When it became the University of Victoria in 1963, librarian Dean Halliwell led a transformation that saw the collection quickly grow to 200,000 volumes and

Dean Halliwell served as the head librarian at the University of Victoria from 1963 until his retirement in 1988, and saw the library grow from the basics to a collection of more than 1,000,000 volumes. In 1971, he served as president of the Canadian Library Association, and in 1977 he was named assistant to the university president. In 1979, he was elected to the American Library Association council. Halliwell died in 2000.

fifty-seven on staff. In 1964 the library's new $1.4-million building, named after Victoria philanthropist Thomas Shanks McPherson, became one of the first buildings to open on the new Gordon Head campus. The University of Victoria library had open stacks, which meant anyone could

The library, centre, was one of the first buildings to go up on the University of Victoria campus in 1963. *University of Victoria Archives 020-0101*

Basil Stuart Stubbs in 1964.
Ray Allan, Vancouver Sun

Basil Stuart-Stubbs started working at the UBC Library in 1956 and was university librarian from 1964 to 1981. He was director of the School of Librarianship, later the School of Library, Archival and Information Studies, from 1981 to 1992. Stuart-Stubbs was one of the founding members of the Alcuin Society, an association concerned with book production and appreciation, in 1965. Six years later he played a key role in the creation of the University of British Columbia Press, the province's first academic book publisher. In 1977 he oversaw the creation of an inter-library lending network for provincial university and colleges on behalf of the B.C. Ministry of Education. He is a member of the Order of Canada and a fellow of the Royal Society of Canada.

browse through the books. And those books saw plenty of use as the university went from 1,000 students in 1960 to 4,000 in 1967.

In 1964, UBC opened its new Woodward Library, with 55,000 volumes of bio-medical books and journals in the first air-conditioned building on campus. It had a capacity of 100,000 volumes. The Woodward Library was the first branch of the Main Library, and the forerunner of a network

of a dozen branches based on subject areas and faculties. The theory was simple: With the campus expanding in all directions, in made sense to put reference material close to the students and the faculty.

"My informal observations led me to believe that students and faculty members were unwilling to walk more than five minutes in the rain to get to a library," says Basil Stuart-Stubbs, who became UBC's head librarian in 1963. As a result, whenever new buildings were constructed for a faculty or department, space was allotted for a branch library. An added benefit was that the branch libraries freed space in the overcrowded Main Library.

The expansion of post-secondary options in the 1960s was triggered by a report on higher education from John B. Macdonald, the president of UBC. Macdonald lobbied for the creation of two-year colleges that would offer a wide range of programs and would be under the control of the local school boards. He recommended the establishment of four-year colleges in Victoria and the Lower Mainland.

His report prompted amendments to the Public Schools Act to permit the creation of colleges following local plebiscites. The institutions were to offer two years of arts and science programming and students would be able to transfer credit to universities. The Universities Act was also changed to create the Academic Board of Higher Education of B.C., which helped develop new colleges and ensured they had consistent standards.

Changes came quickly. Notre Dame University in Nelson came into being in 1963. It had been founded in 1950 as a private university college by the Roman Catholic diocese of Nelson.

In 1964, in response to an earlier report on education by Sperrin Noah Fulton Chant, the British Columbia Institute of Technology was opened at the site of the B.C. Vocational School in Burnaby. The BCIT library was moved to its own building four years later.

When Simon Fraser University was opened in Burnaby in 1965, the first students found a 30,000-volume library ready for their use. Donald Baird, the first librarian, said the library would use "space-age techniques" to give students the best service in Canada. Instantaneous facsimile transmission — faxes, we'd call them later — would give students in the province's three public universities speedy access to books. Baird said that since SFU was 1,200 feet above sea level, it had direct line of sight with UBC, which would make it easier to develop high-speed facsimile transmission. UBC, meanwhile, would be able to establish good contact with the University of Victoria. Baird envisioned a coaxial cable or high-frequency transmission so that pages of a book in one

Simon Fraser University takes shape
on Burnaby Mountain in 1965. *Times
Colonist*

library could be sent almost immediately to another.

That was the plan, anyway. In 1966, it was considered noteworthy that the three university libraries were connected by teletype — basically, typewriters linked by telephone lines — with the physical exchange of books performed by a messenger service.

Baird predicted that reference facilities in Vancouver would someday equal those in Toronto or Los Angeles, thanks to the three university libraries in close proximity. Technology, he said, would enable them to avoid costly duplication, allowing each one to build collections in specific areas. The three libraries set up an informal organization called Tri-University Libraries, or TRIUL, to share ideas.

As a new library, SFU did not bother with old ways. Its books were indexed on IBM cards. The only letters on the cards were SFU; all of the other information about the books was contained in punched holes in 80 columns. The basic system was developed by Herman Hollerith in the 1800s, but it took modern computing power before the cards could be used to keep track of all of the books in a library.

UBC adopted the system as well. Each time a book was taken out, the borrower's library card and the book card were fed into the computer, which kept track of how many books were out, who had them and when they were due back. The UBC Library was one of the first institutions in Canada to apply data-processing machinery to routine operations at a time when entire rooms were needed to house the mainframe computers.

In a major change in 1966, UBC lifted its restrictions on students in first and second year, allowing them to enter the stacks whenever they wanted, rather than only after 6 p.m.

or during the day with a special pass. This granted them the same status as third and fourth year students, who had been allowed unimpeded access for several years. Everyone entering the stacks still had to show a library card. Four years later, the final restrictions were lifted.

The UBC library grew quickly in the 1960s thanks in part to a $3 million gift from H.R. MacMillan, who had made his fortune in the lumber business. The donation inspired a period of rapid change and expansion, with book purchases quickly doubling. By 1966, UBC was getting more than 300 new books every day — 100,000 volumes a year.

It was up to Basil Stuart-Stubbs, the head librarian, to find space to put all of those books. UBC's library was growing as fast as any university library in North America, and his goal was to establish separate subject-area libraries after the pattern of the Woodward Biomedical Library. Over the years UBC established an extensive network of branch libraries, including ones devoted to animal resource ecology, law, education, forestry and agriculture, fisheries, social work, mathematics and music. Divisions were opened for government publications, microfilms and maps.

The Crane Library, a special facility for blind students, was opened in Brock Hall in 1967. A $3,000 grant from the P.A. Woodward Foundation helped pay for materials, tape recorders, cataloguing and staffing. The library had three rooms of books and a reading lounge equipped with tape recorders, pre-recorded tapes, books in Braille and large print and relief maps. The facility was named after Charles

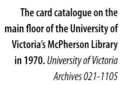

The card catalogue on the main floor of the University of Victoria's McPherson Library in 1970. *University of Victoria Archives 021-1105*

Crane, a deaf and blind man who had collected 2,500 volumes for the blind over forty-four years. Crane's family gave the collection to the university after he died in 1965.

During the 1930s Crane bought a machine for punching Braille and began transcribing books with the assistance of a reader who indicated each letter of each word by touching Crane's fingers. When Crane entered UBC in 1931 he was the first deaf and blind Canadian to undertake university studies. He attended for two years, and was a varsity wrestler, a member of the Classics Club and a reporter for the *Ubyssey* student newspaper. Later he was a publicity agent for the Vancouver Welfare Foundation and an employee of a Canadian National Institute for the Blind workshop.

UBC received a $50,000 grant to establish the first computer system to analyze the use of a large university research library, a project Stuart-Stubbs said would help to improve service and use all library resources more effectively. The information was to be collected and stored on magnetic tape for analysis. The system would answer questions about proper library size, the types of books it should contain, the most desirable loan periods, which books should be moved to storage and the effects of library use on student academic performance.

UBC installed an IBM 1030 data-collection system to control the flow of its 800,000 volumes, providing a central record of all loans and borrowers and a printed list of books most frequently used by undergraduates. The system automatically provided overdue notices and lists of books on loan.

By 1967, the University of Victoria unveiled plans for its own computer system. Each evening, the day's punched-card record of loans and returns would be fed into the computer. The next morning, the library would have an updated record of who had what, along with computer-printed overdue notices to send out. On the horizon was a data retrieval system that would give students lists of books and periodicals in response to a general request.

In 1967, about 100 university, government and public libraries, as well as the National Library of Canada and the National Science Library, were connected by Telex, a system of printers connected to telephone lines that allowed for the transmission of text messages. In a time before e-mail, it was a great advance. A professor requiring a specific article could ask the National Library to check its master lists. The National Library would find it, and the item would be sent on inter-library loan. The plan called for rarely used books to be stored at a central depot and shipped the same day requests were received. This would save money because libraries would not have to stock low-demand books. The number of messages per month rose steadily — UVic reported seventy in June. A typist could operate the small Telex machine after about an hour's instruction.

Alice in Wonderland. University of British Columbia Special Collections

The University of British Columbia received a unique gift in 1965 when the graduating class of 1925 bought a remarkable collection from Victoria book dealer Robert Hilton Smith, who had been a deputy chief librarian at the Toronto Public Library. Hilton Smith had assembled a collection of more than 500 volumes of the works of Lewis Carroll, including more than 200 editions of *Alice's Adventures in Wonderland*, first published in 1865, as well as *Through the Looking Glass and What Alice Found There*. The books featured illustrations by eighty different artists. One book featured the signature of Alice Hargreaves, who had been the original model for Alice. There were also parodies, such as *Adolf in Blunderland*, and novels imitating Carroll's style. The collection included film and stage adaptations as well as foreign-language editions. Hilton Smith had built the collection through purchases from dealers around the world. His book, *Alice One Hundred: A Catalogue in Celebration of the 100th Birthday of Alice's Adventures in Wonderland*, is a comprehensive summary of the Alice books he had for sale in his Adelphi Book Shop.

Students work in the University of Victoria library, 1972. *Times Colonist*

By 1969, SFU's library had a computer that made it easier to find books. Patrons could check the card catalogue for the call number, enter it, and the system would say where the book was, and when it was due back if it was on loan. The system, designed to handle the 250,000 books in the four-year-old library, was accessed through two cathode-ray tube monitors at the loan desks. The screens replaced long computer-typed lists of loaned books that had been produced daily.

Borrowers presented books and their library cards at the loan desks, where an assistant fed the library card and the book's punched card into a reader. The transactions were automatically recorded on another punched card. That system was soon changed, with information transmitted by cable to an IBM terminal reader at the loan desks. The

In February 1982, about 200 protesters shouted at Premier Bill Bennett and his mother, May, when they unveiled a plaque at Simon Fraser University that named the university's library after Bennett's father, former premier W.A.C. Bennett. That did not curb the family's support for SFU; in 1986, they gave the university 110 boxes of the elder Bennett's papers, and archivist Donald Baird set to work cataloguing the tangible evidence of fifty years of the man who had been in power from 1952 to 1972.

The opening of community colleges meant post-secondary students had more choices than ever. Several colleges were combined with existing vocational schools. Libraries were often among the first rooms assigned and librarians the first people hired. College libraries were not like university libraries, which supported research; they were designed to enhance what was being taught in the classrooms. They also complemented public libraries, giving students a wider range and depth of materials.

Vancouver Community College, established in 1965, brought together several organizations serving the lifelong learning needs of adults, including the King Edward Senior Matriculation and Continuing Education Centre, the Vancouver Vocational Institute, the Vancouver School of Art and parts of the night school program. The King Edward centre and the art school were the only two facilities with libraries.

Within five years much of the college was established at its Langara campus and a 25,000-square-foot library had 30,000 volumes. The Langara campus also offered a library technician program, the second post-secondary library course offered in British Columbia. A branch library was opened at the vocational school and a new King Edward library had 13,000 square feet on two floors.

When Capilano College opened in 1968, its library was in a room in West Vancouver Secondary School. After that it was split between the Christian Education Centre at Highlands Church and a building on Welch Street in North Vancouver. In 1974, the main library was opened in the second building erected on the new North Vancouver campus. Called the Media Centre, it included books, periodicals, a circulation desk, audio-visual materials and equipment, and study tables. Branch libraries were established at the Squamish and Sechelt campuses.

Trinity Western University in Langley began as a junior college in 1962. It had seventeen students, seven professors and a librarian who looked after a shelf of books. But the private college grew rapidly. In 1965 a permanent library, with room for 200 students, was built, and an expansion in 1971 gave it room for 10,000 books. By the 1980s the institution had 100,000 books, and a new building was needed.

Selkirk College was opened in 1965 in the former construction camp of a new pulp mill. The library was in a former commissary. The college moved into its permanent quarters a few months later, although the library staff had to share space with college administrators until the administration building was completed in 1984.

Okanagan Regional College enrolled its first university

new system represented a huge step forward from the old microfilm-based Recordak photocharging systems and required huge investments.

Technology marched on. In 1970, UBC librarians at the Woodward Library and the science division were doing subject searches using the collection of magnetic tapes at the National Science Library in Ottawa. Two years later, the expanded Woodward Library was opened with a terminal connected to the U.S. National Library of Medicine's MEDLINE system, for online bibliographic searches in the health and life sciences.

In 1973, UBC opened its new $3.8-million Sedgewick Undergraduate Library. The library under the Main Mall provided seating capacity for 2,000 people and placed the facility close to the Main Library without destroying the mall's trees and lawns. The library won several awards, including the Royal Architectural Institute of Canada award as the finest building of 1972.

Colin William Fraser was director of the British Columbia Medical Library Service from 1961 to 1991. He started library services in thirty-two provincial hospitals, and consulted on medical and hospital library projects throughout British Columbia. He taught courses in librarianship in the field and at the University of British Columbia School of Librarianship. He was a founding member of the Health Libraries Association of British Columbia and a director of the British Columbia Library Association.

studies and career transfer students in 1968. The library opened in March 1969 in the common room of the Kelowna Senior Secondary School, but was soon moved to the main Kelowna campus. Branches were later established in Vernon, Salmon Arm and Osoyoos, then Revelstoke and Penticton.

From 1970 to 1974, the college was melded with the B.C. Vocational School. Okanagan College assumed responsibility for adult education programs. In 1979, the Kelowna library moved to a new building and was renamed in honour of Muriel Page Ffoulkes, the first public librarian in the valley.

Malaspina College opened in 1969 in part of the old Nanaimo regional hospital and moved to a site overlooking the city in 1974. Its library quickly evolved into a learning resources centre with audio-visual materials as well as books.

The College of New Caledonia opened in 1969 in Prince

George, and soon merged with the B.C. Vocational School there. The college's book collection was in the Prince George Senior Secondary library for three years, but in 1972 a portable building was erected on the college grounds to house the library. It was moved to a permanent building in 1978.

In Kamloops, Cariboo College opened in a temporary home, the former Kamloops Indian Residential School, in 1970, with thirty faculty serving 367 full-time and 200 part-time students. It moved to the hill above Kamloops in 1971. In 1976, with 109 full-time faculty serving 1,268 full-time and 1,330 part-time students, Cariboo College's library building was opened.

The Douglas College library was started in 1970, with three locations: New Westminster, Surrey and Richmond. Over the next few years, new branches were opened in Coquitlam, Langley, Newton and Maple Ridge.

Douglas College was split into two in 1981, with Kwantlen College serving the districts south of the Fraser River. In November 1982, the Coquitlam and New Westminster libraries were combined in a new building in New Westminster. Kwantlen College started with the libraries in Surrey, Richmond and Langley that had been established by Douglas College.

In 1971, the Institute of Adult Studies in Victoria became Camosun College, with 10,000 books handled by two librarians in the Young building, built in 1914 as the Provincial Normal School. In 1983 the library was moved to the Ewing Building and two years later a library was opened at the college's new Interurban campus.

Fraser Valley College was opened in 1974, with the

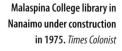

Malaspina College library in Nanaimo under construction in 1975. *Times Colonist*

librarian one of the first two full-time staff members hired. The library was started in a corner of a room above a doughnut shop in Clearbrook and in a section of a Chilliwack high school library. In time, proper libraries were developed and the college provided service to federal correctional facilities. Fraser Valley soon started a library technician school as part of its selection of courses.

The library at East Kootenay Community College was started in 1975 in temporary quarters. In 1982 the 20,000 books were moved to the college's new campus in Cranbrook. The college was renamed College of the Rockies in 1995.

Patti Barnes kept busy. It was not enough to be head librarian at Northwest Community College in Terrace; she also served on the board of the Terrace Public Library and helped establish the Terrace Women's Resources Centre and the North Coast Library Federation. She helped establish the federation's book-delivery system by piggy-backing on the college's delivery system. She was known for her passionate support of the community. Barnes died in April 2009. Six months later, all of the libraries in the North Coast Library Federation paid tribute to her during its annual library week.

Other community colleges started in 1975 included Northern Lights in Dawson Creek; Northwest in Terrace; and North Island in Courtenay and Campbell River. Libraries were essential to their success.

Royal Roads Military College got a dedicated library building in 1974. The Coronel Memorial Library had space for 80,000 books. The move from the old library was accomplished without boxes or professional help: Cadets carried armloads from the old library and deposited them in order on the shelves in the new library.

In the late 1970s, libraries in post-secondary institutions worked together to convert their catalogues to machine-readable form using UTLAS, University of Toronto Library Automated Systems. The catalogues were produced on microfiche, allowing easier access through branches as well as a sharp increase in inter-library loans.

The microfiche catalogue meant the end of card

catalogues. The UBC library, the largest in the province, no longer had to file a million new cards every year. Several public libraries — including Richmond Public Library, North Vancouver District Public Library and Burnaby Public Library — also took part in the microfiche program, with financial help from the provincial government.

Nelson's Notre Dame University enrolled up to 2,000 students in a variety of academic disciplines. Still, it had financial problems. In 1977, at the request of the Notre Dame board of directors, the province assumed control and closed the university for a year. When it reopened it was known as the David Thompson University Centre, under the administration of the University of Victoria. It closed again in 1984.

In 1978, the institution founded in 1925 as the Vancouver School of Decorative and Applied Arts became the Emily Carr College of Art. In 1980 it was moved to Granville Island and the name changed again, to Emily Carr College of Art and Design. Along with books, the college's library had vertical files, art exhibition catalogues and audio-visual materials.

In 1984, when Nelson's university was closed, local residents worried the library collection would be taken from their community. Five senior citizens and two students spent more than three months occupying the library to ensure it would remain in Nelson. The sit-in came to a successful end on July 30, 1984, when the government agreed the collection would remain in the community and open to the public. In 1992 items relating to the region were moved to the Kootenay Museum and Historical Society and the Nelson Municipal Library. In 2005 the library had to vacate the building and much of the collection was dispersed, going to community groups, post-secondary institutions and book dealers.

15

Books, Barcodes and Budgets

On February 1, 1982, a cool Monday, Vancouver Mayor Mike Harcourt walked up to the main desk at Vancouver Public Library's central branch at Robson and Burrard and handed over a book and his new library card. The flickering red line of a laser scanner read the barcodes on the card and on the book.

On the fourth floor, one of the library's four Digital Electronic Corporation PDP11-34 computers whirred, and stored the information about Harcourt's transaction on a plastic disc. The minicomputers cost more than $10,000 each and had less than one per cent of the processing power of an entry-level laptop computer

Opposite: Linda Fargher reads to her daughter Brittany beside the bay window in the children's department of the West Vancouver Memorial Library, 1980. *Glenn Baglo, Vancouver Sun*

Above: Fraser Valley Regional Library director Gordon Ray with book vans, old and new, in 1991. *Ian Lindsay, Vancouver Sun*

Judy Capes of the Vancouver Public Library shows the new barcodes on books and borrower's cards in 1981. *Colin Price, Vancouver Province*

libraries. And once again, the cutbacks came as library traffic increased, with patrons were looking for everything from employment leads to entertainment choices.

The *Vancouver Sun* argued in 1981 that since libraries had only two books for each resident, the government should provide more money to libraries. It said government funding had dropped in 1980 from 1979. Evan Wolfe, the minister responsible, countered that the government was actually increasing funding in a time of general restraint.

Wolfe was challenged in turn by Burnaby North MLA Eileen Dailly, who had been the minister of education in the New Democratic Party government in the early 1970s. She reminded readers that the government had abolished the Library Development Commission in 1978, along with provincial standards and the policy of encouraging strong regional library systems.

In 1980, the provincial government appointed a Library Advisory Committee to help the Library Services Branch, which had replaced the Library Development Commission. The committee's members were Ray Woods of Williams Lake; Dolly Kennedy of Vancouver; Steve Cribb of New Westminster; Don Porter of Delta; Daphne Scott of Prince Rupert; Mike Whittaker of Victoria and Mae Williams of Fernie. The advisory committee soon faded away.

That policy change had increased funding for some libraries at the expense of others. It was felt most severely in the Cariboo-Thompson-Nicola system, which received just $640,000 from the province in 1981, down from $1 million four years earlier. To cope, the system cut services, reduced hours at twenty-seven of its fifty branches, closed a library in the Valleyview area east of downtown Kamloops, and closed its film service.

To save money the library also halved the size of the North Kamloops branch, a move that became an issue in a 1981 byelection to replace MLA Rafe Mair. Even though the reduced library size was a result of Social Credit government cuts, the party rented the unused half as a campaign office. The New Democrats leapt at the chance to remind voters that the library was an example of the meanness of the government's austerity program. (It didn't work; Claude Richmond retained the seat for Social Credit.)

today, but they represented a major step forward for B.C.'s libraries.

Harcourt's library visit marked the official launch of the computerized effort to help the library track the books on its shelves and on loan. Vancouver was not the first public library in B.C. to have such a computer system — that honour went to West Vancouver — and it was certainly not the last. The systems introduced during the 1980s represented a great leap forward from the computer-generated catalogues on microfiche that had been leading edge just a few years earlier.

But while technology was bringing positive changes, a recession was bringing funding cuts and austerity to

The government increased library funding in the 1982 fiscal year, to $5.5 million from $3.4 million. It allocated $4 million for books and other library materials, to be disbursed on a per-capita basis. Additional grants of $8 per square mile were given to the four regionally organized libraries, which had higher costs because they served sparsely settled rural areas. Another $663,000 was to help libraries increase their use of computers.

But libraries were still hurting. To save money, the Greater Victoria system closed its branches on Mondays and parked its bookmobiles. There was still life in one of the vehicles; parked behind the Shop Easy grocery store on Cook Street and staffed by Fairfield Community Association members, it became the smallest branch in the system. The immobile bookmobile was popular at first, but circulation declined and it was closed in 1987.

In August 1984, the thirty-one branches in the Okanagan Regional Library system were closed for three weeks to save money. The closure, forced by a five-per-cent deficit in the $3-million operating budget, followed two years of service

Lesley Dieno started her career as a children's librarian in Windsor, Ontario. She came to British Columbia in 1974 to become the Richmond area manager in the Fraser Valley Regional Library, and moved in 1983 to Prince George to become its chief librarian. In August 1987 she became the executive director of the Okanagan Regional Library — only the third head librarian in the system's 75-year history. In her career there, she has helped the system introduce computers, upgrade branches and expand service.

cuts. Staff members were required to take vacations while the branches were closed. The closure had a positive side: It proved to the public that the library was an essential service.

The era of financial restraint also hit post-secondary libraries, which reduced their acquisition budgets and cut staff. In 1986, the University of British Columbia library stopped subscriptions to 900 journals, the third time it had

Enid Dearing served as the head librarian at North Vancouver District from 1964 to 1991. *Brian Kent, Vancouver Sun*

Jan Pruim passes through the security gate at the Greater Victoria Public Library's main branch in 1984. *John McKay, Times Colonist*

computers. These machines changed the face of libraries and of education itself. At UBC, students could do computer-assisted reference searches, while online bibliographic databases made life easier for librarians. In 1988, UBC introduced an online public catalogue with dial-up access from non-library locations. The library also started offering material on CD-ROM.

The arrival of computer systems in public and post-secondary libraries meant books no longer had cards in pockets; instead, they carried zebra codes similar to the ones on items in grocery stores. Unique numbers identified books and patrons. Libraries gave patrons cards with magnetic strips, and clerks at video-display terminals passed electronic wands over the cards to check account status. Computers kept track of books, and librarians could check catalogues in their own library and elsewhere. The transformations took time; the Vancouver Public Library spent eighteen months converting its collection.

Manual card catalogues were on their way to oblivion because patrons and librarians could use public access computer terminals instead. Librarians expressed hope that computers would make the catalogue more accessible. Some patrons had never been comfortable with the card catalogue, but were too shy to ask for help. They might be willing, however, to admit they couldn't figure out the computer. The technology also meant libraries could finally close an embarrassing information gap: If a book was not on the shelves, it had been almost impossible to determine who had it. Book possession was listed under the borrower's name, not under the book title.

Libraries had several computer systems to choose from, and they were not compatible. That meant patrons on the Lower Mainland had to carry more than one card if they used more than one library. Richmond patrons, for example, could use their cards in libraries in Vancouver, but not in Burnaby or West Vancouver. If they wanted to use the other libraries in the Greater Vancouver Library Federation, they would need a third card. The system chosen by West Vancouver and Burnaby — as well as Prince George and the Cariboo-Thompson-Nicola library — was homegrown, developed by Universal Library Services of West Vancouver. Dubbed Ulisys, the system was adopted by about thirty libraries in North America, including some of the biggest. In time, however, Ulisys faded away.

The transition was not always smooth. In September 1981, the Okanagan Regional Library took delivery of a Datapoint 6600 computer and a Centronics 6300 printer, but serious bugs meant the library could not order books for three months. Once in place, however, the system was

taken a hatchet to ongoing collections. The cuts had a lasting impact; it is virtually impossible to catch up once there has been a break in journal subscriptions.

Despite the restraints, there was a clear demand for library service. At the University of Victoria, a peaceful sit-in by forty students, as well as a 1,000-name petition, resulted in the addition of seven more operating hours every week.

During the bad times, money from the federal and provincial governments helped libraries to embrace

In October 1983, a statue of Terry Fox was unveiled at a new library in Port Coquitlam, part of the Fraser Valley system, which had been named in his honour. Fox died of cancer in 1981 after being forced to abandon his Marathon of Hope fundraising run. Private donors paid for the statue outside the main entrance to the $1.5 million library.

popular, and patrons could finally return a book to any branch in the system.

The Greater Victoria Public Library's $500,000 computer system went into operation in 1986 after two years of planning. The library had ten terminals in the central branch and additional terminals in its other branches. The system helped the library collect an extra $22,000 in fines in its first year, and also helped it determine which books were most popular. "It confirms on paper what most librarians who work with the collections know intuitively," said head librarian Madge Aalto.

Books popular in 1986 included *Borderline* by Janette Turner Hospital, *What's Bred in the Bone* by Robertson Davies, and anything by English romance writer Catherine Cookson.

Within a couple of years the Greater Victoria board spent $82,000 to upgrade the system with a second central processing unit. The original computer had been close to capacity. As soon as the library closed at night, it started reshuffling information, and it finished fifteen minutes before the doors opened the next morning.

Libraries were open to new ways to use technology. In 1980, for example, George Wootton, Vancouver's head librarian, envisioned the day patrons would be able to call the library on a telephone, place the handset in an electronic coupler, and receive detailed information on their television screens.

The Fraser Valley Regional Library set up an experimental telefacsimile service linked to the Vancouver

Public Library and paid for by the Library Services Branch, the successor to the Library Development Commission. For a small fee, documents and reports could be transmitted to the regional library, giving it access to materials not in its own collection.

"These books will not have to be duplicated in the Fraser Valley," said Jim Craven, Fraser Valley's executive director at the time. "It will provide a low-cost answer to the special needs of certain patrons, who up to now have not been able to find the depth in our library system that they wished was there." It was a fine theory, but did not work as well as hoped. Information transmission could be immediate, but the human involvement at either end meant that some requests took weeks to fill.

In Victoria in 1983, library patrons said hello to LUCY, a videotext computer directory of local clubs, societies and organizations. LUCY — for Loosely Unorganized Community Yakety-Yak — hung out at the main desk of the downtown branch.

Another form of new technology was the CD-ROM. In 1987, the Richmond Public Library got a fully electronic encyclopedia with 10,000 pages of printed text from twenty-one printed volumes stored on just twenty per cent of a compact disc. The technology was, according to the *Province*, mind-boggling: You could enter your own birth date and get a list of other people born on that day.

The Richmond library embraced technology. Along with the CD-ROMs, it had a fully computerized catalogue with touch-screen terminals, a computer centre with three

Top left: Madge Aalto served as head librarian in Greater Victoria from 1983 to 1988, and Vancouver from 1988 to 2003. *Vancouver Sun*

Above: In May 1981, Sarah Ellis and Judi Saltman wore hats to entertain children at Vancouver Public Library's Dunbar branch. *Ken Oakes, Vancouver Sun*

Apple IIe and two IBM computers, printers and 240 software programs. It also launched a dial-up system so people at home or school could use modems to search the library catalogue.

In the late 1980s, libraries started offering videocassettes. A 1987 survey in Greater Victoria showed more people would use the library if educational videocassettes were offered. Many people had players, but not many had access to educational material. The only videocassette at the Greater Victoria library at the time was a free film on AIDS produced by the provincial government.

By the next year, patrons could choose from 222 videos, including how-to programs such as cooking, gardening and home repair as well as documentaries, travel, sports, arts, culture and children's titles. The collection did not include feature films, and was only available at the central branch. Most cassettes cost the library between $40 and $50, although the BBC Shakespeare performances had a price of $100.

Hundreds of videos were also available at three branches of the Vancouver Public Library, with an emphasis on instructional and educational titles. Vancouver already offered films and microfilms at selected branches. The six largest libraries also had collections of audiobooks produced by the Library Services Branch, donated in 1981 to mark the International Year of Disabled Persons.

Videocassettes, audiocassettes and phonograph records were never as popular as what came next: CDs and DVDs. Many libraries reported a sharp increase in music and movie loans when these discs became available.

Another major shift was the arrival of literature written for young adults. Starting slowly in the 1970s, more writers were producing books aimed at the people who had outgrown the children's room but were not quite ready for the adult sections. The young adult category exploded in popularity, growing to contain a wide variety of genres. In many cases, these books are more sophisticated and mature than adult books.

In 1987, Culture Minister Bill Reid announced that a task force, created at the request of the Union of B.C. Municipalities and the B.C. Library Trustees Association, would review public library funding and organization, the Library Services Branch and opportunities for joint development. It was the first comprehensive review since the early 1970s.

The report from the seven-member task force — *B.C.'s*

Public Libraries, a New Approach — arrived on Reid's desk in May 1988, and stressed the need to "encourage the development of a strong library in each community and a co-operative approach among all libraries." That would require, the report said, local commitment and initiative, coupled with provincial support, leadership and coordination.

The report said rural patrons deserved the same access to information as city dwellers. It recommended that all public libraries, including small community ones, provide free basic service, and proposed the establishment of a library trust to receive donations and bequests. It recommended that the Library Services Branch close its field offices because modern communications and improved transportation links had made them obsolete. It recommended that Open Shelf, the books-by-mail program, be phased out. It also said the government should end its bulk loans — the travelling libraries.

Ken Haycock came to British Columbia in 1976 as the coordinator of library services for the Vancouver School Board. Later he led the University of British Columbia's School of Library, Archival and Information Studies, and served as president of the Canadian Library Association and the Canadian Association for School Libraries. He has served on the West Vancouver School Board, on West Vancouver council, and on the board of the West Vancouver Memorial Library. He was the author of the 2003 report on school libraries, *The Crisis in School Libraries: The Case for Reform and Re-Investment.*

In response, the Library Services Branch merged its Dawson Creek office with the one in Prince George. Dawson Creek's books were dispersed to the other branch offices and libraries in the Peace. In 1995, the Cranbrook and Prince George offices were closed.

Over the next few years Open Shelf was wound down, with much of the collection given to penitentiaries to support training and literacy programs. Open Shelf had turned over much of its work to the regional libraries in 1985, but still distributed 34,000 books in 1986-87. The service ended in 1995 after seventy-three years. The

In August 1988, a burst water main caused a flood in the basement of the main branch of the Vancouver library, where some of the library's most treasured items were stored. The water flowed for about ten minutes, dumping 46,000 gallons into the stacks. The library had to be closed so staff members could work on a massive cleanup. Not everything in the basement could be saved, but quick action — and freeze-drying — saved many precious books.

One major loss was a collection of bound volumes of the *Vancouver Sun*, dating to the newspaper's earliest days. It did not mean the information was lost, however, because the back issues were still available in several libraries on microfilm.

travelling libraries were phased out after almost a century. The Library Services Branch also started winding down the book acquisition service it performed on behalf of small libraries.

In 1989-90, the government's annual grant to public libraries amount to $7.2 million. The strategy was quite different from the books-only theory embraced a decade earlier. Funding was not tied to book acquisitions; boards were authorized to spend the money as they chose. The Library Services Branch assisted through funding, consultation, training, inter-library loans, special collections and technical services. It provided audiobooks, large print books, French books, books in foreign languages, adult literacy materials, professional library science publications and training support materials. The branch promoted the use of public libraries. It was a role that could only be performed by a provincial coordinating body.

Its financial assistance came in many forms. Grants ranged from $1.60 per capita in large cities to $3.20 per capita for small, remote areas. Consolidated libraries got $3.30 for each square kilometre served. The Greater Vancouver Library Federation received $200,000. The B.C. Library Association and the B.C. Library Trustees Association were given $25,000 each, and the trustees received another $40,000 to develop a trustee training program. The branch also sent libraries the last payments from a $3 million fund that had helped them introduce computers.

Some grants were narrowly targeted. The branch gave the BCLA $5,000 to support publishers' attendance at the annual conference in Penticton, $2,000 for the publication of standards for children's libraries and $2,000 for the development of a display on intellectual freedom. It provided

$4,647 to support the secondment of six library employees to train people at other libraries. Another $10,165 went to twenty-three libraries where B.C. writers offered readings and workshops. A grant to *B.C. Bookworld* magazine supported publication of a directory of B.C. writers.

The renewed interest in libraries led to a government discussion paper in 1990, followed by a public review process in 1993 and a new Library Act in January 1994. The act prohibited boards from charging for basic service and called for free membership to public libraries and free use of materials. The act specified that any new library must be established as a municipal library or as a regional library district. Existing public library associations and integrated library systems were allowed to continue, but no new ones would be allowed.

The act also ended school trustees' involvement in regional libraries; regional district representatives took their places. Library board terms were aligned to the three-year terms of councils and regional district boards, with a three-term limit, and board members became subject to conflict-of-interest laws.

The government continued to encourage collaboration and there were signs of success. In 1992, the Greater Vancouver Library Federation was expanded into InterLINK, which included more libraries, most notably the Fraser Valley regional system. InterLINK's goal was to provide free access to all local libraries. It removed barriers that prevented someone in Surrey, for example, from borrowing a book in Burnaby.

Left: Bob Tharalson of the Vancouver library staff fishes for books after the great flood of 1988. *Vancouver Province*

Nancy Hannum has fought for years for equality of access to information, especially for those who have been marginalized because of culture, race, economic factors, disability, geographic location or other factors. As head librarian at the Legal Resource Centre of the Legal Services Society of B.C., she brought increased access to statutes and legal information to people throughout the province. She helped found the First Nations Interest Group of the British Columbia Library Association and PovNet, an Internet site for people on welfare and for advocates involved in anti-poverty work, and helped create LawMatters, a community outreach program of Courthouse Libraries B.C. that is available through local public libraries. She also served as the BCLA's president.

Vancouver librarian Eleanor Kelly had a regular route through the Downtown Eastside, where she would go in search of books. The Carnegie Centre branch did not charge fines or require a library card, but many patrons still had trouble getting books back. Kelly's pub crawl was through a rough neighbourhood that had the lowest literacy rate in the city, although many people there were fans of western, science fiction and mystery paperbacks. The branch also catered to adult students learning to read and write upstairs at the Carnegie Learning Centre, and had a large collection of Chinese-language books. "They don't always have ID to get a card, so they just give us their name," said Kelly, who retired in 1997.. About 30 per cent of the collection disappeared every year, compared to about five per cent in other branches. The Carnegie branch was funded by the city social planning department but run by the Vancouver Public Library, and is open every day.

Right: Eleanor Kelly from the Vancouver Public Library's Carnegie Centre chats with a client on the Downtown Eastside in 1993. Jeff Vinnick, Vancouver Sun

Efforts were made to extend library service to people in First Nations communities and on Indian reserve lands, which in several urban areas saw an increasing number of non-native residents. In some cases, libraries made financial deals with the bands, although it other cases access has been provided for free.

The era brought major changes to library buildings and even the clientele. The old Carnegie library at Hastings and Main in Vancouver was the subject of intensive efforts by residents of the Downtown Eastside and their supporters. After sitting unused for twelve years, the building was reopened in January 1980 as a community centre for the people in the poorest neighbourhood in Canada.

The centre included a Vancouver Public Library branch, which offered a reading room with 7,000 paperback books. Over the years, the collection has grown to 11,000 books, most of them paperback. The Carnegie Centre branch has relaxed rules to encourage reading. Patrons are allowed, for example, to take books even if they can't prove who they are or where they live. There are limits — drug and alcohol use is banned, and impaired patrons are asked to leave.

The $2-million restoration included major structural changes to meet modern building codes, but the old library retained the dome, spiral marble staircase and stained glass windows that helped make it a landmark in 1903. Designed to serve as an alternative to beer parlours and drug use, the centre was opened with a lounge, exercise room, public washrooms and showers, a cafeteria, a gymnasium, classrooms and a daycare centre in addition to two auditoriums.

A few months after Vancouver's Carnegie library was reborn, the Greater Victoria Public Library closed its Carnegie building. The central branch moved to a building on Broughton Street that offered twice the space. Several options were considered for the old library. Bookstore owner Jim Munro wanted the original building, while the city archives looked at the 1950s addition as a possible home. In the end, the building was sold to a credit union.

Merchants on Yates Street were not happy to lose the library, saying the street started to decline when the library moved away. They later tried to have a library included in a redevelopment proposal. The City of Victoria used the money from the Carnegie sale to upgrade the Royal Theatre, and for many years leased the Broughton Street location of the new central library building. The library bought the property for $5 million in 1995.

Another significant building, opened in 1991, was the Bob Prittie Metrotown Library, which increased the size of the Burnaby system by seventy-eight per cent. The opening of the 61,000-square-foot branch enabled the library to move 80,000 books out of storage. The Metrotown branch was the largest freestanding public library building to open in B.C. in thirty years — although, with a new Vancouver central branch being planned, that record would not last long.

❧

British Columbia's post-secondary system continued to expand in more places than ever before. New libraries were needed to meet the demand. A notable addition at the University of British Columbia was the Asian Studies Library. In Merritt, the Nicola Valley Institute of Technology was created to address low participation and success rates of First Nations students.

Most academic libraries aim for ever-expanding collections, but sometimes common sense dictates that some books should go. In 1985, Simon Fraser University discarded 20,000 books that were rarely used, sending them to wherever they might be of use. Some of the books had never been taken out of the library since it opened in 1965.

In 1989, three colleges — Malaspina, Cariboo and Okanagan — become university colleges to expand degree opportunities outside the Lower Mainland and Victoria. The colleges changed their names to reflect their new status, becoming Okanagan University College, the University College of the Cariboo, and Malaspina University College. The next year, the government created the University of Northern British Columbia in Prince George, and in 1991, Fraser Valley College was converted into a university college. Langara College was formed as a separate institution from Vancouver Community College in 1994, and in 1995 Kwantlen College became a university college. University colleges and two institutions — the B.C. Institute of Technology and the Emily Carr Institute of Art and Design — were all given independent degree granting authority. These changes all resulted in better, and busier, libraries.

Royal Roads Military College near Victoria, which granted its first bachelor's degrees in 1975, was closed in 1995. The site became Royal Roads University, an institution aimed at working professionals.

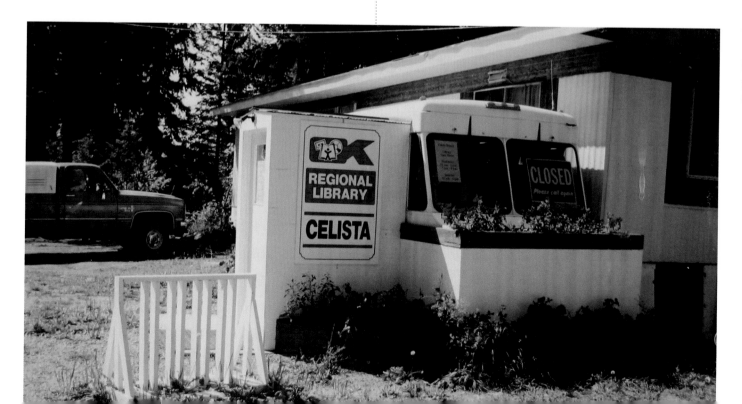

When the Okanagan Regional Library parked its bookmobiles in 1992, Celista gained a library branch.
Okanagan Regional Library

16

FIGHTING FOR INTELLECTUAL FREEDOM

L ois Bewley was working at the literature desk in the Vancouver Public Library when a police officer arrived, ready to take a book off the shelves. The offending title was Henry Miller's *Tropic of Cancer*, which included several graphic descriptions of sex. The book had been banned at the border. It was 1961.

"I remember this Mountie creaking of leather appearing before me, demanding all the copies of it," Bewley says. "I said we should have a look and see what was on the shelf and we did. There was nothing there. The only copy was a circulating copy at my knees, under the desk, waiting to be picked up by the person who had asked for it. I thought, I'm damned if I'll give you a book."

Opposite: Part of the Greater Victoria Freedom to Read display in 2010. *Greater Victoria Public Library*

Above: *Adrian Raeside*

As the saying goes, there is something in the library to offend everyone. Most librarians are proud of the role they play in getting information into the hands of readers — even though not all patrons are happy about it. But a library is not a censor; its role is to provide a wide variety of views on a wide variety of topics to a wide variety of people.

Bewley, who went on to a lengthy career as a professor at the University of British Columbia, says the *Tropic of Cancer* incident sparked her interest in censorship and the role of the Criminal Code in the selection of material for public libraries. Thirty years later, she became the first chair of the Intellectual Freedom, Education and Defence Fund, created by the B.C. Library Association to fight challenges to the right to information.

Lois Bewley in 1972.
Vancouver Sun

Lois Bewley became a faculty member at the University of British Columbia's School of Library, Archival and Information Studies in 1969. She has taught and written extensively about public libraries, library legislation, library architecture and intellectual freedom. She served as president of the B.C. Library Association and the Canadian Library Association. In 1988 she was given the BCLA's highest honour, the Helen Gordon Stewart Award, "in recognition of outstanding lifetime achievement in librarianship in British Columbia."

Intellectual freedom is the freedom of opinion and expression, and it is guaranteed to all Canadians under the Charter of Rights and Freedoms. Bewley says librarians must be increasingly on guard to protect it. "The barbarians are not just at the gates, they are in our communities, and they are in our libraries. And that is the reason for the creation of this fund and this is the reason we must stand as a line in defence against those barbarians."

The determined stand taken by librarians over intellectual freedom has evolved over the years. In 1938 the American Library Association adopted the Library Bill of Rights in reaction to censorship in totalitarian states. Concern grew in the early 1950s, when McCarthyism raged and librarians fought for the right of their patrons to read books about Communism if they chose. As librarians faced increasing challenges, they adopted strong position statements on a local, provincial and national basis.

The censorship fight will probably never end; what is innocent to one person is blasphemous to another. Should a magazine be removed because of one photograph, or a book because of one paragraph? Many complaints have been made about materials dealing with sexuality or containing sexual content, but racism, religion and drug use also trigger protests. Children's books can also be a sensitive topic.

Every year, libraries receive complaints or challenges about what is on their shelves. The fight for intellectual freedom is defensive; libraries respond to protests about the availability of information. Bewley, who chaired the Vancouver Public Library's fiction committee in the early 1960s, says a "sexual pre-selection" helped limit the number of complaints. Controversy was avoided because controversial material was not purchased. Every library makes choices about what to acquire, but ideally, the decisions are based on which materials should be made available, not on which ones should be restricted.

That does not suit all library patrons. "Sometimes they come back horrified and state we have no business to keep such books on our shelves," Margaret Brunette said in 1958, when she was head of the Vancouver Public Library's extension department. Brunette said that if a borrower complained, the librarian would try to show a variety of books, and explain that some readers might benefit from the selection.

At the time, several books were kept behind the counter, some because they were too valuable to leave on the open shelves, but most because they mentioned sex. Eric Partridge's *Dictionary of Slang* was exiled because it contained words considered inappropriate. "I would have thought you had to know the dirty word first to look it up," Bewley says.

It became easier to find things to complain about in the early 1900s when libraries opened their stacks and patrons could browse at will. In 1906, complaints about racy French novels prompted Vancouver library trustee James H. MacGill, a lawyer, to offer to read the books to determine if they were suitable. He soon declared them indecent, immoral and filthy, and hinted that the task of reading the books had robbed him of the pleasure of Vancouver's summer weather. "The books are not fit to be on the shelves of the library," he said. They stayed on the shelves.

Concerns were raised in Victoria in 1908. Alderman William J. Hanna asked that the book *The Decameron*, a fourteenth-century work with bawdy tales, be removed from the library.

"Certainly not," replied Alderman Thornton Fell, a member of Victoria's library board. "This book, which is a relic of the first Victoria public library, has been in circulation for twenty-five years, and it is certainly late in the day to discover that it is unfit to read." The book has endured. Today, the same library has *The Decameron* in print and as a talking book.

In 1913, the Victoria library had a complaint that some poetry in the children's section was more suitable to American children than Canadian children. "There are verses which are calculated to exalt the United States above the rest of the world," the *Daily Colonist* reported, but added that people were being too sensitive.

In 1922, after James Joyce's *Ulysses* was banned in Canada because of its explicit language, the Victoria Public Library locked the book in its vault — and left it there until 1949, when it was put on the open shelves.

Most complaints over the years have been aimed at public and school libraries; post-secondary institutions have usually escaped criticism. One exception came in 1927, when the University of British Columbia library deemed one work — the title is no longer known — unfit for general circulation. In the same year, a department head argued that certain works by Sigmund Freud should be segregated.

In 1937, the International Cultural Promotion Association of Japan offered ninety-seven books to the Fraser Valley library board, but the board sent them back. "The library should not accept such a gift from a country which at the moment is spending millions of dollars in trying to cultivate or maintain international good-will while at the same time waging ruthless war on defenceless women and children," the board decided.

In any event, head librarian Charles Keith Morison determined the books were of "comparatively little value." Since only about half a dozen were worth having, it was deemed unfair to the donors to accept the collection.

Censorship was sometimes not that formal. In Cranbrook in 1937, a library patron borrowed John Steinbeck's *Of Mice and Men*, decided it was not the kind of book that should be read, and destroyed it. The library association ruled it was not up to the library to censor reading material, and asked for $1.70 to cover the cost of replacing the book. The patron paid.

> Once you start limiting what people can have access to, it is very difficult to make those decisions and you put librarians in the role of being a censor rather than providing access.
> *Brian Campbell, librarian*

Libraries try to promote books that might open minds. In 1946, the Public Library Commission noted, the library in Nelson "made a point of recommending any books that will help to break race prejudice, and even fostered a discussion group of teenagers, who have held some exceedingly lively conversations on inter-racial justice and true democracy."

If anyone thought that the choice of reading material did not matter, twenty-two-year-old Harry Medos set them straight. The resident of Oakalla's death row told Rev. W.H. Ross MacPherson that his "start down" the road to ruin was gangster films and cheap detective magazines. Medos continued to read detective stories until October 1, 1947, when he was taken to the gallows for killing a Vancouver police officer in a gunfight.

The Public Library Commission argued crime films and magazines were popular because of the lack of libraries. "News-stands, cigar-stands, drug-stores, and hole-in-the-corner shops abound in the cheap and the tawdry and cater to the youth in an aggressive manner."

The Provincial Parent-Teacher Association wanted cheap fiction and comics censored, but the library commission felt that would not work. "Immediately there develops an 'under-the-counter trade' which is more dangerous than the present system of selling openly. To want what is forbidden is only human nature, and whether it is cheap literature, cheap liquor or Communism, suppression is no solution." The commission pointed out that public libraries offered the most potent antidote to cheap literature.

In 1948, there was concern about crime comic books from Toronto. Canadian import regulations had cut off the supply from the United States, where 250 titles were available, but seventy were being published in Toronto. The Victoria and District Council of the Parent-Teacher Association said crime comic books were "a great menace to the character and development of our children." It said the books "make violence, sadism and crime seem attractive, ignore common morals, and appeal chiefly to the worst in human nature. Certain crime comics ridicule law and order and in our opinion are undemocratic."

Coarse language has prompted book bans. Norman Mailer's *The Naked and the Dead*, a story about the Second World War, was banned in 1949 even though "fug" had been used in place of a similar word.

In 1950, books about sex were kept under lock and key at the Victoria Public Library — for their own protection. Head librarian Margaret Jean Clay said opponents burned them as heretical literature. Clay said the library would like to have the books on open shelves, but to keep the peace and cut costs, kept them locked up.

At Victoria College, Professor E.G. Jones said people were so shy about sex matters they would rather steal a book on the topic than be seen checking it out of the library. These people, he said, had never received proper sex instruction during their youth.

There was a controversy in schools in the early 1950s because of the *Effective Living* curriculum guide. The section entitled Family and Effective Living had information on dating, courtship, engagements, the goodnight kiss, and wearing a boy's or girl's pin. Some parents called the guide a "sexual textbook" that was immoral and sinister, and said parents, not teachers, should tell children about sex. The debate helped establish the role of sex education in B.C. schools.

In 1959, the Vancouver library did not have *Peyton Place*, which dealt with adultery, abortion and incest, because it had not been allowed into Canada. But it did have thirty-four copies of *Lolita*, the story of a middle-aged man's love affair with a twelve-year-old girl. The book had been banned in England and taken out of circulation by the libraries in Windsor and Hamilton. "We are not censors," a library spokesman said. "Whether a book remains on our shelves or not is not based on its subject matter but on the quality of its writing. If the writing is good and meets our standards it goes on the shelves."

The Decameron was not the only vintage title to create a stir long after publication. In 1960, the Vancouver Public Library finally moved the seventeen-volume Sir Francis Burton translation of *The Arabian Nights* to its open shelves. Jack Wasserman, a columnist in the *Vancouver Sun*, suggested that the books needed plain brown wrappers because they would "curl a call girl's hair." He noted with delight that the books were catalogued under the heading of Games, Sports and Amusements.

In 1960, the unexpurgated edition of the D.H. Lawrence book *Lady Chatterley's Lover* was made available in Canada for the first time, thirty-three years after it was first published in Italy. After copies were seized in Montreal, a Quebec court ruled the book obscene. Before that ruling was struck down by the Supreme Court of Canada in 1962, Victoria book dealers said that the ban had prompted an increase in sales. The Victoria library had four copies of the book, but they were revised versions from the 1930s that did not have the offending passages. Librarian John C. Lort said there was less demand for the title than for books on boat-building and gardening. "This could be an indication that Victorians generally are less interested in sex books than other cities," he said.

> I want to congratulate librarians, not famous for their physical strength, who, all over this country, have staunchly resisted anti-democratic bullies who have tried to remove certain books from their shelves, and destroyed records rather than have to reveal to thought police the names of persons who have checked out those titles.
> *Kurt Vonnegut, author*

Sometimes disputes were about quality. In the 1960s, when an Ontario mother launched a campaign to ban the Bobbsey Twins from schools, librarians in Vancouver reacted calmly. "We don't have the Bobbsey books in our public libraries or in our school libraries," said Isabel McTavish, the head children's librarian at Vancouver Public Library. "We try to buy the best children's books and they don't fit on that basis."

In 1964, Helen Bannerman's children's classic *Little Black Sambo* was removed from the open shelves at Vancouver Public Library after a complaint that it was racist. The book was still available, but by request only.

Other books for children were pulled for safety reasons. In 1969, Public Library Commission superintendent Robert Davison sent this warning to all the libraries in the province: "An experiment described in *Safe and Simple Projects With Electricity*, published by Children's Press, is excessively dangerous and in fact illegal in this province. The experiment is on pages 42-45. It describes a hot dog cooker which uses 'line voltage,' i.e. the source of energy available from ordinary receptacles in residential buildings.

The provincial chief electrical inspector requests that all libraries be advised to either remove the pages concerned or obliterate the description of the experiment."

The interest in sex seemed to be timeless. In the 1970s, books dealing with pornography, sexual relations, birth control, courtship and free love were the most likely to be stolen from libraries. They were being stolen from the University of Victoria at the rate of about nineteen per cent a year, compared to one per cent a year for the library as a whole.

In March 1977, school trustees in the Central Okanagan refused to remove *Kane and Abel* from secondary school libraries, despite a complaint that it was pornographic. They removed *For All the Wrong Reasons*, but said it was because the book was dated, not because of pornography. A national organization had complained about both of the books.

Later, a B.C. Supreme Court judge ruled that a Prince George mother did not have the right to go to a high school library to examine books she wanted banned. The mother was upset about *Boys and Sex*, which she said promoted promiscuity, and worried there might be other questionable titles. The judge said he did not want a school's activities disrupted — but told the woman that if she wanted to look at what was available, she was free to use a public library, or buy the book at a store.

Complaints were also made about *The Rapist File*, a book that included interviews with fifteen rapists who said they delighted in torturing women. The books were kept on most library shelves despite protests in Toronto.

In 1978, the Richmond school board banned *Go Ask Alice*, a book about a fifteen-year-old drug addict who dies after an overdose. The concern was that the book could encourage young people to use drugs. After they were removed from the schools, the books were turned over to the Richmond Public Library, which made them available to its patrons.

Playboy magazine caused a stir in the Fraser Valley in 1979, when Matsqui Mayor Harry de Jong led a fight to have the magazine removed from library shelves. "Magazines of this kind are equal to some of the movies provided on the television screen which are in bad taste and not appreciated by the majority," he said.

Ted Dunn, from the Agassiz-Harrison school district, said "salacious and obscene publications imported into Canada produce financial benefit to criminal organizations outside Canada" and that "many parents, women's organizations and school groups consider that the public display of photographs of male and female genitalia, either separately or in deliberately contrived lustful and lascivious

juxtaposition is offensive to the eye." He wanted every work of fiction and every periodical to be screened to identify the pornographic ones.

Langley Alderman Elford Nundal opposed a ban. "I would be very concerned indeed if our intellectual freedom was stamped out as in Germany and Italy during the war, and more recently in countries like Uganda and Russia," he said, adding that libraries should provide materials from all points of view and should not encroach on intellectual freedom.

Library board chairman D.A. Porter told the *Coquitlam Enterprise* that the only solution would be to read all 450,000 books on the shelves, as well as the 60,000 books added every year. "We have complaints about the four-letter words in the Bible, complaints about the *Ladies Home Journal* and other sexist publications and complaints about the poor literary quality of many paperbacks," he said.

The board finally decided in 1980 against banning *Playboy*. It took more than a year to reach the decision, even though only five libraries in the system carried the magazine, and the total cost of the subscriptions was just $60. The Vancouver Public Library had about 10 copies of *Playboy*, and argued that it carried quality articles and interviews with prominent people. Libraries in Surrey had stopped carrying the magazine in 1976 because it was stolen so often.

The most unusual censorship of the era resulted from the colour of a swimming pool. After it was published in 1981, Peter C. Newman's *The Acquisitors* faced a possible ban after a lawsuit was filed by a Toronto couple. The book said that a socialite had wanted the bottom of her pool to be the same shade of blue as her chauffeur's uniform. The publisher agreed to black out the identifying information with a marker pencil.

Librarians supported Little Sisters Book and Art Emporium, a Vancouver store which deals in literature for gays and lesbians, when the store ran into trouble with Canada Customs in 1985. Fifteen years later, the Supreme Court of Canada ruled that the shop had suffered "excessive and unnecessary prejudice" at the hands of Customs officers.

The problems began when 548 books and seventy-seven magazines ordered by the store for resale were seized by Customs, which said they were obscene. When the items were released months later, they were in such bad condition they could not be sold. After that, Little Sisters had to cope with seizures of other books, including one on northwest coast Indian legends that was sold in mainstream stores. A package sent from a domestic publisher in Ontario was diverted to Customs and inspected.

Little Sisters filed suit in B.C. Supreme Court against the

government in 1990. The court ruled against the store, as did the Court of Appeal. The case ended up in the Supreme Court of Canada, which ruled in 2000 that Little Sisters had been treated unfairly. Seven years later, the court ruled that Ottawa did not have to pay the store's legal bills, saying the censorship fight was not of enough public importance. Federal lawyers estimated the case — which had become known as Little Sisters vs. Big Brother — had cost about $2 million.

In 1992, *Sex* was hot. Madonna's provocative 128-page book, a collection of picture and print fantasies, was spiral-backed with metal covers. *Sex* once again raised questions about morality and censorship and children having access to adult books. Every library that obtained a copy of *Sex* had to deal with questions and complaints.

Burnaby kept it on the reference shelves, for viewing in the library only. The Vancouver Public Library had 110 holds on the book before it arrived, but the book was not universally loved. "One runs out of righteous indignation after a while," said Rev. Bernice Gerard, a former Vancouver city councillor. "It seems to me to be so emphatically pornographic. I have not seen the book itself, but I have read some of the descriptions of the book. I just thought it was so pathetic, we've gotten down to the dregs." Vancouver's Catholic archdiocese wanted the book removed from public libraries.

In Kelowna, two anti-pornography groups attended a meeting of the Okanagan Regional Library board for the chance to label *Sex* as "filth." The board agreed to review its acquisition policies, but in the meantime kept Madonna's book in circulation. Three months later, it concluded that there was nothing wrong with its policies and that there was a place for *Sex* in the library system. By that time, 250 people were asking to borrow the book. Executive director Lesley Dieno said it would take four years to meet all of the requests.

In late 1993, librarians were told to censor newspapers with scissors to avoid violating court-ordered bans on media coverage of the Karla Homolka manslaughter trial in Ontario. The ban was imposed in July to ensure that members of the public and potential jurors did not read articles in foreign newspapers that might violate the publication ban.

The ban could not be enforced outside of Canada, so details of the case were published in newspapers such as *USA Today* and the *Washington Post*. The ban also led to problems for police and Customs officials as they tried to ensure that magazines and newspapers that might violate the ban did not cross the border. "It doesn't fit with what public libraries are all about, which is making information available," said Lee Teal, the head of the Greater Victoria Public Library.

In 1995, *The New Joy of Gay Sex* was pulled from the library in North Kamloops as the result of a complaint. It was kept at the administration centre of the Thompson-Nicola library system, and made available by special request. The book had been on the shelves for two years before the complaint was received.

In 1997, a complaint in Winnipeg about *Women on Top: How Real Life Has Changed Women's Sexual Fantasies* prompted the RCMP to check for the book in public libraries on Vancouver Island, in Sparwood and in Merritt. Only Merritt had the book, and the librarians refused to let the police take it. Police decided to forget about it after they spoke to several librarians. "They are more qualified than the RCMP to determine what is on the shelf," RCMP Staff Sergeant Peter Montague said.

In 1997, Surrey school trustees banned three books featuring gay parents. *Asha's Moms*, *Belinda's Bouquet* and *One Dad, Two Dads, Brown Dad, Blue Dads* became a concern because a primary teacher had used the books in a class and was told by the principal that they would need to be approved by trustees.

"We strongly believe in the importance of having a wide range of books available for children," said Sybil Harrison of the B.C. Library Association. "There are probably lots of same-sex parents and families and they need information and stories that represent their point of view and existence." The three books were available in the children's section of the downtown Vancouver Public Library, which had nine books with gay or lesbian parents.

Parents, civil liberties groups and authors joined forces to protest the decision and took the matter to the B.C. Supreme Court. The court ruled against the Surrey school board in 1998, but the Court of Appeal overturned the ruling in 2000. In 2002, the Supreme Court of Canada declared that a ban had no place in the school system. In 2003, the school board once again banned the books, after spending six years and $1 million in a losing defence of its original ban.

Freedom of expression — or, on the other hand, censorship — comes in many forms. It can deal with materials, meetings held in libraries or with the activities of librarians.

The University of British Columbia faced a censorship debate in 1977 over the actions of one of its librarians, Allen Soroka, the previous fall. Soroka had been one of about 250 people who disrupted a series of three speeches given by South African politician Harry Schwarz. He was the only one singled out for punishment.

The argument was that Soroka, a reference librarian in the law library who was not on the job at the time of the protest, had interfered with freedom of speech. He countered that any wrongdoing had taken place outside the jurisdiction of the university — and he was being singled out because of his support for the Communist Party of Canada (Marxist-Leninist).

Soroka also argued that he should have freedom to protest, just as others had freedom of speech. In the end, the university placed a letter of reprimand in his file, which did nothing to resolve the question of competing freedoms. Soroka remained with the law library until he retired in 2001 — and then came back as an adjunct professor in the law faculty.

In 1989 Salman Rushdie's *The Satanic Verses* was front-page news. Iran's Ayatollah Khomeini objected to Rushdie's depiction of Islam, and issued a death threat against him. Canada Customs halted the book at the border, even though it had been available in Canada for six months. Every public library in the Lower Mainland had copies of the book, and every copy was out. Brian Campbell, the chair of the B.C. Library Association's Intellectual Freedom Committee, said judgments by Customs officials were "not made simply on the basis of the material but also on whether it is the Vancouver Public Library, Duthie Books or Little Sisters Book Store who happens to be importing the item."

Sometimes programming can cause problems. In 1995, the Vancouver Public Library had a photo exhibit on the 1945 atomic bombing of Hiroshima. The exhibit, which had been shown at the Smithsonian in Washington, D.C., was graphic, and opened the week before the fiftieth anniversary of Victory in Japan Day. It prompted a backlash from veterans.

Libraries have had other problems as they sought the right balance between freedom of speech and Canadian law. In 1998, the Greater Victoria Public Library board rented a room to the Canadian Free Speech League, despite protests from the Jewish Federation of Victoria and Vancouver Island that the league promoted the hatred of Jews. The board policy was that groups renting space had to agree not to break the Criminal Code. The league did not appear to have a record of violence or promotion of hate, so the meeting was allowed.

In 2009, the Vancouver Public Library refused to rent space for a workshop dealing with assisted suicide because counselling people to end their lives would violate the law. Once again, it raised the question of the library's role in controversial issues and its responsibility to initiate dialogue.

The arrival of Internet access in libraries in the 1990s posed a new problem, because the belief in intellectual freedom applies to computer access as well. People have a right to view what they choose to view, but in a library, their choices might be seen by other people, including children.

Libraries have dealt with the issue in different ways. Some filter content with mixed results — blocking access

In 2003, Brian Campbell, the chair of the B.C. Library Association's Intellectual Freedom Committee, received the Canadian Library Association's top award for outstanding service to librarianship. The award honoured Campbell's work with information policy and intellectual freedom. In 2006 he received the Helen Gordon Stewart award, the BCLA's top honour. Campbell led the introduction of technology to libraries, but devoted much of his career to ensuring that marginalized people had access to libraries and information. He instigated the Working Together Project, which helped connect vulnerable people with library services.

to searches for "breast," for example, would also stop someone from researching "breast cancer." Some have tried to convince patrons interested in pornography to leave, and others have shut down their Internet service when a patron was noticed looking at a porn site. Others have installed privacy screens or partitions or have carefully placed computers to ensure patrons can get their clicks in private.

"Access to the Internet in libraries is for everyone," Sybil Harrison of the B.C. Library Association said in 1997. "It is provided freely, without judgment as to whether someone's particular search is appropriate."

British Columbia's libraries take part in Freedom to Read Week every February. The special week, which was started in the 1980s, encourages Canadians to think about and reaffirm their commitment to intellectual freedom.

The Freedom of Expression Committee of the Book and Periodical Council organizes the week. It also monitors censorship problems and produces an information kit on issues of intellectual freedom. The council is the umbrella organization for associations involved in producing, selling and lending books and periodicals in Canada.

Lois Bewley maintains that librarians must take a personal and professional stand on matters of intellectual freedom and the freedom to read — and she still wears with pride her sweatshirt that says: "There's something in my library to offend everyone."

17

THE TECHNOLOGY TSUNAMI

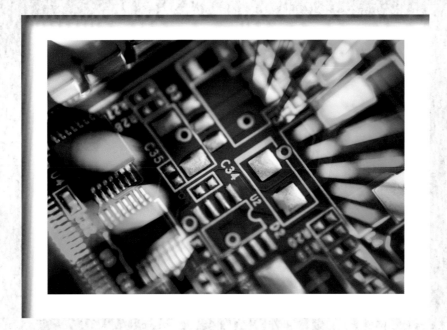

L ibraries have consistently been at the cutting edge of the information technology revolution in British Columbia. They have been among the first to embrace new technologies that would help them serve patrons more effectively, from clunky dial-up systems to the most modern computer databases. They have helped introduce British Columbians to computers, the Internet and the riches of today's online world, and still play a major role in offering training and public access.

Librarians have also been among the first to grapple with the emerging issues technology has brought, from censorship to the risk of a fundamental social divide between those who have access to the latest technology and the skills to use it, and those being left behind.

Technology hit the world like a tsunami, and libraries were ready to help.

In August 1989, the big news at Greater Victoria Public Library was that the catalogue would be available to anyone anywhere — if they had a computer with a modem. Online users could search remotely through a database of 500,000 items. "People who don't have time to come to the building will be able to dial in through their computer," chief librarian Lee Teal said.

David Sheldon updates the database at the Burnaby Public Library in 1987. *Ian Lindsay, Vancouver Sun*

There were catches. The system was limited to two callers at a time. They had to set their computers to the right combination of data bits, stop bits, parity, duplex and baud rate. A pamphlet helped explain all that. The online service, available when the library was open, let patrons see if a book was in the collection and whether it was on loan. Patrons could not reserve the book online; they could only print the entry, probably with a humming dot-matrix printer, and take it to a library staff member who would reserve it for them. Still, in its first month, the system recorded an average of fourteen searches a day. Over the next six months, the daily average rose to thirty.

Other large public libraries offered similar systems. It had been a breakthrough when they had been able to use microfiche to produce duplicate copies of their catalogues; now, fiche seemed dated. Gradually, the work assigned to bits and bytes increased. They helped keep track of where books were, helped patrons place holds, and enabled access to the catalogue from outside the library. Computers did not reduce the need for staff. They saved time but increased activity and demand. More books and other materials moved through libraries quicker than before.

In the early 1990s many libraries offered information by telefacsimile machine, at no cost, for up to four pages. There was a fee of $1 per page after the first four. The libraries generally tried to meet requests within twenty-four hours, except on weekends, but warned that because of copyright laws it could not send sheet music or pages from directories by fax.

Vancouver's new system went live in October 1990. Gordon Campbell, Vancouver's mayor, was the first person to reserve a book when he sat at one of eighty public terminals in the central library and requested, legend has it, *How to Win An Election* by Anthony Gargrave and Raymond Hull. The Vancouver system, provided by a company called Dynix, was an improvement over the Victoria model. In Vancouver, people dialling from home could reserve books, as if they were in the library. The project helped shape systems throughout British Columbia because Dynix developed it to meet the demands of Vancouver's librarians.

Vancouver also launched a community database with information on groups and organizations, including meeting times and contact details. About 4,000 local groups were included, thanks to money from the Library Services Branch and the Vancouver Foundation.

The computer systems allowed access to book titles, but not content. In 1989, Douglas Sagi of the *Vancouver Sun* imagined how wonderful a library could be for people with a home computer. "You would sit at your monitor screen, dial a phone number, and have access to all the books, papers, magazines, pamphlets, even picture books, works of art, movies, videos and recordings, from as many other libraries in the world that we could afford."

Madge Aalto, Vancouver's head librarian, envisioned

Computers have brought many more people into libraries. *Vancouver Public Library*

satellite branches connected by computer, as well as an "online public access catalogue" — known as OPAC — that would make it easier to get a book. Patrons could order a book at a branch terminal and have it delivered within hours.

The conversion to computers took time. The entire Vancouver Island Regional Library system was closed for three weeks in 1990 so an inventory could be completed, barcode labels affixed to 600,000 books, computers installed and staff trained. The full conversion of the Island system was not finished until 2001.

Computers and automated systems were of great value to the regional libraries. For the first time, Okanagan chief librarian Lesley Dieno points out, they could overcome the problems of time and distance. Branches had up-to-date catalogues and books could be moved around quickly. If the books were still around, that is; when the Okanagan system started using computers to track its items, it discovered that 20,000 books had vanished over the years.

The Okanagan Regional Library went to an automated system in 1990, starting in Vernon in June and Kelowna in October. It took almost three years before every branch had computers to handle barcodes. The request system was closed for several months and branch collections were

frozen for much of the year. The seven largest branches were shut for a week so the barcodes could be added. Circulation dropped by three per cent during the transition.

But the automated system helped increase activity later, because patrons could get books faster than before. Dieno said at the time that chasing after overdue books and fines would be easier. "It can be more expensive now to send out an overdue notice than the money we might get from a person who has an overdue book. The computer will take over all that." Delinquent patrons who had been able to escape fines for overdue books could not beat the computers.

Staff members no longer had to search for requests, so they spent more time on inter-library loans using a service run by the Library Services Branch. New technology made it much easier to share resources. For years, if a patron had asked for a book not available locally, the library would use the post or telephone to contact others nearby, gradually moving farther afield. The search often ended at the Vancouver Public Library, which had the largest collection. The government used lottery funds to make a special $250,000 grant for a province-wide electronic inter-library loan network. By March 1990, all seventy public libraries had a computer, printer, modem and software so they could take part.

A province-wide catalogue, the backbone of the modern inter-library loan system, first appeared on CD-ROM in 1991. Called Outlook, it made it easy to find which public or post-secondary libraries had titles, so librarians could obtain books from elsewhere. Outlook did not include the three big university libraries; it would have taken too many CDs. Originally published on three CD-ROM discs, Outlook was updated annually through the 1990s and shifted to the Internet in 1998.

Pat Sifton came to Fraser Valley College in 1980 from Fanshawe College in London, Ontario, where she taught in the library technology program. She developed the Fraser Valley's library technology program and all of its courses, and for many years she was the only instructor. Sifton became a self-taught expert on the then-fledgling personal computer and on many application programs that she would subsequently incorporate into student assignments. She remained program head until she retired in 1995. Sifton died in 2009, but her memory lives on in the Pat Sifton Endowment Leadership Award, given annually to students in the library and information technology program.

Above: Computer centre at the University of Victoria in 1974.
University of Victoria 125-0504

Outlook was one of many changes that resulted from a new spirit of collaboration, one of the most dramatic behind-the-scenes changes in B.C. libraries.

In 1989, the British Columbia Electronic Library Network — BC ELN — was created as a partnership between the province and the post-secondary libraries. It was housed at the Open Learning Agency; the first manager was Lynn Copeland, later the head librarian at Simon Fraser University. BC ELN enabled universities and colleges to work together on a joint collection of online journals. The collective approach led to better deals with suppliers, which vastly increased the amount and range of material available. Today, all public post-secondary libraries are partners in BC ELN and offer access to the collection through their websites.

BC ELN initially offered databases providing listings of the media and serials holdings of about twenty post-secondary libraries, and has been expanded with

contributions from member libraries. The government provides core funding for the BC ELN office and the member libraries pay for their share of database licences negotiated by the province. BC ELN places an emphasis on undergraduate material; two other collective efforts, the Council of Prairie and Pacific University Libraries and Canadian Research Knowledge Network, deal with research-level material for faculty and graduate students.

The University of British Columbia introduced a new online catalogue in 1992, with a common search interface for all files and links to circulation information so patrons would know whether an item was available. The next year Internet access was added; patrons could search catalogues and websites around the world. In 1994 the library launched its own website and made its first full-text database available. The UBC library was the first Canadian university library, and one of only four worldwide, to provide networked full-text access to material published by the institutes of electrical

McPherson Library was a key building as
the University of Victoria expanded in the
1980s. *Times Colonist*

engineers in the United States and the United Kingdom.

The provincial government boosted public libraries in 1995 with a $1-million program to connect them to the Internet. British Columbia was the first jurisdiction in North America with that goal.

The government then announced a high-tech network that would link schools, colleges and libraries. The Provincial Learning Network — PLNet — was designed to radically change how education and teaching were delivered, bringing email, fax service, the Internet and video conferencing to all communities. It was based on universal student access to learning opportunities and educational programs.

PLNet grew to include more than 1,800 schools and post-secondary and other institutions — but few public libraries. The heavy Internet filtering needed to make PLNet acceptable for school use went against the commitment to intellectual freedom that drives most public libraries. Libraries not yet online looked for other means to hit the information superhighway.

The arrival of CD-ROMs allowed libraries, public and academic, to offer unprecedented access to publications.

The first periodicals CD-ROM held 1.5 million entries from about 200 business magazines, ten U.S. publications and seven Canadian newspapers including the Toronto *Globe and Mail* and the *Vancouver Sun*. Released in 1990, the CD-ROM had publications from the previous eight years.

New technology meant less space would be needed for collections. Telephone books had filled shelves, but by 1998 telephone numbers from across Canada and the United States were available on CD-ROMs and would soon be available through the Internet. A library's entire reference section could take up a fraction of the space of a decade earlier. In time the space was filled with computers and workstations.

As British Columbians started going online, public libraries provided the first access to the Internet for many communities. The first Internet access in schools was usually in the school library.

Canada's first public computer network — a FreeNet —

Below: In 1992, Ken Roberts of the Richmond Public Library showed off a compact disk that held as much information as a 21-volume encyclopedia. *Vancouver Province*

Below right: Libraries have made the Internet available for free. *Vancouver Public Library*

was launched in Victoria on Monday, November 16, 1992. It was the eleventh such system in the world, and it gave anyone with a computer and modem the ability to plug into information bulletin boards, discuss issues, search library catalogues and connect with other computer network systems around the world.

"This is like what happened when public libraries were developed in the nineteenth century," Gary Shearman, chair of the Victoria FreeNet Association, said. "Books were hard to get until public libraries opened. Now we expect to have them. It's the same with computer networks." The association launched the FreeNet with a computer donated by Sun Microsystems Canada and $200,000 in private and government money. The Greater Victoria Public Library was the first institution to install a public terminal to access the FreeNet, which meant that even people without homes could have email accounts.

A FreeNet was started in Vancouver in September 1994 to provide a free, publicly accessible computer utility in the Lower Mainland. FreeNet callers were allowed thirty minutes per visit. The problem was getting through, because the modem lines were usually busy. Thousands of users accessed the FreeNet at the public library.

One of the builders of the Vancouver Community Network, as the FreeNet was later known, was Brian Campbell, the Vancouver Public Library's director of information and planning. He was concerned that access to information would increasingly demand access to technology.

"We are increasingly building powerful transmission systems for electronic information, but those systems are concentrated in the hands of people who can afford them," he said. "If we don't move quickly to create a public utility for information, we'll find ourselves in a situation with the information-rich on one side, and those that don't have the information on the other." Libraries, he said, help people make knowledgeable decisions about their lives and take part in discussions about the way they want society to go. "Technology can cut people out of the information loop."

The Vancouver Public Library introduced Internet access in the early 1990s. When its new central branch opened in 1995, it had 130 Internet-ready workstations

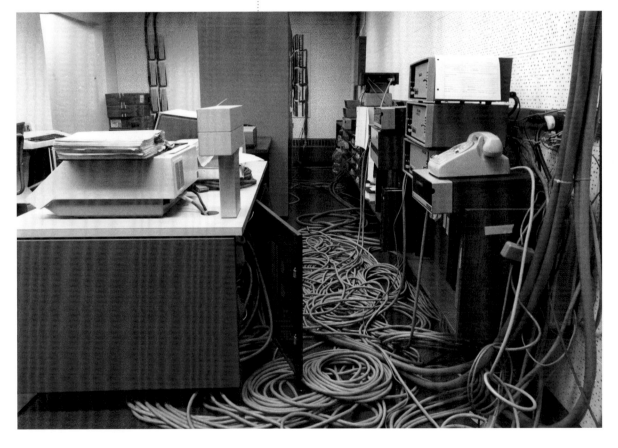

Above: Cables fill the floor of the computing centre at the University of Victoria in 1977.
University of Victoria Archives 124-0126

and all branches had Internet access. High demand meant restrictions, with some computers limited for library work or e-mail, and some with time limits. Within a few years, more patrons had home computers or laptop computers, so library computer lineups were reduced.

Campbell also warned that libraries were being asked to pay for information each time they used it, rather than owning it. Government agencies were selling or giving information to private companies, which then repackaged the data and sold it at a high price.

The B.C. Library Association set up an information policy committee because of the risk that technology would erode the public's right to information. The committee, chaired by Campbell, sponsored its first conference on the issue in 1992, and launched Information Rights Week to bring more attention to its concerns.

In 1996, the library association became part of the B.C. Coalition for Information Access, along with the B.C. Teachers' Federation, the Telecommunications Workers Union and other groups. The organization was formed to challenge a B.C. Telephone Company proposal to reduce residential rates and limit users to thirty free local calls a month. As Campbell said, that was a sign of a metered local telephone service, which could restrict access for some users.

Paul Whitney, then chief librarian in Burnaby, expressed concern about possible charges for local calls. They would "significantly suppress institutional and individual use of the Internet," he said, and challenge the fundamental public library principle of free access to information.

In 1997, the information policy conference focused on the theme Making the Links: A Critical Look at Community and the Internet. The concern was that more information was being placed online, but some people might not have access. Different standards for software meant some documents could only be printed on specific kinds of printers or with compatible software, which further restricted information access.

The information policy committee had successes. For several years it pushed to have more government publications made available, for free, in public libraries. Only two libraries, the legislative library in Victoria and the library at the University of British Columbia, had all information the government produced. The association wanted the University of Victoria, Simon Fraser University, the University of Northern B.C. and the Vancouver Public Library to also get a full set of government publications automatically.

A pilot project saw fifteen publications going to forty-

British Columbia Library Association works to ensure that information is available to everyone. *B.C. Library Association information policy committee*

three libraries, but dozens of libraries were unserved. "The government never did catch on to the idea of making information available instead of forcing people to ask," Campbell says. In time, the Internet changed everything. The government could post documents on its website, and when library patrons asked to see those documents, librarians could just go get them — or teach the patrons how to do it themselves. The system was not perfect, however, because while printed reports last for years, reports can be deleted from an Internet site with a couple of keystrokes.

Libraries continued working to ensure that everyone in their communities would have access to computers if desired. Libraries also provided training on computers and the Internet.

The Vancouver Public Library received $675,000 from Microsoft in 1997 to widen access to the Internet and multimedia computers. The donation — one of three made by Microsoft in Canada that year — provided sixteen computers, software for in-library reference, public circulation and library administration, as well as technical training and support. Three years later, the Bill and Melinda Gates Foundation gave $2.5 million to B.C. libraries for computer equipment, improved Internet access and training facilities for library staff and the public. The theory, according to the foundation, was that anyone who could get to a public library should be able to get on the Internet. The money was administered by the Library Services Branch.

Jim Looney spent his career working for the Library Development Commission, which became the Library Services Branch and then the Public Library Services Branch. He was a co-author of the strategic plan, *Libraries Without Walls: The World Within Your Reach*.

He helped the branch — and the entire library community — embrace technology. Looney was responsible for, among many other things, the Youth@BC program, which gave young people a chance to help others learn new skills and make money. He was also part of the team responsible for Wormsworth, a mascot that encouraged children to read. Since retiring from the government, he has continued to work for the library community on a volunteer basis.

> The challenge now is for public libraries — particularly in low-income communities — to stay connected. Libraries need support to maintain quality technology services so they can effectively serve the millions who count on them for their only access to computers and the internet.
> *Bill Gates, billionaire*

Grants from the federal and provincial governments helped bring the Internet to libraries. The provincial government also helped make library patrons more capable computer users. In 1998, it announced a $36-million plan to create jobs for youth, including a program called Youth@ BC. It created eighty jobs in public libraries so young people could teach others how to access the Internet and create websites — including sites for some of the libraries.

By this time, universities and colleges were providing email and Internet access to students, and their library catalogues were online with links to other post-secondary libraries. Students could dial into the Internet from their home computers, using portals provided by their institutions.

Technology marched relentlessly on. In 1995, the Greater Victoria Public Library stopped providing access to typewriters and ditched its sixteen-millimetre movies and vinyl long-play records. Head librarian Sandra Anderson said libraries weren't museums — they needed to make way for new technology that would someday offer "the virtual library, or library without walls."

The revolution was hitting public education as well. In 1997, a dozen Langley schools worked together on an Internet-based communications program for students, teachers and parents. Each student could have a personal web page and homework could be assigned over the Internet, with links to suggested websites. Students could place assignments on a web page for their teacher. If they had a computer with a modem, they could submit their work from home, and could even have discussions with teachers over the Internet.

The federal government helped libraries by providing Internet access grants in the late 1990s. The Okanagan

Wormsworth helped bring books to young readers.
Vernon branch, Okanagan Regional Library

Regional Library gave the program credit when it referred to 1997 as "the year of the Internet," with access in nineteen of twenty-nine branches. The following year the regional system started offering "Internet Only" membership cards. For $2, non-residents would be allowed Internet access in library branches. The cards were popular with tourists and itinerant workers such as fruit pickers.

> The prestige of the library of the future will not be the size of the collection, but the number of clicks to its website.
> *Thornton Tibbals, librarian*

Most public libraries started to offer, through their websites, a wide selection of online databases that ranged from encyclopedias to a special children's site — Searchosaurus — to auto repair manuals. Patrons could print pages, take them under the car with them, and recycle them when their work was finished. These electronic databases allowed libraries to save space and money — most of the time. There was a problem with these digital resources because a library would have nothing if it dropped the

subscription. With print copies or CD-ROMs, the back issues would still be available. There would always be the Internet, however — and in 1999, the Library Services Branch launched its Virtual Reference Desk to give library patrons and staff quick access to more than 1,000 websites.

New technology increased library access for people with disabilities. In 1999, the federal government paid for computer equipment that would enable the blind to make use of library databases and the Internet. "Equipment like this is making an incredible difference in many blind people's lives," said Oriano Belusic, a Victoria member of the National Federation for the Blind.

In 2000, Stephen King released his novella *Riding the Bullet* only on the Internet, resulting in a stampede of about 400,000 downloads in the first 24 hours. These electronic books were the start of something big, although it was not immediately obvious.

Public libraries in Vancouver, Richmond and Surrey signed deals in 2001 to get ebooks from netLibrary, a Colorado company that secured publishing rights to books, digitized them and distributed them online. The Vancouver library started its ebook collection with 500 titles, mainly

Modern libraries are designed to provide access to information for all users.
Vancouver Public Library

self-help, career, business and classic literature titles. The ebooks would never need to be rebound or replaced, did not take up shelf space, and readers could borrow them without leaving their homes, although only one patron at a time could check out each book.

In 2005, the Fraser Valley Regional Library was the first library in Canada to introduce netLibrary's downloadable audiobooks. The library provided its patrons with home access to 764 unabridged audiobooks, with 30 new titles added every month. It was also the first in Canada to offer Live Homework Help, an online tutoring service that connected students to expert tutors in math, science, social studies and English.

Finding enough money was a never-ending concern. For decades, libraries had been trying to balance the desire to provide access to materials with the harsh reality of tight funding. The arrival of new technology made matters worse, because it took a lot of money to get connected, add equipment and add resources.

In 1997 and again in 1999, the Vancouver Public Library closed its branches for a week to deal with funding shortfalls. The library's online catalogue and Internet connections were also closed. The library in Smithers was briefly closed in 2000 for the same reason. And the money woes have continued: The library in Fernie was closed for six weeks in 2009.

Cuts to school libraries put greater pressure on public ones. Resources for school libraries had been dropping since the 1980s, and public libraries were under greater pressure to fill in the gaps. Librarians have played an important role in helping children learn. They teach students how to use a library catalogue and indexes, to mine Internet databases, to conduct research, to evaluate sources and to take effective notes. Students also need to know how to navigate the Internet, and determine what information is valid and what is not.

> The Internet is marvellous, but to claim, as some do now, that it's making libraries obsolete is as silly as saying shoes have made feet unnecessary.
>
> *Mark Y. Herring, librarian*

The Internet has also forced special libraries — the ones serving businesses, associations and professions — to reinvent themselves. They no longer need shelves filled with reference works in a reading room; they need to provide access to digitized resources over the Internet, and often do research for patrons as well.

Along with the benefits provided by the Internet, there were challenges as well — for librarians and for patrons. The World Wide Web helped remind us of the need for experienced librarians. It can be a problem to sort through millions of potential sources of information, and weed out the inaccurate or trivial sources from the ones that offer quality.

That's where librarians can help; they have been trained in finding, using and evaluating resources, and can guide patrons to the ones that should be the most useful. The role of the librarian has not changed all that much in a century. It's the medium that has been transformed, but the need for a qualified guide remains.

Libraries are one of the few long-standing institutions in our society thriving in
both physical and virtual space. They will endure.
Paul Whitney, librarian

18

LIBRARIES
WITHOUT WALLS

For more than a century British Columbia's libraries have provided a comfortable, welcoming environment for people searching for information, entertainment or conversation with other people. What will the future hold? Given the pace of change, it's difficult to say for sure — although we can count on the continuing evolution of the library experience, both physical and virtual.

We don't use libraries the way we used to. They are still extensions of our homes and still enrich our lives, but our tastes and our needs are not the same as a century ago — and the world we live in has changed dramatically as well. Information was

The library is the mother ship: It's vast, it's warm, it hums, you can sleep there if you need to, head on your arms in a carrel, and no one will bother you.
Annabel Lyon, writer

once available to us primarily through the printed page, but now we can find what we want in several other ways. Sometimes, we don't even look at books when we visit the library. And thanks to the Internet, a library can be open virtually, twenty-four hours a day and seven days a week.

The theory behind library service remains the same today as it was a century and a half ago: By sharing our resources, we all benefit. All ten major reports in library service in British Columbia have stressed the need for local involvement, for provincial co-ordination, and for collaboration.

The ever-changing ways we use libraries have been reflected in physical changes over the decades. Public libraries have taken bold leaps forward in communities

such as Vancouver, Surrey, Langford, Richmond, Langley, Kelowna, Port Moody, Burnaby, North Vancouver (both city and district), Port Clements and Kamloops, and most post-secondary libraries have been transformed as well.

The province's most visible library is Vancouver Public Library's central branch, which brings to mind the Coliseum of Rome. The building — basically a square within an elliptical outer shell — was completed in 1995 and quickly became a landmark on the east side of downtown Vancouver. It is the largest public library development the province has ever seen, and makes a bold statement about the importance and value of libraries.

"It doesn't look like a library, but everybody knows it's a library," says Lois Bewley, a former librarianship professor who served on one of the planning committees. She says the branch reflects good library design, with easy access for patrons and staff — and people and materials are able to flow through without being restricted by pillars, steps or wasted space.

Bewley notes that at one time, libraries put books around perimeter walls and people in the middle, but Vancouver's coliseum, like many other new buildings, switches that. Books and other resources are in the middle and people are on the outside, enjoying natural light or feeling connected to the outside world rather than isolated from it.

The building opened on May 26, 1995, with scanners

Vancouver Mayor Gordon Campbell at the ground-breaking ceremony for the new Vancouver central library in 1993. *Greg Osadchuk, Vancouver Province*

Vancouver Public Library's 1995 move from the old central branch at Robson and Burrard took five weeks, with a fleet of five-tonne trucks making about 600 trips between the old building and the new. In the old branch, books were shifted into movable bookcases so they could be placed in the new building with a minimum of fuss and reshelving. Forty movers worked seven days a week transferring the books, newspapers, microfilm, videocassettes, audiocassettes, compact discs, pictures, paintings, filing cabinets, tables and chairs.

Above: Paul Andre Fortier performs as part of "Dancing on the Edge," an event at Vancouver's central branch in 2009. *Steve Bosch, Vancouver Sun*

Left: Members of the Aeriosa Dance Society touch the sky at the Vancouver Public Library in 2010. *Vancouver Public Library*

Two unsuccessful designs for Vancouver's new central library. *David Clark, Vancouver Province*

for self-serve checkout, card-operated photocopiers, 216 computer terminals, and wired study carrels for patrons with laptop computers. It quickly proved to be a huge success, and welcomes about 2.3 million visitors a year. It has 1.3 million items; at least 6,000 are checked out each day it is open.

The $100-million building, designed by Moshe Safdie in partnership with Vancouver architect Downs/Archambault, has been a planning magnet on the eastern edge of downtown and an example for new libraries everywhere. Safdie also designed, with local partners, the new Salt Lake City Public Library, which opened in 2003. It is strikingly similar to Vancouver's library, and indication of the success of the concept.

Critics of Vancouver's design — and yes, there were some — could take pleasure in the 2001 Arnold Schwarzenegger movie, *The 6th Day*, which featured the building being destroyed. *The 6th Day* was one of several movies to feature the library; others include *88 Minutes*, *Personal Effects*, *Mr. Magoo*, *The Imaginarium of Doctor Parnassus*, *Battle in Seattle* and *Ballistic: Ecks vs. Sever*, widely considered one of the worst movies of all time. Television series filmed there include *Smallville*, *Battlestar Galactica*, *Stargate SG-1*, *Caprica* and *The Dead Zone*.

The library was designed with expansion and evolution in mind, and today has more space for laptop computers, more electrical outlets and more ways to connect to the Internet. The library made extensive use of computers and databases when it opened, but the notion of wireless Internet access in 1995 would have sounded as plausible as the plot of a Schwarzenegger movie.

The technological revolution has breathed new life into old buildings. Libraries with large stacks of books and small study areas were suddenly outdated when patrons started looking for computer access, or bringing their own laptops to connect to the Internet. Renovations were needed in libraries across the province to make way for the new technology.

Libraries rarely have landmark buildings or high profiles in small communities, with Fernie and Hazelton being two notable exceptions. Some small libraries make do as best they can — in the community hall in Hedley, in the school in Port Renfrew, in a trailer park in Anahim Lake, and in other premises that are a world apart from Vancouver's coliseum. But in every library, no matter its shape or size, technology has changed the way patrons are served.

More libraries are embracing or testing the concept of the "learning commons," which promotes learning, research and social engagement in several ways. A learning commons includes computer workstations, work areas for individuals and groups, support from staff members, comfortable chairs and ready access to food and drink. It helps reinforce the notion that we are not individuals using resources on our own; we are part of a shared experience and can learn from and help those around us. The learning commons idea has been introduced in many post-secondary libraries, school libraries and public libraries.

Rapidly changing technology has created challenges for library planners. Buildings are supposed to last forty or fifty years, but it is impossible to predict the pressures that will be created by technological change in the next decade. With every new or renovated library, flexibility has been a top priority. Walls might need to be moved and wiring almost certainly will need to change.

> Our libraries are a great investment in community, learning and literacy. They open doors of opportunity for minds hungry for knowledge and adventure. They are the front lines of the effort to make British Columbia the most literate place in the world.
> *Gordon Campbell, premier 2001 – 2011*

British Columbia was the first province to commit to providing Internet access in all public libraries, and those libraries helped push and pull us into the Internet age by offering access, training and resources. In 1998, for example, Richmond's 12,000-square-foot Ironwood branch opened with as much space for electronic information stations as for books. It had an Internet café, a computer centre, fifty-five desktop computers, a motorized projection screen, digital reference stations, mobile computer stations and scanners for quick self-service checkout.

Ten years later, the new North Vancouver City Library offered a media room with viewing and listening stands, an outdoor reading room with views of the Lions Gate Bridge, an outdoor children's room with an "ouchless" floor and fun seating, and a room devoted to teenagers that has study tables, game gear and a fifty-two-inch television set. The library, which won the 2009 B.C. Lieutenant Governor Award for Architecture, includes environment-friendly features such as efficient heating and lighting systems and solar shading.

The Comox branch of the Vancouver Island Regional Library has a lounge area with leather chairs, end tables, a large LCD screen and local works of art. The Greater Victoria Public Library's John Goudy branch in Langford offers a technological twist: Patrons can borrow a laptop computer, and then use it in the municipality's free wireless Internet area along Goldstream Avenue.

In 2009 Burnaby opened its Tommy Douglas branch, named after a former local MP who is best known as the father of Canada's health-care system. The open, airy building has lots of natural light and comfortable seating, about two dozen computers, two public multi-purpose rooms and a special area for children. It is a green building with a green roof and geothermal exchange system.

There have also been major changes behind the scenes. The District of North Vancouver's new Lynn Valley branch, which opened in 2007, features an automated system designed to sort books, using microchips and radio signals, into carts destined for different departments. Many other libraries are introducing similar systems. The Lynn Valley branch is part of a $41-million complex with retail outlets, community gathering spaces, a restaurant and an outdoor plaza.

These aren't the only libraries being connected with their surroundings. Vancouver's central branch complex, known as Library Square, has small retail shops in an enclosed courtyard where people are encouraged to relax and enjoy the ambience. The North Kamloops library, opened in 2010, is the anchor tenant in a development — also known as Library Square — with two commercial units and 140 residential condominiums.

Top left: Artist's conception of the new Surrey City Centre Library, designed by Bing Thom, opening in 2011. *Surrey Public Library*

Above: Burnaby Public Library's McGill branch, opened in 2001, features striking architecture. *Burnaby Public Library*

Below: Richmond Public Library's Brighouse branch, extensively renovated in 2006, looks like an upscale bookstore. *Richmond Public Library*

Right: North Kamloops library branch, which opened in 2010, is on the ground floor of a residential condo complex. *Dave Obee*

Bottom: Surrey's Semiahmoo branch has a unique "living wall" filled with vegetation. *Surrey Public Library*

The downtown Kamloops branch opened in 1998 in a building it shares with the Thompson-Nicola Regional District's administration offices and the city's art gallery. Surrey's Semiahmoo branch is with the police station, but one of the branch's most notable aspects is its outdoor green wall, the largest of its kind in North America. The 3,000-square-foot vertical garden has more than 100,000 plants and 120 species, with everything from ground covers to large perennials. It's a highly visible reminder that libraries strive to be both technologically and environmentally friendly.

Major changes have taken place inside libraries. Many are striving to look like upmarket bookstores, with subject categories rather than Dewey decimal numbers on prominent shelves and bookcases. There are comfortable chairs and vending machines for those who get hungry or thirsty while browsing the books or using the wireless Internet connection. Computer workstations offer access to electronic resources, library catalogues, Internet, email and software applications. Self-service reserve shelves and checkout stations mean patrons can borrow a book without fear of being judged, and without waiting in line.

British Columbians place high value on libraries, with 2.7 million people holding public library cards. Public library service locations circulate almost 220,000 items every year on average, more than twice the number in Alberta or Ontario. In total, B.C. public libraries have more than 12 million items on their shelves, and each item circulates, on average, more than four times during the year. Public libraries record about 52 million visits each year — in-person and virtual — and the number increases every year.

Post-secondary libraries are also as busy as ever, supporting research and learning at all levels, from undergraduate students to doctoral researchers. Fifty campus libraries serve 177,000 full-time or equivalent students and 14,000 faculty. They have 20 million items in their physical collections and another 24 million electronic products. Every year, post-secondary libraries answer more than 700,000 reference questions and record about 17 million in-person visits.

A $60-million renovation at the University of British Columbia's old Main Library included the first robotic book retrieval system in Canada as well as innovations in the laptop computer loan program, computer labs and high-tech classrooms. The project, completed in 2008, helped make the 1925 building one of the most modern on campus. The library also gained a new name: The Irving K. Barber Learning Centre, in appreciation of the man who donated $20 million, the biggest single capital contribution in the university's history.

Irving K. (Ike) Barber.
Dominic Schaefer, University of British Columbia

Irving K. (Ike) Barber became a student at the University of British Columbia in September 1945, and graduated with a forestry degree in 1950. In 1952, he qualified as a professional registered forester. He founded Slocan Forest Products Ltd. in 1978 and retired in 2002.

Barber is committed to projects that will strengthen the province and improve the quality of life for its residents. He helped establish research programs such as the I.K. Barber Enhanced Forestry Laboratory at the University of Northern British Columbia, the Irving K. Barber Diabetes Research Endowment Fund at the University of British Columbia, and the Ike Barber Human Islet Transplant Laboratory at Vancouver General Hospital in partnership with the University of British Columbia.

The Barber Learning Centre is designed to work for the "intellectual, social, cultural and economic development of the people of British Columbia and beyond." It includes collection space for 2.1 million volumes including open stack shelving and 1.8 million items with its automated storage and retrieval system. It also has the Chapman Learning Commons, with more than 1,500 study seats and a 157-seat learning theatre as well as classrooms, seminar rooms, project rooms and boardrooms.

The Irving K. Barber Learning Centre at the University of British Columbia includes an automated storage and retrieval system that helps keep the collection accessible while addressing the demands on space and the need for preservation. The system has a capacity of about 1.8 million items, equivalent to 15 years of collection growth for the UBC library. It consists of bins stored on a rack system that are retrieved by automated cranes. To retrieve materials, users make a request through the library's online catalogue. Using the book's barcode as the locating device, the automated mini-load crane identifies the bin that holds the item and delivers it to the circulation desk within two minutes. A staff member retrieves the requested item from the bin and holds it for pickup.

Automated storage and retrieval system in the Irving K. Barber Learning Centre. *University of British Columbia Library*

Opposite: Mearns Centre at the University of Victoria features several work areas with natural light. *Times Colonist*

John Ridington, the university's first librarian, is remembered in the Ridington Reading Room, and Ike's Café pays tribute to Barber. The centre provided new space for the School of Library, Archival and Information Studies, the Centre for Teaching and Academic Growth, the Office of Learning Technology, the UBC Archives, Rare Books and Special Collections and university programs.

The Barber name is also associated with scores of digitization projects that place materials online so they can be accessed from anywhere. UBC, Simon Fraser University and other library, museum and archive partners have been heavily involved in digitization projects such as West Beyond the West, an Internet portal into a vast amount of historical resources. Some projects are much smaller — Vanderhoof's Bill Silver Digital Newspaper Archive is one example — but are just as important.

The Barber centre was opened a decade after UBC opened the Walter C. Koerner Library, which links the former Sedgewick Undergraduate Library's underground space to a new five-storey tower. Koerner Library brought together collections in the humanities and social sciences, government publications and microforms.

UBC also has the Xwi7xwa (pronounced whei-wha) Library in the First Nations Longhouse. The name comes from the Squamish Nation word meaning "echo." The library has 12,000 items relating to First Nations in British Columbia, and resources on indigenous peoples from across Canada and internationally. The library began in the Indian Education Resource Centre, which was established in the 1970s, and became a branch of the UBC Library in 2005.

In 2001, UBC opened a branch library at its Robson Square campus in downtown Vancouver. UBC also has a branch library at the Okanagan campus in Kelowna.

The McPherson Library at the University of Victoria was transformed with a $20-million expansion, becoming the William C. Mearns Centre for Learning. Mearns was a 1927 graduate of Victoria College, the predecessor to the university, and in the early 1960s helped assemble the land for the new campus. Mearns died in 1998. In 2005, his family donated $5 million to the university.

The Mearns Centre opened in 2008 with enhanced technology to increase access to information within UVic and around the globe. It includes a digital access area known as the Information Commons, classrooms and computer workstations. Its Bessie Brooks Winspear Media Commons brings together music, audio and video collections. The university's archives are also in the centre. The library expansion included seating areas next to floor-to-ceiling windows and created room for the BiblioCafé, a cafeteria that would never have been allowed in the early days of the McPherson library — or any other library, for that matter.

In 2002, SFU opened a Surrey branch campus in temporary quarters. The permanent location opened four years later with wireless Internet access throughout and a high-speed Internet connection to the main library in Burnaby. The library at SFU Surrey is called the Fraser Valley Real Estate Board Academic Library, or Fraser Library for short, in recognition of a donation made by the real estate board. It was the university's second branch library; the Samuel and Frances Belzberg Library, opened as part of the Harbour Centre branch in downtown Vancouver in 1989, was developed with the help of a donation by Vancouver businessman Samuel Belzberg and his family.

SFU is a leader in digitization work, helping to provide an online home for resources such as old newspapers from Prince George. It is involved, with eleven other partners, in Multicultural Canada, a website with 1.5 million pages including the *Chinese Times* from 1915 to 1992 as well as photographs, records, Chinese Benevolent Association documents and more. SFU and UBC also work together, with Stanford University in California, in the Public Knowledge Project, which is designed to use technology to improve the professional and public value of scholarly research.

Several other post-secondary institutions have seen major changes in recent years. In 2005, Thompson Rivers University was formed through the amalgamation of the University College of the Cariboo and the B.C. Open University. Okanagan University College was split to become UBC Okanagan and Okanagan College. In 2007, the Institute of Indigenous Government was merged with the Nicola Valley Institute of Technology. In 2008, five institutions became full universities. They were Kwantlen Polytechnic University, formerly Kwantlen University College; Vancouver Island University, formerly Malaspina University-College; the University of the Fraser Valley, formerly the University College of the Fraser Valley; Capilano University, formerly Capilano College; and the Emily Carr University of Art and Design, formerly Emily Carr Institute of Art and Design.

That meant there were eleven universities, eleven colleges, and three institutes in the B.C. public post-secondary system — a dramatic change from fifty years earlier, when B.C. had one university and one college. Over the years, most post-secondary libraries have been moved, expanded, squeezed and moved again. To meet rising demand, they have worked together to provide access to hundreds of online databases — and millions of digital files — covering many disciplines.

Access has been improved in many ways. Buildings have been modified to make it easier for patrons with physical disabilities. B.C. College and Institute Library Services, based at Langara, provides accessible learning and teaching materials to students and instructors who cannot use conventional print because of disabilities. The Provincial Resource Centre for the Visually Impaired and the Accessible Resource Centre — British Columbia provide a similar essential service for students from kindergarten to Grade 12. Many formats are available to suit different needs.

Public libraries also offer services to people with learning disabilities or who cannot use printed books. They have built collections of audiobooks and DAISY books, for example, to help patrons with limited vision or dyslexia, or who are unable to hold a book. These collections might never be large

enough to provide true equity, but the ever-quickening pace of putting content into digital form is sharply increasing the amount of accessible resources available. Libraries also offer outreach programs, designed to make materials available to people who are homebound.

Libraries have adapted to the changing face of the province, building multilingual collections for patrons who increasingly speak languages other than English. Their shelves and their websites reflect their communities: The Richmond Public Library has a large collection of works in Chinese, for example, while West Vancouver has a substantial Persian collection. In Lillooet, songs and stories in First Nations languages have been placed online in an effort to help preserve those languages. Burnaby offers songs and stories in foreign languages, helping new arrivals feel comfortable as they struggle to learn English. Other libraries are working on similar projects.

In the 1990s the British Columbia Library Association set up a diversity committee to help librarians provide better service in multiple languages. New immigrants often visit libraries within days of their arrival, looking for information on their new home and for a way to check in with friends or relatives in their old one. This is not a new phenomenon. Margaret Brunette, the former head of Vancouver Public Library's extension department, said in 1958 that new Canadians saw the public library as a "privilege such as the parks."

Libraries come in all shapes and sizes. Along with the public, school and post-secondary libraries, there are

hundreds of special ones. Courthouse libraries, which are open to the public, include major resource centres in Vancouver and Victoria, regional libraries in Kamloops, Kelowna, Nanaimo, New Westminster and Prince George, and twenty-three small branches. The Workers' Compensation Board of B.C. has a library in Richmond that specializes in occupation health and safety and related issues. The Health Libraries Association of B.C. has more than ninety members.

Libraries serve the disadvantaged and the vulnerable. The best example is the Carnegie Centre in the old Carnegie library building at Hastings and Main streets in Vancouver's Downtown Eastside. The Vancouver Public Library branch on the main floor takes the concept of a library back to its roots, providing a safe refuge, an alternative to the streets, and resources to people who could not afford their own books. It welcomes more than 300 people a day.

The Vancouver Public Library was a partner, with libraries in Regina, Toronto and Halifax, in the Working Together Project, building connections and relationships with communities that are traditionally excluded from public libraries. It helped identify and tear down barriers in low-income areas with ethnic and cultural diversity.

At the other end of the economic spectrum, major benefactors have made large donations to public libraries. These included Robert Leslie Welsh's bequest of $2.2 million to the West Vancouver Memorial Library. The gift allowed a major expansion of music programs — including concerts, collections and the purchase of a grand piano.

Greater Victoria's Saanich Centennial branch includes the Saanich municipal archives. *Times Colonist*

Ultimately, however, libraries are not just buildings. They are patrons and staff members; they are ideas and enlightenment; they are facts and information; they are fun and entertainment. Their ability to deliver on their potential depends on their ability to use technology and to collaborate with each other.

The role of libraries was clear in the name of a major strategic plan unveiled in 2004: *Libraries Without Walls, The World Within Your Reach.* The plan helped transform service, establishing a new provincial context for public libraries. The plan specified that access to core library services and information should be free and equitable. It challenged library leaders to think regionally and provincially to ensure that small libraries could benefit from emerging technology, and stressed the need for collaboration for the benefit of all.

With the plan's encouragement and the example of the successful library federation in Greater Vancouver, new federations were set up in the northeast, north-central, and north coast regions, as well as the Kootenay and Vancouver Island. The six federations, which represent eighty per cent of the population, allow local boards to retain control of libraries while sharing resources and expertise with others.

In 2004, Premier Gordon Campbell — who as Vancouver's mayor had helped to unveil a computerized library catalogue just fourteen years earlier — endorsed *Libraries Without Walls.* Speaking to 130 educators and literacy experts at the Premier's Literacy Summit in Vancouver, he promised $12 million for public libraries to implement the plan. "There isn't anything more important than giving … that gift of literacy," Campbell said.

As part of the emphasis on collaboration, *Libraries Without Walls* helped bring about BC OneCard, which provides basic service at all 243 public library branches. Patrons still need a local card as well, but BC OneCard is a big step toward seamless access to all publicly funded library resources.

Libraries Without Walls included several collaborative technological initiatives, including:

- Sitka, a shared catalogue that uses open source software. Full implementation of Sitka will make a single-card province a reality.
- Access to databases with everything from car repair manuals to periodicals to encyclopedias and much more.
- Library-to-Go, downloadable ebooks in various electronic formats.
- The AskAway reference service offering real-time chat service via computer, which meant a person with

Libraries growing together

a question could get an answer without visiting the library in person. A parallel AskAway service was started by post-secondary libraries.
- Website templates to help small public libraries establish a professional Internet presence, a critical extension of physical service.

In 2005 the government gave $1.8 million to public libraries to support literacy programs. Libraries have been heavily involved in the promotion of literacy for years, and often work with other organizations to support local initiatives. In keeping with the goal of increasing literacy rates, Education Minister Shirley Bond announced Books for B.C. Babies, which gave 42,000 kits a year to new parents to encourage and support reading to newborns. Bond also provided every kindergarten student with a copy of *Down at the Seaweed Café* by Robert Perry, a Victoria poet.

Once upon a time, libraries did not serve children, but that changed with the realization that an investment in young readers makes sense. Reading skills are crucial to learning ability and learning potential. Children develop rhythm and rhyme when books are read to them, and their oral language skills are enhanced as well.

When the Vancouver Public Library started storytimes for babies in 1980, former children's librarian Janice Douglas says, "people thought we were crazy, absolutely crazy. Now all the research shows you have to read to babies." Being read to at an early age helps children bond with their parents, helps them develop early language skills which are the basis of reading readiness, and has enormous implications for their well-being for the rest of their lives.

Programs for babies teach them different skills, and Douglas says touch, sound and smell can build the scaffolding for learning. "If every single preschooler could have quality picture books in their life, they would go to school ready to learn, have a sense of empathy, compassion, tolerance, understanding and respect. It's all there in those

Logo for Sitka, the shared catalogue, is made up of trees drawn by participants at the organizational meeting in 2007. *Public Library Services Branch*

Janice Douglas retired in 2008 as Vancouver Public Library's Director of Youth Services and Programming. Her contributions to library service and children's literacy have been recognized by the B.C. Library Association and the International Reading Association. She received the Queen's Jubilee Medal and was given the Certificate of Commendation by the Writers Union of Canada in 2001 in recognition of the outstanding series of public readings she conducted at VPL. Premier Gordon Campbell named Douglas as British Columbia's 2008 recipient of the Council of the Federation Literacy Award.

Janice Douglas of Vancouver Public Library, photographed in 1984 with a selection of books for children. *David Clark, Vancouver Province*

and parents might read four or five in one evening. A few books will become favorites, and parents might decide to buy their own copies. Others will be read once or twice, and the children will not shed tears when they are returned to the library.

"Parents cannot afford to buy it all and have it all in their homes," Taylor McBryde says. "Even people who buy lots of books would never be able to satisfy that ability of children to plow through books." A stack of books for one child for one week might cost $200 at a store, but is free from the library.

Taylor McBryde also notes that a child's tastes can change overnight. Their book choices will change as their knowledge grows and their interests develop. "With a library, children can sample all kinds of books and decide which ones they love. They have the power to choose whatever they want at a library, and it is the only place where they can do that."

Adult choices have much more lasting appeal. The same book can be borrowed by a twenty-year-old one week and a seventy-year-old the next.

Public libraries offer literacy outreach programs in daycares, preschools and kindergartens as well as the Summer Reading Club to ensure that the benefits of reading reach as many children as possible. Libraries have comprehensive sections for school-age children and teens, and these resources can complement the libraries found in schools. Many are open in the evenings, and six or seven days a week all year long. That means they offer reading choices, homework support and resources for self-directed learning when school libraries are not accessible.

While libraries have computers and electronic games for teenagers, teens are reading more books than ever before. And they are getting more involved in the books than their parents did, using technology to talk about them, find them, look up authors and post reviews online.

Children who read through the summer are more prepared to learn when they arrive at school in the fall; children who do not read will lose ground in both reading and mathematics. Summer reading clubs offered by public libraries motivate children to continue to expand their minds.

In schools, teacher-librarians play a crucial role. They help teachers and students in finding and using the many sources of information available, and how to cope with the rapidly changing ways that information is being presented. They support the formal education system and play an essential role in the self-directed learning of students. Teacher-librarians teach students how to evaluate sources and apply what they learn to their lives.

books," she says. Children who are read to, taught to value books, get books as gifts and are allowed to choose their own books will have an advantage when they get to school.

Douglas says preschool children can learn eight to ten words a day, and talking, singing and reading from books can help them to absorb the structure of the language and develop the roots of literacy. Reading books at home has been linked to success in school, and reading aloud has been identified as the single most important factor in teaching children to read.

Allison Taylor McBryde, the co-ordinator of children's and young adult services at North Vancouver District Public Library, says preschoolers can devour twenty books a week,

Libraries have also been increasing the range of adult programming offered. These programs bring adults into the library to hear authors and other people of interest, and encourage exposure to information and intelligence. Some people might not have the literacy skills to read books, but they can benefit from hearing speakers and seeing exhibits.

Word on the Street, a September event at Vancouver's central branch, has been Western Canada's largest celebration of words and reading since the 1990s. Word on the Street promotes books and authors with free exhibits, author readings, book dealers, performances and hands-on activities. It attracts about 35,000 visitors a year, and the streets around the library are closed to accommodate its tents, booths and crowds.

There is also One Book, as in One Book One Vancouver and One Book One Kootenay. Inspired by an event started in Chicago in 1991, these programs encourage people to read and talk about topics by spotlighting one remarkable book, usually of local interest. Wayson Choy's *The Jade Peony* was the choice in Vancouver when the program started in 2002. Almost 2,000 people attended One Book One Vancouver events that year and the book was checked out of the library 7,000 times. About 6,000 copies were sold in B.C., and the book was on the B.C. bestseller list for thirteen weeks.

Events such as One Book help bring people together in person or through technology. That makes sense; libraries are high-quality public spaces where people come for information and to be entertained, for contact with others and for a better sense of self. They can collaborate with others, develop their own voices and content or realize a

dream of lifelong learning. Many people who never borrow a book will still be regular patrons.

Libraries are true information portals; what is on their shelves does not matter as much as the way they open doors. More information is available now to more people in more ways than ever before. The Internet enables library patrons to access library resources without setting foot in a physical library branch.

B.C. Books Online, a collaboration of libraries and publishers, has been launched as a pilot project. Through B.C. Books Online, a collection of non-fiction books by B.C. publishers is accessible through the websites of public, school and post-secondary libraries. When the pilot service was launched in 2010 it was the first time that publishers and libraries had worked together to deliver digital content to an entire province.

New technology might not result in smaller libraries, even though less space will be needed for books; the space once used for multi-volume reference works will be devoted to people, and they will be sharing, learning, discovering, creating and collaborating. That is because libraries are safe, welcoming environments where people can read, study, meet and explore, in person or online.

Jacqueline van Dyk, the director of the Public Library Services Branch, is confident that libraries will stay relevant, and will even thrive in the technology-driven global economy. "Strengthened relations between libraries of all kinds and between libraries and other public services, as well as continued sharing of services and resources, will encourage greater levels of collaboration and technical

Summer Reading Club has encouraged school students to keep their minds active during July and August — a crucial step for their success in September. *Summer Reading Club*

In 1982, Gene Joseph, Wet'suwet'en Dakehl, was the first First Nations person to graduate from library school in British Columbia. She helped develop First Nations libraries for years and was the first head librarian of the Xwi7xwa Library at UBC. Joseph also manages First Nations litigation research for cultural and legal issues. She served as the librarian for the Gitxsan Wet'suwet'en in the precedent-setting Delgamuukw-Gisdaywa case, which affirmed the inherent meaning of aboriginal title. Ruling on the case in 1997, the Supreme Court of Canada decided that oral history or oral evidence should be placed on equal footing with that given to historical documents. Since 2002 Joseph has been doing historical research for the Haida aboriginal title case.

libraries need to be ready for whatever comes next. Mobile access, in whatever form it takes, will be important. Libraries will continue to provide public access to computers and other technology, and to trusted information of every description.

In 2010, the New Westminster Public Library introduced a social network catalogue, which extends the regular Internet catalogue by allowing patrons to comment on and rate books and interact with others with like interests. Since the user-created content is aggregated across many libraries, the benefits will grow as more libraries offer the service.

Today, information comes in all shapes and sizes. Along with books, libraries offer movies, music, research databases, audiobooks, video games, websites and more. The library experience is also being transformed by ebooks and e-audiobooks, which can be downloaded to a patron's computer or portable device from a library website. The patron can adjust the appearance of the printed word and carry several books at once. It's impossible to be late returning one of these books; when they are due, they just disappear.

innovation," she says. "This is all for the benefit of the patrons." Van Dyk notes that seamless library access for all citizens was the goal of library pioneers such as Helen Gordon Stewart and William Kaye Lamb, and it remains a key goal today.

Libraries will continue to serve as community hubs and sources of civic pride. More libraries are becoming part of true multi-purpose facilities, linked to everything from daycares to senior centres, from police stations to schools, art galleries and much more. They are evolving inside their walls as well — working with other agencies to provide job training and placement or training in English as a Second Language. Libraries even share space with other organizations. The Vancouver Island Regional Library branch in Port Clements, in the Haida Gwaii, is a prime example, since it is linked with other essential community services such as the elementary school, town hall, seniors' centre and daycare. In some small communities, libraries provide the primary contact with government.

Libraries are also community living rooms, especially in urban areas where smaller living quarters encourage people to step outside their own walls. They provide space for groups large and small, and people without regular offices can use them for occasional work or meeting space. Children can use them to do homework or research, or meet with tutors or other students.

And again, technology helps make contact possible. After making way for laptop computers and smart phones,

Digitization projects enable libraries to put more material into the hands of more people. They include hard-to-find or fragile materials such as old newspapers and historic documents. These items are scanned from the original documents or from microfilm, then posted online in a common format such as a portable document file, or PDF. They can be text-searchable, which allows for a level of access that would have been unimaginable even a decade earlier. And, since they are placed on websites, you don't need to visit a library to use the material — it comes to where you are, in an instant, without risking damage to the original document. Libraries were key partners, for example, in the *British Colonist* website, which digitized the first fifty years of the oldest newspaper in the province, the Victoria *Daily Colonist*.

LOOK AT THIS, VICKY. I CHECKED OUT AN "E-BOOK" FROM THE LIBRARY.

HOW LONG HAVE YOU HAD IT OUT?

TWO MONTHS.

I THINK IT'S OVERDUE.

Adrian Raeside

Librarians will continue to organize digitization projects, and will help people navigate through information and the countless sources to be tapped. Individual patrons have easy access to information in vastly greater quantities than ever before, but we still benefit from people who can guide us and help us filter the good from the bad. Many of these librarians will continue to come from the School of Library, Archival and Information Studies at the University of British Columbia, which has been helping people earn library degrees for half a century. Our libraries will also be staffed by technicians trained in the library and information technology programs at Langara College and the University of the Fraser Valley. The provincial Public Library Services Branch provides training to community librarians as well.

What will the future bring? We can be sure that librarians will continue to fight for equitable access, intellectual freedom and improved literacy. They will deal with constant technological change and help the public adapt. They will represent the benefits of working together and collaborating — principles that are at the very heart of what libraries are all about.

Librarians have always been resourceful, creative and passionate. They have set up libraries in wooden huts, in construction camps, in schools and hospitals, and in doughnut shops. They have offered book service through meat markets, service stations and at the side of muddy roads. They have worked in partnerships of many descriptions. They have battled snow, rain, and budget cuts, always with the goal of putting books and information into the hands of eager readers.

We might eventually see libraries that do not have books on paper, just digital resources with an emphasis on community engagement. That day might not come soon — not with more than 50 million books being circulated through British Columbia's public libraries every year — but if it happens, librarians will be ready. They have always changed with the times.

"People seem to think that librarians are synonymous with the book form, but we have gone from clay tablets to scrolls to papyrus to vellum and so on — and now we are in electronic forms," says Samuel Rothstein, the founding director of the School of Librarianship at the University of British Columbia.

Rothstein is confident that libraries are here to stay. As long as we need materials of the mind and of the emotion, he says, libraries will be collecting these materials and dispensing them to the waiting public. Libraries exist to satisfy the endless curiosity in all of us.

With their casual atmosphere, comfortable chairs, coffee bars, wireless Internet access and digital offerings, libraries are nothing like those of a half-century ago. The pioneers such as Helen Gordon Stewart and Ethelbert Olaf Stuart Scholefield might not recognize today's libraries, but odds are that they would approve.

In 1958, Joyce Wilby decided that Alert Bay needed a public library, so she started one. At first the library was open just ten hours a week, but it was so popular it became a vital part of the community. After fifty years — with Wilby still in charge — the library offers public access computers as well as the best selection of books on Cormorant Island. The Alert Bay library never joined the Vancouver Island Regional Library, but in 2009 it became part of IslandLink, a federation of independent libraries that also includes Powell River, Salt Spring Island and Victoria. The federation enabled the little library — annual budget $25,000 — to bring in a computerized catalogue and improve staff training.

1960	B.C. Ferries starts service
1960	Beaver Valley Public Library started by Teen Town; serves Montrose and Fruitvale
1960	Chase Women's Institute Library opens
1960	Documentary *Journey from Zero* filmed in the Peace River district
1960	Fraser Valley and Vancouver Island headquarters expanded
1960	Greenwood library moves to McArthur Centre
1960	Kimberley library opens in city hall
1960	Library associations formed in Cassiar and Marysville
1960	UBC and Public Library Commission offer training to staff from small public libraries
1960	UBC Library's south wing completed
1960	Vanderhoof library moves to municipal office
1961	Burnaby's McGill branch is opened
1961	Fraser Valley opens Ladner branch
1961	Salmo library becomes a public library association
1961	Graduate School of Librarianship opens at the University of British Columbia
1961	Nanaimo gets a new library building
1961	Okanagan Regional Library expands its headquarters
1961	Public Library Commission comes under Provincial Secretary
1961	Sechelt library started by Parent Teacher Association
1961	Vernon library moves to old city hall
1962	Burnaby's Kingsway branch is opened
1962	East Kootenay libraries form association
1962	Fraser Valley opens branches in Port Coquitlam and Clearbrook
1962	Westview library (at Powell River) moves to municipal hall
1962	Rose Vainstein starts a major library survey
1962	Trans-Canada Highway is opened at Rogers Pass
1962	Trinity Western University opens as a junior college
1963	Fort St. James public library association founded
1963	Fraser Valley opens new Ladner, White Rock and Haney branches
1963	Fraser Valley launches Helen Gordon Stewart bursary
1963	Invermere library re-established
1963	Notre Dame in Nelson becomes a university
1963	Qualicum Beach library gets new home
1963	Salt Spring Island Library gets its own building
1963	University of Victoria established
1963	Vancouver opens Mount Pleasant branch and new Kitsilano branch
1963	Vancouver Island opens branches in Colwood and Sooke
1964	British Columbia Institute of Technology library established
1964	Franklin P. Levirs completes report on school libraries
1964	B.C. Lions win the Grey Cup
1964	Burnaby becomes third library in B.C. to circulate one million books in a year
1964	Fraser Valley opens Seafair branch in Richmond and Newton branch in Surrey
1964	Grand Forks opens new library as a centennial project
1964	North Vancouver District library becomes a municipal library
1964	Toll removed from George Massey Tunnel
1964	Sayward library started by Women's Institute
1964	Tidal wave sweeps up Alberni inlet
1964	UBC opens Woodward Biomedical Library
1964	McPherson Library at the University of Victoria opens
1964	Beatles play in Vancouver
1964	Valemount library opens
1964	Vancouver Island Regional Library opens Port Renfrew branch
1965	100 Mile House library started
1965	Fraser Valley opens Hope branch
1965	Vancouver Island's Ladysmith branch gets larger quarters
1965	North Vancouver City library gets municipal status
1965	Okanagan opens new branch in Penticton
1965	Sidney and North Saanich join Vancouver Island Regional Library
1965	Simon Fraser University library opens on Burnaby Mountain

1965	UBC starts automation of book-lending process
1965	UBC opens library for the School of Social Work
1965	Vancouver Community College founded
1966	Fernie opens its centennial library
1966	Fort Nelson library moves to provincial government building
1966	Fraser Valley opens Shellmont and Langley Centennial branches
1966	Gold River joins Vancouver Island Regional Library
1966	Houston and Fruitvale start library associations
1966	Hudson's Hope library formed
1966	Okanagan system opens new library in Vernon
1966	Province creates regional districts
1966	Langara College starts library technician program
1966	Selkirk College library opens in former mill construction camp
1966	UBC opens library for Institute of Fisheries
1966	Vainstein Report urges more co-operation and regional service
1966	Victoria opens Town and Country branch in Saanich
1966	Victoria Public Library adds "Greater" to its name
1967	Centennial libraries open in Abbotsford, Campbell River, Castlegar, Chetwynd, Creston, Fernie, Haney, Houston, McBride, Pouce Coupe, Sidney, Smithers and Terrace
1967	Charles Crane Memorial Library for the Blind opens at UBC
1967	Cumberland quits Vancouver Island system
1967	Greater Victoria circulates one million books
1967	Vancouver school board severs ties with Vancouver Public Library
1967	Kamloops and North Kamloops municipalities amalgamate
1967	Okanagan opens new library in Oliver
1967	Okanagan Regional Library opens branch at Mica Dam construction site
1967	Okanagan Regional Library starts bookmobile service in the northern areas
1967	Sechelt library gets its own building

1967	UBC opens libraries for Mathematics, Forestry/Agriculture, and Music
1967	Williams Lake library moves to larger quarters
1968	Capilano College library opens
1968	Granisle collection started by the Public Library Commission
1968	Kinnaird library obtains a charter
1968	Lake Cowichan branch gets new home
1968	Okanagan College opens, with branches and libraries in Kelowna, Vernon and Salmon Arm
1968	Okanagan opens new branches in Armstrong and Summerland
1968	Port Moody Centennial Library opens
1968	Prince Rupert library destroyed by fire
1968	Provincial Museum (now Royal B.C. Museum) opens
1968	Public Library Commission is renamed the Library Development Commission
1968	Library Development Commission starts a consultant service
1968	Vancouver Public Library starts Sunday service
1968	Vancouver opens branch in Killarney school
1968	Vancouver Island Regional Library starts boat service on west coast
1969	College of New Caledonia library opens
1969	Coquitlam opens a library in Centennial High School
1969	Fraser Valley opens new branch at Port Kells in Surrey
1969	Neil Armstrong takes "one small step" on the moon
1969	Malaspina College library opens
1969	John Church completes school library report, finds that forty-six districts have district librarians
1969	Library Development Commission starts correspondence courses for community librarians
1969	Penticton withdraws from the Okanagan Regional Library
1969	Victoria opens Esquimalt branch
1970	Ashcroft public library association formed
1970	Douglas College library opens
1970	Fraser Lake public library association formed
1970	Fraser Valley opens Matsqui Prairie and Pitt Meadows branches

1970   Hudson's Hope gets new library

1970   Provincial Archives move to museum complex

1970   Sergey Yesenin ship and Queen of Victoria ferry collide in Active Pass

1970   Ucluelet joins Vancouver Island Regional Library

1970   Vancouver Community College opens its Langara campus

1970   Vancouver opens Grandview branch

1970   Vancouver Canucks join the National Hockey League

1971   Burns Lake, Fort St. James, Fraser Lake, Vanderhoof get libraries to mark the centennial of B.C.'s entry into Confederation

1971   Victoria's Camosun College created from Institute of Adult Studies

1971   Centennial conference on libraries is held in Victoria

1971   UBC School of Librarianship shifts to a two-year masters program

1971   Proposal for Province-Wide Organization of Library Services released, based on Vainstein report

1971   Community libraries open at Glacier and Elkford

1971   Cranbrook moves to Balment Park location

1971   Fraser Valley opens Brighouse Centre, Whalley, Broadmoor, Guildford, Agassiz, and Aldergrove branches

1971   Okanagan Regional Library adds second bookmobile

1971   Pierre Trudeau marries Margaret Sinclair in Vancouver

1971   Port Hardy, Port Alice and Port McNeill join Vancouver Island Regional Library

1971   Prince Rupert opens new library building

1971   Vancouver opens Fraserview branch

1971   Victoria opens Oak Bay branch

1971   Albert Bowron completes a study of Greater Vancouver library service

1972   Alberni and Port Alberni libraries merge in new premise

1972   Comox rejoins Vancouver Island Regional Library

1972   Elkford library opens with donated books

1972   Fraser Valley opens Mission, Ocean Park and North Delta (George Mackie) branches; Hammond branch is closed

1972   Gibsons library moves into municipal complex

1972   New Democrats elected; Dave Barrett becomes premier

1972   Port Moody becomes a municipal library

1972   Vancouver opens branch in Strathcona school

1972   Vancouver Island Regional Library opens branch at William Head prison; closed in 1977

1972   Vancouver Community College opens a library at the King Edward campus

1972   Victoria opens Victoria-Saanich branch

1972   Williams Lake library gets a new home

1972   Albert Bowron completes a study of Greater Victoria library service

1973   Douglas Lake library opened by the Ladies' Club

1973   Fort Nelson public library association founded

1973   Programme for Library Development in the Province of British Columbia is published

1973   Okanagan closes Westbank branch, with bookmobile service planned until a new location could be found

1973   Okanagan provides a book deposit at Boat Encampment for crews working on the Mica Dam

1973   Okanagan opens new branches in Winfield and Coldstream

1973   Fraser Valley opens bookmobile service at Agassiz Mountain Prison

1973   Fraser Valley opens South Delta and Newton branches, closes Bridgeport and Harrison Hot Springs

1973   Volunteers open Lillooet library in basement of museum

1973   Port Edward branch opened by Prince Rupert

1973   Powell River district library formed with merger of Townsite, Westview, Wildwood Heights and Cranberry Lake libraries

1973   Quesnel library moves to old bank building

1973   Sparwood library opens in Greenwood Mall

1973   Vancouver Public Library starts audiobooks service

1973   Vancouver Community College opens a library at the Vancouver Vocational Institute

1974	Burnaby's Central Park branch is opened
1974	Burnaby's Crest Neighbourhood Library is opened; closed 1982
1974	Castlegar and Kinnaird libraries amalgamate
1974	University of Victoria opens the Diana Priestly Law Library
1974	Kootenay Library System Committee formed
1974	Elkford, Fort Nelson, Lillooet, Mackenzie, and Queen Charlotte City and Sparwood library associations formed
1974	Fraser Valley College opens
1974	Insurance Corporation of B.C. started
1974	Okanagan College opens a branch library in Penticton
1974	Granisle public library association formed, library opens in old store
1974	Okanagan Regional Library opens new headquarters on KLO Road
1974	Provincial Library becomes the Legislative Library of British Columbia
1974	Okanagan Regional Library opens new Westbank branch
1974	McPherson Library at the University of Victoria is expanded
1974	Royal Roads library moves to a new building
1974	Tahsis joins Vancouver Island Regional Library
1974	Thompson-Nicola Library System started, with existing libraries in Kamloops, Merritt and Ashcroft, and new ones in Barriere, Clearwater, Cache Creek and Clinton
1974	Vancouver opens Richard Marpole branch
1975	Cariboo votes to join the Thompson-Nicola system
1975	Central Saanich leaves the Greater Victoria system to join Vancouver Island
1975	Cumberland rejoins Vancouver Island system
1975	East Kootenay Community College library opens
1975	Greater Vancouver Library Federation established
1975	B.C. Law Library Foundation formed to manage courthouse libraries
1975	Library Development Commission offers audiobooks
1975	North Vancouver City moves to new building

1975	Okanagan opens branches in Golden, Lumby, Salmon Arm, Osoyoos, and Okanagan Falls
1975	Okanagan opens paperback deposit stations in Cawston and Seymour Arm
1975	Social Credit elected; Bill Bennett becomes premier
1975	Sooke branch of Vancouver Island Regional Library gets a new location
1975	Sparwood library moves to church basement
1975	Thompson-Nicola opens branches in Blue River, Logan Lake, North Kamloops and on the Kamloops Indian Reserve
1975	UBC opens new law library
1975	Vancouver opens Britannia and South Granville branches
1976	Victoria opens Nellie McClung branch
1976	Forest magnate H.R. MacMillan dies
1976	Hudson's Hope library moves to log building overlooking the Peace River
1976	Writer Roderick Haig-Brown of Campbell River dies
1976	Libraries opened in Lytton, Lillooet, Shalalth, Hendrix Lake, Bridge Lake, Canim Lake, Lac la Hache, McLeese Lake, Nazko, Big Lake, Eagle Creek, Narcosli, Alexis Creek, Alkali Lake, Forest Grove, Riske Creek, Nemaiah Valley, Horsefly, Likely, Anahim Lake and Tatla Lake
1976	Library Development Commission comes under the Ministry of Recreation and Conservation
1976	Princeton joins the Okanagan Regional Library
1976	Okanagan opens new branch in Peachland
1976	Richmond leaves the Fraser Valley Regional Library, taking five branches
1976	Salmo library moves to main street storefront
1976	Vancouver opens Joe Fortes branch; closes Grandview
1976	Vancouver Island opens Langford and Brentwood Bay branches
1976	Williams Lake library moves to larger quarters
1976	Legal Services Society starts offering funding, training and support to public libraries in aid of getting legal information to the public
1977	Ladner Pioneer branch in Delta destroyed by fire in March; reopened in November

1977	Notre Dame University in Nelson closed by the provincial government
1977	British Columbia Library Trustees Association is formed
1977	Okanagan's Revelstoke and Rutland branches move to new locations
1977	Queen Charlotte City library moves to new home
1977	Post-secondary libraries adopt UTLAS (University of Toronto Library Automation System) cataloguing products
1977	Singer Elvis Presley dies at 42
1977	Speed limits go metric
1977	Star Wars opens in movie theatres
1977	Cariboo-Thompson-Nicola opens branch in Spences Bridge
1977	UBC closes its card catalogue
1977	Whalley branch opens in Surrey
1978	Camosun College opens branch on Carey Road in Saanich
1978	College of New Caledonia library moves to permanent building
1978	Comox library moves to larger premises
1978	Coquitlam's Cottonwood and Ridgeway branches opened
1978	David Thompson University Centre in Nelson takes the place of Notre Dame
1978	Kamloops opens new library
1978	Library Services Branch replaces Library Development Commission; moved to Ministry of Provincial Secretary and Government Services
1978	New Westminster's expanded library opens
1978	Cariboo-Thompson-Nicola opens branch in Savona and moves Quesnel branch to bigger quarters
1978	Health Libraries Association of B.C. formed
1978	University, college and select public libraries create a union catalogue on microfiche
1978	Vancouver opens West Point Grey branch
1978	Vancouver School of Decorative and Applied Arts becomes the Emily Carr College of Art
1978	Justice Institute of B.C. Library opens
1979	Fraser Valley opens new headquarters in Abbotsford

1979	Fraser Valley opens branches in Boston Bar and Yale schools
1979	Okanagan opens new Revelstoke branch
1979	Former premier W.A.C. Bennett dies
1979	Report sparks upgrading of libraries in provincial jails
1979	Free B.C. Resources Investment Corp. shares for all of us
1979	UBC School of Librarianship offers a two-year masters program in archival studies
1979	Vancouver Island's Gold River and Cowichan branches move to larger locations
1979	Kinnaird moves to a larger location
1979	Midway Public Library started as a reading centre in Boundary Central Secondary School
1979	Kamloops library lost in a fire
1979	Cariboo-Thompson-Nicola opens branches in Strathnaver and Wells
1979	Okanagan College library moves to new building and is renamed in honour of pioneer librarian Muriel Ffoulkes
1979	Kootenay Library System Committee collapses
1979	Pemberton library association formed
1979	Port Hardy, Port McNeill branches of Vancouver Island get new locations
1979	Second Vancouver Island branch opens in Nanaimo; known as Wellington
1980	Burnaby's Cameron branch is opened
1980	Fraser Valley opens Surrey Centennial and Guildford branches
1980	Jessie Simpson library opens in Masset
1980	Kimberley opens its new library
1980	Wildwood library at Powell River closes
1980	Okanagan opens new branches in Kelowna, Enderby, Westbank and Sicamous
1980	UBC opens Asian Studies Library
1980	Richmond expands Brighouse Centre branch
1980	Library technicians course started by Fraser Valley College
1980	University of Victoria Law Library moves to Begbie Building
1980	Victoria central branch moves to new library building
1980	Valleyview library in Kamloops closes due to a financial crunch

1980 Vancouver opens Kensington and Champlain Heights branches; closes Killarney

1980 Vancouver opens Carnegie Community Centre branch

1980 Vancouver starts story times for babies

1981 Bowen Island reading centre opens

1981 Chilliwack branch moves to larger location

1981 Coquitlam's Burquitlam Plaza and Lincoln branches opened

1981 Douglas College splits into Douglas and Kwantlen

1981 Marathon of Hope's Terry Fox dies

1981 Okanagan opens new branches in Golden, Peachland and Naramata

1981 Prince George opens its new library

1981 Selkirk College opens a branch in Nelson

1981 Vancouver Island system starts Bella Coola library

1981 Vancouver opens Riley Park branch

1982 East Kootenay Community College library moves to new campus

1982 Grand Forks, Kaslo, Sidney-North Saanich and Tahsis libraries move to new locations

1982 Prince Rupert opens expanded, renovated building

1982 Okanagan's Cawston paperback station closed because of budget cuts

1982 Okanagan opens new Summerland branch, and moves Silver Creek to a school classroom

1982 Okanagan College Vernon campus library moves to new location

1982 Cranberry library at Powell River closes

1982 Cariboo-Thompson-Nicola opens branch in Avola

1982 Mackenzie library becomes a municipal library

1982 Victoria's old Carnegie building sold; proceeds go to renovate a theatre

1983 Nicola Valley Institute of Technology opens in Merritt

1983 Queen Charlottes (Haida Gwaii) joins Vancouver Island Regional Library, with branches in Masset, Sandspit, Port Clements and Queen Charlotte City

1983 Surrey leaves the Fraser Valley system

1983 Townsite library at Powell River closes

1983 Fraser Valley system opens Terry Fox branch in Port Coquitlam and George Mackie branch in North Delta, and moves Clearbrook branch

1983 Vancouver Island gets new headquarters

1983 Okanagan's Keremeos, Rutland and Mica Creek branches get new quarters

1983 School librarians' association becomes the B.C. Teacher Librarians' Association

1984 Budget cuts force libraries to scale back

1984 David Thompson University Centre in Nelson closed, leading to a sit-in to save the library

1984 Dawson Creek becomes a municipal library

1984 Fort St. John moves to larger premises

1984 Fraser Valley's Hope branch moves to larger premises

1984 Okanagan opens Oyama branch

1984 B.C. Law Library Foundation becomes the British Columbia Courthouse Library Society

1984 Rossland library moves into old service station

1984 Tumbler Ridge main library opens in recreation centre

1984 Vancouver Island's Colwood, Sooke and Ladysmith branches move to larger premises

1984 Vancouver Island opens Bella Coola branch

1984 Woss branch established by Vancouver Island

1985 Camosun College opens branch on Interurban Road in Saanich

1985 Fort Nelson public library is in the Village Complex

1985 Greater Victoria's Esquimalt branch moves to new premises

1985 Kamloops library moves into old Woodward's store

1985 Bowen Island reading centre becomes a public library association

1985 North Vancouver District opens renovated Capilano branch

1985 Okanagan's Enderby branch destroyed by fire, and re-opens in a new location five weeks later

1985 Okanagan opens Okanagan Falls branch

1985 Steve Fonyo completes cross-Canada run

1985 Vancouver Island's Courtenay and Sooke branches move to larger premises

1986	British Columbia Institute of Technology library merges with Pacific Vocational Institute library
1986	Salmo Public Library moves to new premises
1986	Fraser Valley opens South Delta and Maple Ridge branches
1986	Library Services Branch moved to Ministry of Tourism, Recreation and Culture
1986	B.C. College and Institute Library Services starts at Vancouver Community College's Langara campus, providing books in alternate formats
1986	Okanagan opens new Westbank and Winfield branches
1986	Vancouver Island expands Wellington, Lake Cowichan and Parksville branches
1986	Vancouver hosts Expo 86
1986	Whistler opens library
1987	Bookmobiles are parked on Hornby, Quadra and Gabriola Islands as small branches
1987	Bowen Island, Burns Lake and Castlegar open new libraries
1987	Fraser Valley's Mount Lehman branch is closed for two months due to fire
1987	Loonie goes into circulation
1987	Okanagan's Winfield branch destroyed by fire
1987	Okanagan's Enderby branch gets a new home
1987	Okanagan drops its Mica Creek branch
1987	Cariboo-Thompson-Nicola opens branches in Lillooet, Shalalth, and Gold Bridge
1987	Vancouver Island expands Campbell River, Sandspit and Ucluelet branches
1987	Vancouver starts Outreach Services for people who cannot get to branches
1988	Fraser Valley opens Pitt Meadows branch, closes Matsqui Prairie
1988	Library Services Branch moves to Ministry of Municipal Affairs
1988	Library Services Branch's Dawson Creek office closes
1988	Okanagan opens Peachland and Winfield branches
1988	Report on public libraries, *New Approaches*, calls for province-wide electronic interlibrary loan system

1988	Valemount opens new library
1988	Vancouver Island expands Lake Cowichan branch, parks bookmobile
1989	British Columbia Electronic Library Network is created to assist in sharing resources
1989	Coquitlam opens Poirier branch
1989	Fraser Valley moves Aldergrove branch
1989	Malaspina, Cariboo and Okanagan colleges become university colleges
1989	Lillooet, Shalalth and Gold Bridge leave the Cariboo-Thompson-Nicola system
1989	Okanagan opens expanded Vernon branch
1989	Richmond opens Steveston branch
1989	Simon Fraser University's Samuel and Frances Belzberg Library opened
1989	Sparwood opens new library
1989	Victoria's Nellie McClung branch destroyed by fire
1989	Vancouver Island opens South Cowichan and Brentwood/Central Saanich branches
1990	Hazelton District opens new library, shared with the museum
1990	Lillooet library destroyed by fire
1990	University of Northern British Columbia opens
1990	Vancouver Island opens Sointula branch
1990	Okanagan replaces Coldstream branch with two bookmobile stops
1990	Okanagan opens new Winfield branch
1990	Vancouver Island moves its Chemainus and Port McNeill branches
1990	Vancouver Island replaces Quadra and Hornby bookmobiles with small branches
1991	Province-wide Summer Reading Club launched
1991	Bowen Island, Elkford, Lillooet and Pouce Coupe open new libraries
1991	Burnaby opens the Bob Prittie Metrotown branch
1991	Okanagan College Salmon Arm campus library moves to new location
1991	Fraser Valley College becomes a university college
1991	Federal goods and services tax takes effect
1991	Okanagan opens new Falkland, Sicamous and Armstrong branches

1991	Greater Victoria opens new Nellie McClung branch after fire
1991	New Democratic Party elected; Mike Harcourt becomes premier
1991	Outlook, a province-wide CD-ROM catalogue, released
1991	Vancouver, Fraser Valley end bookmobile services
1992	Vancouver opens Firehall branch, shared with the fire department; closes South Granville
1992	Creston, Nelson and Fort St. John open new libraries
1992	First B.C. Library Association information policy conference held
1992	Canada's first public computer network started in Victoria
1992	InterLINK library federation expands Greater Vancouver federation
1992	Lillooet opens Goldbridge branch, shared with post office and fire hall
1992	Okanagan opens new branches in Lumby, Cherryville, Hedley, Oyama and Kaleden
1992	Okanagan parks its bookmobiles, making them temporary mini-branches in Celista and Sorrento
1992	Richmond opens new Brighouse branch
1992	Surrey opens new Newton branch
1992	Vancouver Island opens new Gold River, Sayward, and Sooke branches
1993	Cariboo-Thompson-Nicola system splits into two
1993	Kim Campbell becomes prime minister
1993	Public computer networks started in Vancouver and Prince George
1993	Okanagan College opens North Kelowna campus and library
1993	Okanagan opens new Salmon Arm and Sorrento branches
1993	West Vancouver opens expanded library
1994	Fraser Valley opens Walnut Grove branch
1994	Radium Hot Springs establishes a community library
1994	Greater Victoria opens new Bruce Hutchison branch in Saanich
1994	Internet service arrives in public libraries
1994	Langara College splits from Vancouver Community College
1994	New Library Act is passed, defining core free library services and dropping school board representatives from library boards; they were replaced by regional district directors
1994	North Vancouver District opens Parkgate branch
1994	Okanagan opens Celista branch
1994	University of British Columbia launches its website
1994	Vancouver Island opens new Ladysmith branch
1994	Vancouver opens Renfrew branch, the largest branch in Vancouver
1994	Whistler opens new library
1995	Fraser Valley opens new Clearbrook branch
1995	Kitimat, Port Moody open new libraries
1995	Kwantlen College becomes a university college
1995	Justice Institute of B.C. Library moves to New Westminster
1995	Library Services Branch closes Prince George, Cranbrook offices
1995	Okanagan opens new Winfield branch
1995	Open Shelf books-by-mail program ends
1995	Royal Roads Military College closes, becomes Royal Roads University
1995	Surrey opens new Fleetwood branch
1995	Terrace opens expanded library
1995	Vancouver opens new central branch
1996	Colwood, Langford and Metchosin switch from Vancouver Island system to Greater Victoria system
1996	Fraser Valley opens new Agassiz branch
1996	Gibsons and District opens new library
1996	Okanagan opens new Kelowna, Westbank branches
1996	Victoria's Carnegie Library featured on a postage stamp
1997	Delta votes to stay in Fraser Valley system
1997	Fraser Valley moves its Hope branch
1997	Greater Victoria opens Juan de Fuca branch in Colwood
1997	Invermere becomes a municipal library

1997 Library Services Branch ends distribution of blocks of books to libraries – the last of the travelling libraries

1997 Midway and Squamish open new libraries

1997 Thompson-Nicola opens Blue River branch

1997 Vancouver Island opens Nanaimo Harbourfront, Sooke, Tofino, Qualicum Beach and Cortes Island branches

1997 Youth employment program provides Internet training

1998 Coquitlam opens new City Centre branch

1998 Fraser Valley expands its Ladner branch

1998 Okanagan opens new Keremeos branch

1998 Greater Victoria buys its central branch building

1998 Thompson-Nicola system opens new Kamloops branch and administration centre

1998 Outlook catalogue moves to the Internet

1998 Richmond opens new Ironwood branch

1999 Harrison Hot Springs joins Fraser Valley

1999 Victoria-Saanich branch library is renamed to honour artist Emily Carr

1999 Vancouver opens new Outreach branch

1999 Okanagan opens new Peachland and Oliver branches

1999 Vancouver Island opens new Gabriola Island branch

1999 Virtual Reference Desk launched

2000 Fraser Valley opens new Langley City branch

2000 Surrey opens new Strawberry Hill branch

2000 Computer and Internet grants made by Bill and Melinda Gates Foundation

2000 Library Services Branch gets a national award for innovative use of Internet

2001 B.C. Liberals elected; Gordon Campbell becomes premier

2001 Burnaby opens new McGill branch

2001 Central Saanich withdraws from Vancouver Island system

2001 Fraser Valley opens new Agassiz, Maple Ridge branches

2001 Library Services Branch renamed Public Library Services Branch; moved to Ministry of Community, Aboriginal and Women's Services

2001 Thompson-Nicola opens new Merritt branch

2001 Smithers becomes a municipal library

2001 Vancouver opens Champlain Heights branch

2001 Vancouver Island opens new Courtenay, Parksville branches

2001 UBC opens branch in Robson Square in downtown Vancouver

2002 Cranbrook and Kimberley become municipal libraries

2002 Fraser Valley opens new Langley Township branch

2002 Greater Victoria opens new Brentwood Bay branch

2002 Simon Fraser University opens Surrey campus

2002 One Book One Vancouver program started

2002 Thompson-Nicola opens new Lytton branch

2002 Vancouver Island opens new Nanaimo Wellington branch

2003 Greater Victoria opens new Esquimalt branch

2003 Squamish becomes a municipal library

2003 Surrey opens new Semiahmoo branch

2004 *Libraries Without Walls: The World Within Your Reach*, a provincial strategic plan for libraries, calls for equitable access, collaboration and partnerships

2004 Powell River becomes a municipal library

2004 Okanagan opens new Okanagan Falls branch

2004 Richmond opens new Cambie branch

2004 Thompson-Nicola opens new Barriere branch

2004 Vancouver Island opens new Lake Cowichan branch

2004 Google launches its Google Books service

2004 Kootenay Library Federation started

2005 Fraser Valley opens Willowbrook branch

2005 New Westminster Public Library completes major renovations

2005 Okanagan opens new Kelowna branch

2005 Okanagan University College split into Okanagan College and UBC Okanagan, with North Kelowna campus library becoming part of UBC

2005 Books for B.C. Babies program started

2005 Public Library Services Branch moved to Ministry of Education

2005 Thompson Rivers University created from University College of the Cariboo and B.C. Open University

2005	Teen Summer Reading Club started
2005	Xwi7xwa Library becomes a branch of UBC Library
2005	Thompson-Nicola opens new Savona branch
2005	Tofino library moves to a new home
2006	AskAway, a virtual reference service, is introduced in public and post-secondary libraries
2006	BC OneCard offers patrons access to all public libraries in the province
2006	Radium Hot Springs library becomes a municipal public library
2006	Fort St. James opens new main library
2006	Richmond completes Brighouse branch renovations
2006	North Coast Library Federation evolves from the Northcoast Libraries Association
2006	Okanagan opens North Shuswap branch, formerly Celista
2006	Taylor establishes municipal public library
2006	Simon Fraser University opens new branch library in Surrey
2007	Greater Victoria opens new Tillicum (Saanich Centennial) branch
2007	Library federations started in the North Central and North East regions
2007	North Vancouver District opens new main library
2007	Library2020 conference looks at future
2007	Okanagan opens new Osoyoos branch
2007	Pouce Coupe opens a library in the school to service public and students
2007	Prince Rupert is first B.C. library to use the Evergreen catalogue system
2007	Institute of Indigenous Government merges with Nicola Valley Institute of Technology
2007	Courthouse Libraries BC initiates LawMatters, which helps public libraries provide legal information
2007	Langara College opens new library
2007	Kuugin King Naay Haida children's library established in Skidegate

2008	Capilano University, Emily Carr University of Art and Design, Kwantlen Polytechnic University, University of the Fraser Valley and Vancouver Island University officially designated as universities
2008	Greater Victoria opens John Goudy express branch in Langford
2008	North Vancouver City opens new main library
2008	William C. Mearns Centre for Learning opens at the University of Victoria
2008	Irving K. Barber Learning Centre opens at UBC
2008	Cranbrook opens new main library
2008	Okanagan opens new headquarters
2008	Pemberton and District main library moves into new community centre
2008	Vancouver Island opens new Comox and Bowser branches
2008	IslandLink federation started, serving Greater Victoria, Salt Spring, Alert Bay and Powell River
2008	Whistler opens new library
2008	UBC's Koerner Library is featured on a postage stamp
2009	B.C. Libraries Cooperative formed
2009	One Book One Kootenay program launched
2009	Books for B.C. Babies and AskAway public library service ended
2009	Burnaby opens Tommy Douglas branch
2009	Vancouver opens new Kensington and Mount Pleasant branches
2009	Vancouver Island opens new Port Clements branch as part of community multiplex
2010	Thompson-Nicola opens North Kamloops branch in Library Square
2010	100 Mile House Library opens in new location
2010	Bowen Island community library gets municipal status
2010	New Westminster launches a social networking library catalogue
2011	Surrey City Centre Library replaces Whalley branch
2011	Librarians deal with explosion of interest in ebooks
2011	Vancouver opens Terry Salman branch in Hillcrest Centre

APPENDIX

1. Chairs of the Public Library Commission (1919-1968) and the Library Development Commission (1968-1978)

1919-1920	Malcolm Bruce Jackson
1920-1923	Helen Gordon Stewart
1926-1928	Norman Fergus Black
1929-1944	Hugh Norman Lidster
1945-1946	Edgar Stewart Robinson
1947-1948	William Kaye Lamb
Dec. 1948	Hugh Norman Lidster
1949-1950	Margaret Jean Clay
1951-1952	William Crossley Mainwaring
1953-1954	Cecil Hacker
1955-1956	Hugh Norman Lidster
1957	Edgar Stewart Robinson
1958-1959	Margaret Jean Clay
1960-1961	Winfield Scott Pipes
1962-1967	Daphne Parr
1968-1972	Robert D. Ferguson
1973-1978	Ray Culos

2. Superintendents and directors of the Public Library Commission (1919-1968), Library Development Commission (1968-1978), Library Services Branch (1978-2001) and Public Library Services Branch (2001-)

1919-1935	Arthur Herbert Killam
1936-1940	William Kaye Lamb
1940-1956	Charles Keith Morison
1956-1980	Robert L. Davison
1980	Mary Leask (acting)
1980-1987	Peter Martin
1987-1988	Chris Peppler (acting)
1988-2001	Barbara Greeniaus
2001-2003	Chris Peppler
2003-2006	Maureen Woods
2006-	Jacqueline van Dyk

3. Legislative Library directors

1885-1888	William Atkins
1888-1889	Nevil Edgar Graves
1891-1892	Joseph E. Bridgman
1893-1898	R. Edward Gosnell
1899-1919	E.O.S. Scholefield
1919-1926	John Forsyth
1926-1934	John Hosie
1934	Alma Russell (acting)
1934-1940	William Kaye Lamb
1940-1942	Willard E. Ireland
1942-1946	Madge Wolfenden (acting)
1946-1973	Willard E. Ireland
1973-1982	James G. Mitchell
1982-1985	Margaret E. Hastings (acting)
1985-2003	Joan A. Barton
2003-2009	Jane Taylor
2009-	Peter Gourlay (acting)

4. Provincial archives directors

1908-1910	R. Edward Gosnell
1910-1919	E.O.S. Scholefield
1919-1926	John Forsyth
1926-1934	John Hosie
1934	Alma Russell (acting)
1934-1940	W. Kaye Lamb
1940-1942	Willard E. Ireland
1942-1946	Madge Wolfenden (acting)
1946-1974	Willard E. Ireland
1974-1979	Allan R. Turner
1979-1998	John A. Bovey
1998-	Gary A. Mitchell

5. Major surveys, plans and programs

1927-28	British Columbia Library Survey
1940	Libraries in British Columbia
1945	Programme for Library Development in British Columbia
1950	Programme for Library Development
1956	Programme for Library Development
1966	Public Libraries in British Columbia: A Survey with Recommendations (Rose Vainstein)
1971	Proposal for Province-Wide Reorganization of Library Services
1973	Programme for Library Development
1988	British Columbia's Public Libraries: A New Approach
2004	Libraries Without Walls: The World Within Your Reach

6. Helen Gordon Stewart Award winners
(Given by the British Columbia Library Association to honour members who have made, or are making, an extraordinary contribution to librarianship)

1962	Helen Gordon Stewart
1963	Margaret Jean Clay
1970	Samuel Rothstein
1973	Alice Simpson
1975	Mary Leask
1984	Sheila Egoff
1985-86	Margaret Burke
1987-88	Lois Bewley
1988-89	Harry Newsom
1991-92	Basil Stuart-Stubbs
1992-93	C. William Fraser
2002-03	Nancy Hannum
2004-05	Ken Haycock
2005-06	Brian Campbell
2005-06	Jim Looney
2008-09	Greg Buss
2009-10	Lynn Copeland

7. Presidents of the British Columbia Library Association

1911-1913	Robert W. Douglas
1913-1914	John J. Shallcross

1914-1917	Ethelbert Olaf Stuart Scholefield		1979-1980	James C. Scott
1917-1919	Helen Gordon Stewart		1980-1981	Mary Beth MacDonald
1919-1920	Annie B. Jamieson		1981-1982	Maureen Willison
1920-1921	Arthur Herbert Killam		1982-1983	Harry Newsom
1921-1922	John Hosie		1983-1984	Margaret Freisen
1922-1923	John Ridington		1984-1985	Garth Homer/Margaret Friesen
1924	Alma M. Russell		1985-1986	Jack Mounce
1925	Margaret Jean Clay		1986-1987	Linda Hale
1926-1927	Edgar Stewart Robinson		1987-1988	Linda Kabush
1927-1928	John Hosie		1988-1989	Brian Owen
1928-1929	Samuel Tilden Dare		1989-1990	Paula Pick
1930	Frederick William Howay		1990-1991	Paul Whitney
1931	Jean Elisabeth Whitman		1991-1992	Nancy Hannum
1932	Helen Gordon Stewart		1992-1993	Sylvia Crooks
1933	John Ridington		1993-1994	Gordon Ray
1933-1934	Marjorie C. Holmes		1994-1995	Leonora Crema
1934-1935	Julia Carson Stockett		1995-1996	Nancy Levesque
1935-1936	Alma M. Russell		1996-1997	Ron Clancy
1936-1937	Hugh Norman Lidster		1997-1998	Frieda Wiebe
1937-1938	Charles Keith Morison		1998-1999	Greg Buss
1938-1939	Edgar Stewart Robinson		1999-2000	Sybil Harrison
1939-1940	William Kaye Lamb		2000-2001	Julie Spurrell
1940-1941	Anne M. Smith		2001-2003	Carol Elder
1941-1942	Ruth Emiline Cameron		2003-2004	Alison Nussbaumer
1942-1943	Jeannette Sargent		2004-2005	Diana Guinn
1943-1944	Jessie Marion G. Hotson		2005-2006	Melanie Houlden
1944-1945	Muriel Carruthers		2006-2007	Inba Kehoe
1945-1946	Irene McAfee		2007-2008	Deb Thomas
1946-1947	Christine McNamee		2008-2009	Lynne Jordon
1947-1948	Bessie Greenwood		2009-2010	Kenneth Cooley
1948-1949	Willard E. Ireland		2010-2011	Marjorie Mitchell
1949-1950	Amy Hutcheson		2011-2012	Chris Kevlahan
1950-1951	Eleanor Mercer			
1951-1952	Marjorie Sing			

8. Honorary presidents of the British Columbia Library Association (Provincial cabinet ministers responsible for libraries)

1952-1953	Thressa Pollock		1911-1912	Dr. Henry Esson Young
1953-1954	Ronald Ley		1913-1916	William John Bowser
1954-1955	Anne Berry		1917-1919	John Wallace deBeque Farris
1955-1956	Margaret Brunette		1919-1925	John Duncan MacLean
1956-1957	Muriel Laing		1926-1928	William Sloan
1957-1958	Robert L. Davison		1928-1934	Samuel Lyness Howe
1958-1959	Peter Grossman		1934-1941	George Moir Weir
1959-1960	Samuel Rothstein		1942-1945	Henry George Thomas Perry
1960-1961	Dorothy Salisbury		1945-1947	George Moir Weir
1961-1962	John C. Lort		1948-1952	William Thomas Straith
1962-1963	Doreen Fraser		1952-1954	Tillie Jean Rolston
1963-1964	Theodora G. Rhodes		1954-1956	Ray. G. Williston
1964-1965	George Turner (resigned); Lois Bewley		1957-1961	Leslie Peterson
1965-1966	Dean Halliwell		1961-1966	Wesley Black
1966-1967	Enid Dearing			

9. Presidents of the British Columbia Library Trustees Association

1967-1968	Aileen Tufts		1976-1977	Bill Parker
1968-1969	Anna Leith		1978-1979	Dolly Kennedy
1969-1970	Joy Scudamore		1980	Nora Stocks
1970-1971	Sheila MacDonald		1981	Bunne Hoffman
1971-1972	Robert Harris		1982	Gordon Hoglund
1972-1973	Del Affleck		1983	Emil Gobes
1973-1974	Margaret Burke		1984-1985	Allan Blair
1974-1975	Don Miller		1986-1987	Gordon Wainwright
1975-1976	John Backhouse		1988	Sue Granger
1976-1977	William Watson		1989	Mae Williams
1977-1978	Fred White			
1978-1979	Ron Willey			

1990-1991	Chuck Haddock
1992-1993	Chad Whyte
1994-1995	Barry Lynch
1996-1997	Dan Greene
1998-1999	Ernest Neumann
2000	Colleen Chambers
2001-2002	Blair Qualey
2003-2003	Sally Gibson
2005-2006	Lawrence Lavender
2007	Peter Wainwright
2008-2011	Andy Ackerman

10. British Columbia presidents of the Pacific Northwest Library Association

1911-13	Ethelbert Olaf Stuart Scholefield
1915-16	Arthur Herbert Killam
1918-19	John Ridington
1920-21	Helen Gordon Stewart
1923-24	John Ridington
1928-29	Edgar Stewart Robinson
1934-35	Margaret Jean Clay
1941-42	Julia Carson Stockett
1945-46	William Kaye Lamb
1949-50	Anne M. Smith
1953-54	Willard Ireland
1958-59	Ronald Ley
1963-64	Samuel Rothstein
1981-82	Joy Scudamore
1997-98	Gordon Ray
2010-2011	Michael Burris

11. British Columbia presidents of the Canadian Library Association

1948	William Kaye Lamb
1953	Edgar Stewart Robinson
1954	Peter Grossman
1956	Willard Ireland
1961	Neal Harlow
1962	Robert M. Hamilton
1968	Amy Hutcheson
1972	Dean Halliwell
1977	Anne Piternick
1978	Ken Haycock
1984	Lois Bewley
1990	Beth Barlow
1992	Marnie Swanson
1998	Paul Whitney

12. British Columbia presidents of the Canadian Association of Public Libraries

1974-75	Fred White
1979-80	Heather Harbord
1982-83	Don Miller
1983-84	Madge Aalto
1985-86	Gordon Ray
1986-87	Stan Smith

13. British Columbia winners of the Canadian Library Association's award for outstanding service to librarianship

1983	Sheila Egoff
1986	Samuel Rothstein
1989	Lois Bewley

1991	Ken Haycock
2002	Paul Whitney
2003	Brian Campbell
2010	Lynn Copeland

14. Presidents of the British Columbia School Librarians Association (1939-1983) and the British Columbia Teacher-Librarians Association (1983-)

1939-1940	Muriel Carruthers
1940-1941	Margaret (Rathie) Ginther
1941-1942	Jean Woodrow
1942-1943	Margaret Cook
1943-1944	Jean (Witbeck) Vick
1944-1945	Mary Coleman
1945-1946	Cordy Mackay / Myrtle Batchelor
1946-1947	Myrtle Batchelor
1947-1949	Lucy Howell
1949-1951	Margaret Murray
1951-1953	Hilda Smith
1953-1955	Christine Sutherland
1955-1957	Josie MacDonald
1957-1958	May Martin
1958-1959	Dorothy McLellan
1959-1960	Dorothy Williams
1960-1961	Marion Wylie
1961-1962	Ed Burchak
1962-1963	Harry Newsom
1963-1964	Grace d'Arcy
1964-1965	Mary Coggin
1965-1966	Ed Albrecht
1966-1967	Robert Brown
1967-1968	Margaretta Rice
1968-1969	Alan Fraser
1969-1970	Elsie Wagner
1970-1971	Roger Behn
1971-1972	Fran Sbrocchi
1972-1973	Gerry Constable
1973-1974	Mel Rainey
1974-1976	Angela Thacker
1976-1977	Blair Greenwood
1977-1978	Doug Trounce
1978-1979	Mel Maglio
1979-1980	Glen Pinch
1980-1982	William Scott
1982-1984	Alan Knight
1984-1986	Liz Austrom
1986-1988	Barbara Hall
1988-1990	Diana Poole
1990-1992	Patricia Finlay
1992-1994	Kristina Nellis
1994-1995	Judith Kootte
1995-1998	Gerald Soon
1998-2001	Mark Roberts
2001-2003	Joan Eaton and Kaye Treadgold
2003-2005	Mary Locke
2005-2007	Pat Parungao
2008-2009	Bonnie McComb and Heather Daly
2009-	Heather Daly

15. British Columbia winners of the Margaret B. Scott Award of Merit (for outstanding contribution to Canadian school librarianship)

1979	Ken Haycock
1981	Mary Coggin
1986	Grace Funk
1988	Donald Hamilton
1998	Willa Walsh
2005	Karin Paul
2007	Marlene Asselin

16. British Columbia winners of the teacher-librarian of the year award (given by the Canadian Association for School Libraries)

1998	Willa Walsh
2001	Kay Treadgold
2003	Bonnie McComb
2005	Hazel Clark
2006	Karen Cordiner
2007	Mary Locke
2009	Michele Farquharson
2010	Pat Parungao

17. British Columbia presidents of the Canadian Association of College and University Libraries

1967-68	Dean Halliwell
1970-71	Inglis Bell
1974-75	Helen Rodney
1989-91	Pat Appavoo
1997-99	Melody Burton

18. British Columbia presidents of the Canadian Association of Research Libraries

1987	Doug McInnes
1991	Ted Dobb
1997	Marnie Swanson

19. British Columbia presidents of the Western Canada chapter of the Special Libraries Association

1993-94	Jan Wallace
1994-95	Linda Everett
1995-96	Grace Makarewicz
1996-96	Diana Broome
1997-98	Rita Penco
1998-99	Carol Williams
1999-2000	Barbara Holder
2000-01	Debbie Millward
2001-02	Patricia Cia
2004-05	Keith Low
2005-06	Christina Zeller
2007	Robyn McDowell
2009	Debbie Schachter
2010	Frances Main

20. Vancouver head librarians

1887-1889	George Pollay
1889-1910	Edwin Machin
1910-1911	A.E. Goodman
1911-1924	R.W. Douglas
1924-1957	Edgar Stewart Robinson
1957-1970	Peter Grossman
1978-1978	Morton Jordan
1979-1983	George Wootton
1983-1988	Aileen Tufts
1988-2003	Madge Aalto
2003-2010	Paul Whitney
2011-	Sandra Singh

21. Victoria head librarians

1889-1897	James McGregor
1897-1905	Henry Goward
1905-1912	J. Griffith Hands
1912-1924	Helen Gordon Stewart
1924-1952	Margaret Jean Clay
1952-1954	Thressa Pollock
1954-1970	John C. Lort
1971-1983	Don Miller
1983-1988	Madge Aalto
1988-1995	Lee Teal
1995-2006	Sandra Anderson
2006-2010	Barry Holmes
2010	Lee Teal (acting)
2010-	Maureen Sawa

22. New Westminster head librarians

1865	William Edward Wynne Williams
1866	George Ramsay
1866-1867	John B. Harris
1867-1868	W.E. Cormack
1874	J. Dawson
1882-1884	Henry W. Hughes
1887-1890	Donald McGregor
1891	Julian Peacock
1899	Edward Z. Whyman
1905-1912	Susan Gilley
1912-1913	Annie T. O'Meara
1914-1921	Mabel Macmillan
1921-1923	Pearl Hale
1923-1936	Samuel Tilden Dare
1936-1954	Ruth Cameron
1954-1973	Amy Hutcheson
1973-1991	Alan Woodland
1991-2003	Ron Clancy
2003-	Julie Spurrell

23. University of British Columbia head librarians

1915-1940	John Ridington
1940-1948	William Kaye Lamb
1948-1949	Anne Smith (acting)
1949-1950	Leslie W. Dunlap
1950-1951	Anne Smith (acting)
1951-1961	Neal Harlow
1961-1962	Samuel Rothstein (acting)
1962-1963	James Ranz
1964-1981	Basil Stuart-Stubbs
1982-1989	Douglas McInnes
1989-1990	William Watson (acting)
1990-1997	Ruth Patrick
1997-2007	Catherine Quinlan
2007-2009	Peter Ward (pro tem)
2009-	Ingrid Parent

24. University of Victoria head librarians

1963-1987	Dean Halliwell
1987-	Marnie Swanson

25. Simon Fraser University head librarians

1965-1978	Donald Baird
1978-1998	Ted Dobb
1998-2010	Lynn Copeland
2010-	Charles Eckman

26. Fraser Valley Demonstration / Union / Regional Library head librarians

1930-1934	Helen Gordon Stewart
1934-1940	Charles Keith Morison
1940-1945	R. Bruce Carrick
1946-1948	Peter Grossman
1948-1970	Ronald Ley
1971-1980	Howard Overend
1981-1984	James Craven
1984-1986	James Scott
1986-1993	Gordon Ray
1993	Paul Hinton (acting)
1994-1996	Judith Hare
1996-2004	Jean Dirksen

2004-2007	Saul Amdursky
2007-2008	Rob O'Brennan (acting)
2008-2009	Maureen Woods
2009-	Rob O'Brennan

27. Okanagan Union / Regional Library head librarians

1936-1964	Muriel Page Ffoulkes
1964-1987	Peter Lofts
1987-	Lesley Dieno

28. Vancouver Island Union / Regional Library head librarians

1936-1938	Jean E. Stewart
1938-1939	Peter Grossman
1939-1942	Marjorie Largue
1943-1949	Jean G. Fannin
1949-1951	John C. Lort
1952-1955	Robert L. Davison
1956-1961	William Reid Taggart
1961-1986	Fred White
1986-1997	Don Meadows
1998-2007	Penny Grant
2008-	Rosemary Bonanno

BIBLIOGRAPHY

British Columbia Library Association: *British Columbia Libraries: Historical Profiles*. Vancouver: British Columbia Library Association, 1986.

Gilroy, Marion and Samuel Rothstein: *As We Remember It*. Vancouver: University of British Columbia School of Librarianship, 1970.

Donnelly, F. Dolores. *The National Library of Canada*. Ottawa: Canadian Library Association, 1973.

Holmes, Marjorie C.: *Library Service in British Columbia*. Victoria: Public Library Commision, 1959.

Hutcheson, Amy. *New Westminster Library History*. In *British Columbia Library Quarterly*, 1965.

Marshall, John Douglas. *Place of Learning, Place of Dreams*. Seattle: University of Washington Press, 2004.

Morison, C.K.: *A Book Pedlar in British Columbia*. Victoria: Library Development Commission, 1969.

Murray, Stuart A.P. *The Library: An Illustrated History*. New York: Skyhorse Books, 2009.

Overend, Howard. *The Library Commission*. In *British Columbia Historical News*, Spring 2004.

Overend, Howard. *Book Guy*. Vancouver: Touchwood Editions, 2001.

Sawa, Maureen. *The Library Book: The Story of Libraries from Camels to Computers*. Toronto: Tundra, 2006.

Vancouver Island Regional Library: *The Key*, 2006.

ACKNOWLEDGEMENTS

A project of this size is not the work of one person. Credit goes to dozens of people, alive and dead, who took the time to record their thoughts on library services and library development. Some of these contributors are anonymous; their words appeared in newspaper accounts or official reports written many years ago. Other contributors are well known. All of these people made *The Library Book* possible. More than that, they helped to make it comprehensive, accurate and entertaining.

It is important to note the special contributions of three people. Former Lieutenant-Governor Iona Campagnolo and Sarah Ellis, who won a Governor-General's Award for Children's Literature, helped introduce the subject to our readers. Cartoonist Adrian Raeside kept us laughing, and with luck, thinking as well.

Jacqueline van Dyk, the director of the provincial Public Library Services Branch, is a passionate advocate for library service. She provided valuable context for this book, explaining the vision for libraries in general as well as for specific types of libraries, and provided historical background as well. As the provincial librarian, she pushed to ensure this book was as collaborative and inclusive as possible.

Several people offered an exceptional level of service, going far beyond what was asked of them. People such as Ian Baird, Lesley Dieno, Peter Gourlay, Chris Hives, Andrew Martin, Debbie Millward, Basil Stuart-Stubbs, Marnie Swanson and Paul Whitney represent the best of library service, and help fulfill the most optimistic goals of Helen Gordon Stewart, Ethelbert Olaf Stuart Scholefield and the other pioneers. Our libraries were left in good hands.

The information gathered on these pages came from a wide variety of sources. More than 2,000 newspaper articles were consulted, and helped to add life to the story through the exact words used by library pioneers. The newspaper index at the Legislative Library was invaluable in the search for stories about libraries; it is fitting to note that the index was started by Alma Russell, the first trained librarian in the province, in 1908. Annual reports came from the Public Library Commission, the Library Development Commission, the Library Services Branch and the Public Library Services Branch. Reports from the British Columbia Library Association, reports from the regional library systems and the university libraries were also consulted. There were also ten province-wide library development plans, two regional ones and Maxwell Cameron's report on education, which had a huge impact on school and public libraries. Publications of the British Columbia Teacher-Librarians Association also helped as this book came together.

These materials came from several institutions, including the Legislative Library, the Mearns Centre at the University of Victoria, the Vancouver Public Library and the libraries of the *Times Colonist*, *Vancouver Sun* and *Province* newspapers. Other repositories were not quite as formal. One of the most important sources, the minute book of the original Nanaimo literary institute, was retrieved from a rummage sale.

Printed sources had much to offer, but the nuggets they contain need to be brought together by people who can explain the reasons for decisions, and the impacts they had. Several people, including working and retired librarians, politicians and relatives of prominent figures in library history, agreed to interviews in person or on the telephone.

They included Alice Bacon, Sam Bawlf, Lois Bewley, Brian Campbell, Lynn Copeland, Sylvia Crooks, Ray Culos, Lesley Dieno, Janice Douglas, Barbara Greeniaus, Gene Joseph, Mary Leask, Jim Looney, Dr. Stuart Madden, Dr. John Marshall, Howard Overend, Samuel Rothstein, Basil Stuart-Stubbs, Allison Taylor McBryde and Carol Williams.

Words without pictures can be boring. Photographs provide valuable information, and help connect us with the past. A special thanks is due to all of the libraries and librarians, archives and archivists who provided the images that grace these pages.

Major sources of photographs were the Vancouver Public Library, the Pacific Newspaper Group, which publishes the *Vancouver Sun* and the *Province*, the Royal B.C. Museum -

B.C. Archives, and the *Times Colonist* newspaper in Victoria. The University of British Columbia provided photographs from its library, its archives, its special collections department, and its communications department.

More photographs came from the public libraries in Burnaby, Greater Victoria, Kitimat, New Westminster, Richmond and Surrey, as well as the West Vancouver Memorial Library and the regional libraries in the Fraser Valley and the Okanagan Valley. Other sources included Library and Archives Canada, the University of Victoria Archives, the City of Vancouver Archives, the Legislative Library and the Langley Museum. The files at the Public Library Services Branch provided early colour slides. Photographs were also provided by individuals such as Bette Cannings, Hazel Lynn, Sherri Robinson, and John Maitland Marshall's children, Dr. John Marshall and Kathleen Heron. Other images came from the author's own collection.

This project would not have been possible without the support of people in the Public Library Services Branch, including Jacqueline van Dyk, Ben Hyman and Dawn Stoppard.

Further help came from Andy Ackerman, Kirsten Andersen, Katherine Anderson, Tina Artuso, Rita Avigdor, Beth Barlow, Jenny Benedict, Johanne Blenkin, Ursula Brigl, Jim Bruce, Dorothy Cameron, Bette Cannings, Steven Chan, Virginia Charron, Shelley Civkin, Sheila Coe, Laurie Cooke, Ken Cooley, Leonora Crema, Maureen Curry, Heather Daly, Mandy Davies, Annette DeFaveri, Ann Doyle, Emma Dressler, Corinne Durston, Moira Ekdahl, J. McRee (Mac) Elrod, Kim Feltham, Audrey Fennema, Shelagh Flaherty, Kyrstin Floodeen, James Fournie, James Gemmill, Linnea Gibbs, April Haddad, Val Hamilton, Nancy Hannum, Aphrodite Harris, Sybil Harrison, Ken Haycock, Susan Henderson, Joan Holzer, Melanie Houlden, Faith Jones, Lynne Jordon, Katherine Kalsbeek, David Karppinen, Jean Kavanagh, Eva Kelemen, Kevin Kierans, Kathleen Larkin, Barbara Jo May, Virginia McCreedy, Anne Morgan, Errin Morrison, Jack Mounce, Ron O'Brennan, Marla O'Brien, Anne Olsen, Chris Petter, Cheryl Reaume, Kate Russell, Stephen Ruttan, Andrew Seary, Tom Shorthouse, Cheryl Siegel, Sandra Singh, Julie Spurrell, Deb Thomas, Diana Thompson, Sheila Thompson, Gordon Ray, Edel Toner-Rogala, Denise St. Arnaud, Wendy Turnbull, Paul Tutsch, Ross Tyner, Frederike Verspoor, Amy Veysey, Virginia Walker, Adrienne Wass, Betty Weaver, Fran Welwood, Ron Welwood, Paul Whitney, Lara Wilson, Michelle Wong and Emily Yearwood-Lee. It's also important to thank Marion Gilroy and Charles Keith Morison, who in the 1960s had the foresight to record the memories of some pioneer librarians.

Good editors are essential to the creation of a book. This book was edited by Sarah Obee, Paul Willcocks, Lucinda Chodan and Jacqueline van Dyk. Others who read the manuscript and helped make it better were Patrick Dunae, Percilla Groves, Karen Parrish and Maureen Sawa. Ron Welwood and Basil Stuart-Stubbs were inspirational. That said, I take full responsibility for any errors or omissions.

All of the elements in this book were brought together by designer Roger Handling. His can be a thankless task. A reader will notice bad book design, but great book design is invisible, although it certainly helps to make the author look good.

Many people contributed indirectly. Special thanks go to professionals such as Don Bourdon, Neil Firkins, Gary Mitchell, Pauline Rafferty, Steve Roome and Ann ten Cate, friends such as Melanie Arscott and Sherri Robinson, and family members such as Dixie Obee, Will Obee, Judy Obee and Stephen Decarie. They, among others, put up with me through the many months it took to bring *The Library Book* together.

All of this makes it sound as if this book is the work of a small army of people — but this list barely scratches the surface. Think of the professional librarians over the years. Think of the volunteers, the staff members, and the trustees. Think of the people who wrapped up books for mailing, or the ones who drove the trucks, day after day, to ensure that library patrons could get the books they were eagerly waiting for. Think of the people who are scanning material today, preparing yet another digital file for a library website. This book recognizes, in a small way, the contributions made by thousands of people over the decades.

The Library Book is dedicated to the memory of Ruth Mould, the librarian at the Smithers Public Library from 1957 to 1978. The lessons she taught me about the value of libraries in opening a person's mind have lasted a lifetime. She encouraged my interest in British Columbia's history, and helped me to respect the work of librarians everywhere.

Thank you for reading this book. Libraries are as important today as they ever were. Spread the word.

Dave Obee
Victoria, 2011

INDEX

Edited by Lucinda Chodan, Sarah Obee, Jacqueline van Dyk and Paul Willcocks.
Designed by Roger Handling, Terra Firma Digital Arts.
Photography for front cover: Image I-00531 courtesy of Royal BC Museum, BC Archives; Image A-09542 courtesy of Royal BC Museum, BC Archives; Fraser Valley Regional Library; and Vancouver Public Library.
Photography for back cover: Dave Obee collection; Fraser Valley Regional Library; Image A-02828 courtesy of Royal BC Museum, BC Archives; Leonard Frank, Vancouver Province; Don McLeod, Vancouver Province; Vancouver Public Library; and University of British Columbia Archives 41.1/2712-4.
Cover back flap photography by Debra Brash, *Times Colonist*.
Printed in Canada.

Published the British Columbia Library Association
150 – 900 Howe Street, Vancouver, BC V6Z 2M4

British Columbia
Library Association

The B.C. Library Association gratefully acknowledges the support of the Province of British Columbia.

BRITISH
COLUMBIA
The Best Place on Earth

Library and Archives Canada Cataloguing in Publication

Obee, Dave, 1953-
    The library book : a history of service to British Columbia / Dave Obee.

Includes index.
ISBN 978-0-9692614-9-0

    1. Libraries—British Columbia—History. I. British Columbia Library Association II. Title.

Z735.B7O34 2011   027.0711   C2011-901351-7